EMPIRE MADE

Fiction by Kief Hillsbery

WAR BOY

WHAT WE DO IS SECRET

EMPIRE MADE

My Search for an Outlaw Uncle Who
Vanished in British India

KIEF HILLSBERY

HOUGHTON MIFFLIN HARCOURT
BOSTON NEW YORK
2017

For information about permission to reproduce selections from this book, write
to trade.permissions@hmhco.com or to Permissions, Houghton Mifflin Harcourt
Publishing Company, 3 Park Avenue, 19th Floor, New York, New York 10016.

www.hmhco.com

Library of Congress Cataloging-in-Publication Data is available.
ISBN 978-0-547-44331-7

Book design by Martha Kennedy

Map by Mapping Specialists, Ltd.

Printed in the United States of America
DOC 10 9 8 7 6 5 4 3 2 1

ONCE AGAIN
to David

What I mean is, that if I had some more detective stories instead of Thucydides and some bottles of claret instead of tepid whisky, I should probably settle here for good.

— ROBERT BYRON, *The Road to Oxiana*

CONTENTS

Nigel Halleck's India, 1845

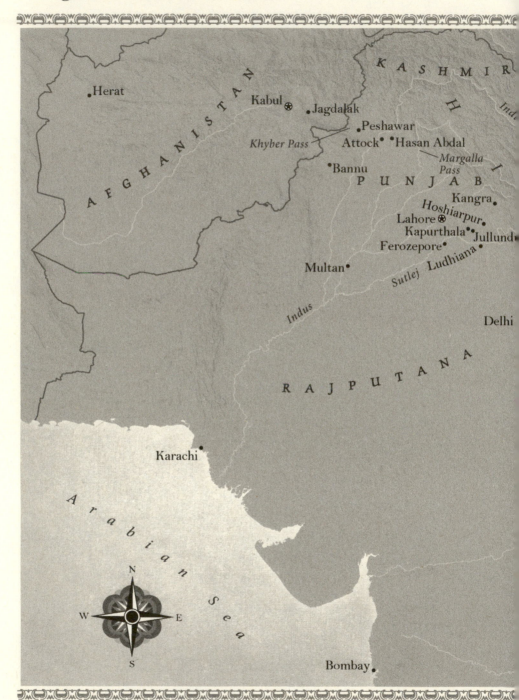

K A S H M I R

Herat

Kabul ⊗ •Jagdalak

Peshawar•
Khyber Pass   Attock• •Hasan Abdal

A F G H A N I S T A N

•Bannu   P U N J A B   *Margalla Pass*

Kangra•

Hoshiarpur•
Lahore ⊗
Kapurthala• •Jullund

Ferozepore•
Multan•   *Sutlej* Ludhiana•

Indus   Delhi

R A J P U T A N A

Karachi•

A r a b i a n   S e a

N
W   E
S

Bombay•

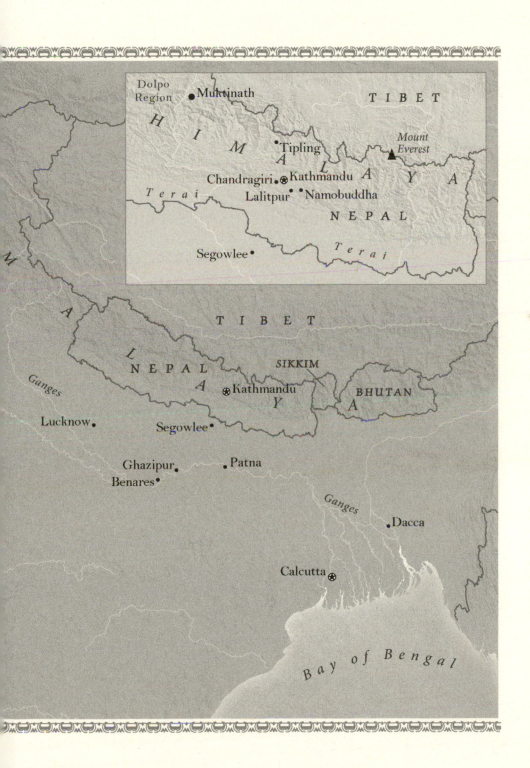

Dolpo
Region
Muktinath
TIBET
HIMALAYA
Tipling
Mount
Everest
Chandragiri
Kathmandu
Terai
Lalitpur
Namobuddha
NEPAL
Segowlee
Terai

HIMALAYA
TIBET
NEPAL
SIKKIM
Ganges
Kathmandu
BHUTAN
Lucknow
Segowlee
Ghazipur
Patna
Benares
Ganges
Dacca
Calcutta
Bay of Bengal

TIMELINE

NIGEL HALLECK

1822

Born in Coventry, England

1839

Visits France and Italy
Secures nomination for writership with East India Company

1840

Enrolls at Haileybury College in Hertfordshire

1841

Graduates from Haileybury
Visits Egypt and Aden en route to India

1842

Settles in Calcutta
Hires native tutor and reads for honor in languages at College of
*   Fort William during Company probationary period*

1843

Posted to Dacca on temporary assignment as assistant in Company
*   revenue office*
Appointed to Accountant General's Office, Calcutta

1844

Sponsored for election to the Bengal Club
Requests transfer to the Company's revenue office in Patna

1845

Audits tax receipts of native squires appointed by the British to oversee
*   opium croplands surrounding Patna*

1846

Conducts field audit in Ghazipur and meets Major Henry Lawrence
"Borrowed" on Lawrence's recommendation to assist with settlement of
*   tax revenues in the newly annexed Jullundur Doab territory bordering*
*   the Punjab*
Meets Lieutenant John Nicholson at Lawrence's headquarters in Lahore

1847

Assesses tax revenues in Hoshiarpur district

1848

Continues tax assessment work in Kapurthala district

1849

Meets Sa'adat ul-Mulk at Ludhiana Cantonment
Visits John Nicholson at Hasan Abdal en route to assignment training
*   revenue clerks in Yousafzai district, near Peshawar*
Accompanies Sa'adat on ride out of Lahore to visit Afghan ruby
*   mines at Jagdalak*

1850

Visits Kathmandu, Nepal, with Sa'adat after Company approves
*   application for home leave*
Returns to England

1851

Chooses not to renew employment with East India Company after returning to India and settles in Nepal as guest of Maharaja Jang Bahadur Rana

1854

Travels to Peshawar with Sa'adat and visits Nicholson at Bannu

1856

Joins Jang Bahadur on tiger shoot in Terai jungle

1878

Dies at Namobuddha, Nepal

Prologue

THIS BOOK TELLS the story — often shadowy, sometimes perplexing, frequently eccentric — of an English gentleman who went out to India in the era of Kipling's "white man's burden" and found that its weight was more than he could bear. Like his ten thousand countrymen who dispensed justice and imposed taxes on one-fifth of the world's population in the 1840s, he was neither a civil servant nor a soldier, but a salaried employee of a joint stock company whose shares were traded on the London exchange. "It is the strangest of all governments," said the Whig politician Thomas Macaulay in the House of Commons in 1833, "but it is designed for the strangest of all empires."

For the first two hundred years of the Honourable East India Company's existence after its charter by Elizabeth I in 1600, its men on the ground in India fit the mold of ruffians and buccaneers more than rulers. But powerful forces back home eventually worked to refine the behavior of Company employees and transform the role of the Company itself. The first was the rise of the Evangelical movement within the Church of England. Until 1813, missionary work was against the law in colonial India, on grounds that it caused disaffection among the natives and undermined British political authority. But when the Company's charter came up for renewal that year, it was obliged by Parliament to welcome missionaries as the price of retaining its trading privileges.

The second was the propagation of Jeremy Bentham's philosophy of utilitarianism, which held that moral, social, and political action should be directed toward achieving the greatest good for the largest number of people. The idea that Indians were a backward race who should be ruled by Englishmen for their own good replaced the profit motive as the engine of colonial administration. By the time a wide-eyed twenty-year-old named Nigel Halleck debarked from a packet steamer onto the teeming docks of Calcutta in 1842, the East India Company was no longer involved in commerce at all. Its mission was to civilize, and Christianize.

Nigel was my mother's grandfather's great-uncle. The first time I heard of him I was a child, on a visit to my aunt's home in the old Midlands market town of Coventry. On the rainy afternoon of a gray English day, I sat on the floor of her dressing closet and watched my sister bedeck herself with cast-off jewelry, culled from heirlooms my aunt thought too hideous to wear but too ancient to discard. I rummaged through her leavings and held up a heavy silver brooch, black with tarnish. It was particularly old and particularly ugly. The shield was fussily chased, and the large, gaudy stone gleamed pink as candy floss.

Its facets caught the light from the dim bare bulb overhead and sparked with lurid fire. I turned the brooch in my hands and read out the spidery text engraved on the back:

Your loving Nigel

"Who was Nigel?" I asked my aunt.

That would be my uncle, she said, many times removed. He had gone out to India.

I asked why.

To help those poor people, she said. "Many men did in those days."

India, she explained, had figured in the lives of several of my ancestors. A consulship in Burma was mentioned, and there had been a couple of vicars, and someone in railway administration — no, not an engineer, of either sort. Driving a train, she informed me, was common, and as for devising a railway's route — grades and bridges, tunnels, beds for track — a head for such figures never sat on the shoulders of anyone who bled our blood, she was absolutely sure of that.

How long were they in India, I wondered, and what was it they did afterwards, back in England, and after she told me — two or three

years for the consul and the clergymen, five she supposed for the rail-
wayman, and more or less the same as what they did in India, practiced
their professions — I returned to Uncle Nigel: what did he do?

"Do?"

"In England. After India."

Actually, she said, he never came back. He stayed in the East.

"His whole life?"

"Indeed he did."

"He must have liked it."

"I suppose he must."

"Was he the only one ever? Who stayed?"

"Heavens, no. Many have. Why, Mother Teresa—"

"In our family."

No others came to mind, she said. Not for India. There was my
mother, of course, who married my American father after the war and
decamped across the pond.

"Did Nigel get married? Was that why? To an Indian?"

"Certainly not. Of course not."

"He never had a wife?"

"I'm afraid not."

The brooch had been a gift to his mother, she said.

Then she changed the subject, leaving me with both a clear sense
that she disapproved of Nigel and the vague notion that there was
more to his story than my aunt thought suitable for sharing with my
ten-year-old self. A decade later, when I was on the verge of heading
East myself for a college year abroad in Nepal, my mother confirmed
my suspicions. Nigel, she confided, had separated from the East India Company under some sort of cloud. Afterwards he had supposedly "gone native" in Nepal and lived until his death in 1878 as one of a
handful of Europeans admitted to the then-forbidden Himalayan kingdom.

According to family legend, his exile was forced — he couldn't stay
in India or come back to England. But no one quite knew why. He

might have been a jewel thief, he might have been a spy. He was, everyone agreed, a hunter of big game, and one story had it that he met his end in the mouth of a man-eating tiger in the Terai jungle, on the border of Nepal and India.

My mother was less troubled by the manner of his reputed demise than by its loneliness. On the eve of my departure in the spring of 1975, she entrusted me with a sheaf of pages from letters written by Nigel in the 1840s and early 1850s. Some were reproduced on vintage copy paper, slick and vaguely toxic. Others were transcribed from the originals. Only a few of the letters were complete. She said that most of his correspondence had been lost in the Nazi bombing of Coventry, as had the whereabouts of his grave. To her way of thinking, it was nothing short of scandalous that in all those years none of Nigel's relatives — not even those who spent years in India themselves — had ever had the bottle to find his gravesite and pay their respects.

I promised I would do my best to be the first. I had never been to Asia. I thought it would be simple — an inquiry here, a walk through a graveyard there. I had no idea that the very concept of bureaucracy was invented by the Mughal rulers of India in the fifteenth century, only to be raised to impenetrable perfection by the British who supplanted them as imperial masters.

TWENTY-ONE YEARS LATER, nursing a glass of sweet milky tea in a café in Kathmandu, at the end of my third sojourn in Nepal, I had so far succeeded only in prolonging the scandal. By 1996 I had traipsed across a half dozen colonial cemeteries, forgotten ossuaries of empire where epitaphs alluded to epidemics, massacres, and the shimmer of moonlight upon the freshet Clyde. I had come to navigate the stacks of several British Council libraries with the same hard-won sureness I felt after mastering the subway maze beneath Times Square. I had devoted time and trouble to near-forensic examination of vermin-chewed ledgers in the archives of the family that had long ruled Nepal, and more conversations than I could count with persons and personages in

India, Nepal, and Pakistan deemed likely to know where all manner of bodies were buried. For more than half my life, I had tried and failed to find out exactly what became of Nigel Halleck.

But it was other unfinished business in Nepal that occupied my thoughts on that day in the Unity Restaurant. At a nearby table, a Japanese in his late twenties pored over a binder of black-and-white photographs encased in plastic sleeves. I couldn't make out what they depicted, but I recognized the title on the spine of the book he referred to as he leafed through them.

In my college days, *Himalayan Pilgrimage* had amounted to my Bible. Published in 1961, it recounted one of the first journeys undertaken by a European, David Snellgrove, into the remote region of the Nepal Himalaya called Dolpo. The highest permanently inhabited place on the planet, it was the last redoubt of practitioners of Bön, the ancient religion of Tibet.

My independent undergraduate research project in Nepal had focused on nature reverence among the Bön-po, mostly because I was a mountaineer, and studying people who lived nowhere but the high country seemed the best way to ensure that I spent most of my time there. As it turned out, though, I never managed to visit their homeland. The trails into Dolpo were treacherous, I was told, and there was hardly any food. Nor would I care for the inhabitants, who were surly and dirty. Left unspoken by the authorities at the Ministry of Home Affairs in Kathmandu was their real reason for saying no, which was the lingering presence in Dolpo of Tibetan resistance fighters, who had harassed the People's Liberation Army from bases there until President Nixon's visit to China put an end to their sponsorship by the CIA. Three years after the last American airdrop, the Khampas, as they were known, had no intention of giving up their guerrilla raids; the Nepalese government, unable to evict them, chose to pretend they did not exist. Keeping out foreigners who might produce evidence to the contrary was part of the charade in 1975.

I decided to recalibrate my research project. But Dolpo had never lost its allure for me. Twenty years later, I still wanted to go there. Travel restrictions had gradually been relaxed with the dispersal of the guerrillas, and though some of the most enticing areas remained off-limits, I knew that trekking permits were now occasionally granted on a case-by-case basis. I asked my neighbor with the photographs if he was one of the lucky ones.

Not yet, he said.

Still trying.

The problem, he said, was the exorbitant fee for a permit. The Nepalese had lately made the happy discovery that they could charge tens of thousands of dollars apiece to mountaineers for permission to climb eight-thousand-meter summits like Everest and Annapurna. They were currently operating on the assumption that trekkers who wished to be among the first into Dolpo had pockets just as deep. But there he was, a graduate student on a spartan budget. Even the Unity — an oasis of hygiene where salad greens were washed in boiled water and cutlery was sterilized to ward off hepatitis — was a stretch. Usually he dined at one of the dives in Thamel where out-of-work Sherpas ate their fill of buckwheat noodles for a rupee or two a bowl.

I told him of my interest in the Bön-po. He said he found them fascinating, too. Not that he was a Tibetologist himself, or even a scholar of religion. His field was East Asian history, and for several years he had been researching the travels of Ekai Kawaguchi, a Buddhist monk and amateur Japanese spy who in 1899 became the first foreigner to enter Dolpo. Like the Khampas seventy-five years later, Kawaguchi was not supposed to be there. Disguised as a Tibetan lama and accompanied by two loyal Mongolian servants, he passed through Dolpo, sketching and mapping, and returned to his base of operations in Tibet. Some years later, Kawaguchi discharged the servants, a married couple who then decided to return to Nepal on pilgrimage before journeying home to Mongolia.

It was the servants, he said, whose lives he was researching now. He actually found them more interesting than Kawaguchi. The arc of the secret agent's story was predictable; the arc of the story of his devout retainers was anything but. They never went back to Mongolia, for one thing. When they learned that a Buddhist shrine in the Himalayan foothills east of Kathmandu was without a caretaker, they took the job and settled there.

"Do you know Namobuddha?" he asked.

I said that I did. I had visited the shrine myself, twenty years before.

"I remember it well," I said.

But I barely knew the place at all. He spun one yarn after another about the antics, sacred and profane, of the pilgrims who made their way there over the course of several generations, as reported by the estimable Mongolians, who for decades told and retold everything they saw and heard with Chaucerian relish, over endless cups of black brick tea, to travelers from as near as you could spit and as far as you could go, from as far as England, even, like the one poor sahib who stopped at the *chautara* at the top of the hill to take one breath and never took another, back when most Nepalis had never seen a live sahib, let alone a dead one.

Wait, I said.

A *chautara*, he explained, was a resting platform for porters, built up with stones to take the weight of the heavy baskets they carried off their necks and shoulders.

I know, I said.

But the Englishman—he died there?

What was his name?

He had no idea.

But yes, he died there, a long time ago.

He said that upkeep of the *chautara* was among the couple's duties, so they were mindful of the story, which they had heard from the previous caretaker.

And there was a remembrance, with English writing.

The first photograph he passed me was an image of the shrine itself, a bas-relief, black with antiquity, worn almost smooth from devotion, depicting the scene played out in that spot by a Buddha of the past, feeding his own arm to the starving cubs of a tigress killed by a hunter.

The second showed the *chautara* from a distance, built up around the massive trunk of the grand old tree that shaded it. The third was a close-up of two roots of the tree, exposed beneath the platform, with a star-shaped mosaic tile inset between them. It was chipped and weathered, and at first I discerned no English in the stylized calligraphy. It took a while to puzzle out what remained legible:

> *stars of tears . . .*
> *night remains dark . . .*
> *shining stars . . .*

It seemed to be a fragment of a poem.

"I know this poem," I said.

I couldn't place it, though.

There was something about the tile, too.

It looked foreign — and not just the lettering. You saw faience mosaic like that on the Mughal monuments of India and Pakistan. You saw it on the mosques and tombs and madrassas of Iran and Afghanistan. You didn't see it in Nepal, which in those days qualified as the world's only Hindu kingdom. When I lived in Kathmandu, I had been told that the only Muslims in the city had been imported from India to serve as butchers.

It looked foreign, but also familiar. Star-shaped mosaic tiles like that were unusual, but I was sure that I had seen one before.

It would take some time to remember where.

EVEN AS I dodged cycle rickshaws and cow patties after leaving the Unity that day, wondering if the memorial could be Nigel's, I saw how susceptible the story was to reversal. How readily, in retelling over the years, the tigress killed by the hunter became the hunter killed by the tigress. No surprise there. By then I had learned enough about Nigel's life in India to doubt the particulars of most of the stories about him. But it always seemed clear to me that something definite was responsible for his exile.

Something had to be. He had gone East at twenty—the same age as me. He was the dutiful son of a respectable family in provincial England who assured his parents after he arrived in Calcutta that he would keep his distance from the alluring, beguiling, enveloping East. He would confine his circle of acquaintance to gentlemen like himself, and, whatever the obstacles posed by the climate and his official responsibilities, he would read a chapter from the Holy Bible every day. Ten years later, he was happily ensconced as the permanent houseguest of a highborn Hindu in a kingdom where a young girl was worshiped as a living goddess, and each October, on a date determined by the phase of the moon, the streets ran ankle-deep with blood from buffalo, goats, pigeons, and ducks, sacrificed by the hundreds of thousands to propitiate Kali, "the black one."

Even if Namobuddha answered the question of Nigel's death, what brought him to Nepal in the first place—and kept him there—remained a mystery. My struggle to solve it became this book. Nigel dominates the stage, with a supporting cast worthy of Shakespeare. There is the fugitive queen mother of the boy king of the Sikhs, described by another Englishman who knew her as "a strange blend of the prostitute, the tigress, and Machiavelli's Prince." There is a dispossessed Afghan prince, whose father poisoned his grandfather and maintained a pride of lions to which he fed his enemies alive. There is the maharaja of Nepal, a cavalry officer who came to power by way of imprisoning the king and slaughtering the aristocracy, then held on to it by making nice to Queen Victoria at Buckingham Palace.

And then there are the British. Before his break with the East India Company, Nigel cast his professional lot with a cadre of officials whose enlightened approach to governance went against the imperial grain. Some of their names endure today, on plinths of heroic statuary in England and chiseled into monuments astride the Khyber Pass.

Men such as Henry Lawrence and John Nicholson are counted among the greats of British India. Yet Nigel went on to abandon them, just as their policies began to pay off.

The first great question, then, is why Nigel turned his back on the empire, and his story begins with the man who forced it on his countrymen to begin with, whether they wanted it or not.

PART I

1

An Empire

AT THE DAWN of the nineteenth century, in the second year of his reign over more of humanity than any Englishman had ever ruled before him, Richard Wellesley decided to found a school for imperialists. It was the forerunner of the institution that prepared Nigel for his career in India.

None of Wellesley's predecessors as governors general of India would have thought of such a thing. They contented themselves with shoring up "John Company's" trade monopolies in tea and silk and opium—attaining sovereignty over Bengal and the Carnatic region, surrounding Madras, through smooth talk, bribery, and, when all else failed, force of arms. For forty years, since the Company's army defeated the troops of the last nawab of Bengal at the Battle of Plassey, its territorial holdings had fluctuated. But the trend, when Wellesley took up residence at Government House in Calcutta in 1798, was toward contraction. It seemed likely that the British footprint in India would be reduced to the environs of Bombay, Madras, and Calcutta.

This prospect delighted the Company's Court of Directors. They had always seen their business as business, not empire building. Looming over them when they met round a horseshoe table at their headquarters in the City of London was an ornate marble chimneypiece adorned with a bas-relief panel, *Britannia Receiving the Riches of the East*. Yet territorial conquest had brought the Company to the verge of bankruptcy. A loan of £1.5 million from the Treasury kept it afloat, but by no means would it suffice to finance further military adventure. Before Wellesley set sail for India, he was told in no uncertain terms that he must hew most strictly to a policy of non-intervention.

Wellesley, a great-great-great-grandfather of Elizabeth II whose portrait hangs today in the Throne Room at Buckingham Palace, had other ideas. With the tacit support of Henry Dundas, war secretary under Prime Minister William Pitt, his goal was nothing less than subjection of the entire subcontinent. It was a daunting task, to be sure, one that had proved the undoing of no less a personage than Alexander the Great. But Wellesley seems never to have doubted that he was up to it. He was a haughty Old Etonian whose excessive vanity caused him to wear his medals and decorations even in bed.

History, moreover, proved that unification of India into one state was possible. Chandragupta Maurya, a native of Patna on the river Ganges, had managed it in 322 B.C., founding an empire that lasted for five hundred years and extended beyond the Indus to encompass much of what is now Afghanistan and southeast Iran. A millennium and change later, a Turko-Mongol named Babur — who claimed descent from Genghis Khan on his father's side and Tamerlane on his mother's — swept down from Central Asia to pick up the pieces; though his Mughal Empire had largely disintegrated by 1750, it lived on in the vicinity of Delhi under an emperor looking for British protection to preserve his dynasty.

Less than two years after Wellesley's arrival, he was well on his way to emulating his imperial predecessors. He had already waged three wars on his own initiative, destroying the last pockets of French influence in Mysore and Hyderabad. Most of the subcontinent south of the fifteenth parallel was in British hands, along with Bengal, the lower Ganges, and Bombay.

Much of the rest was ripe for the taking. It was largely a matter of securing the loyalty of native princes, who were promised protection from their enemies. Once British troops were stationed near their seats of power, Wellesley bullied the nobles into adopting policies of provincial administration dictated by Calcutta. The East India Company became ruler in all but name.

As word of his conquests filtered back to London, the outraged di-

rectors issued orders forbidding further expansion. Since these direc-
tives were transmitted by sailing ship around the Cape of Good Hope
and took as long as four months to reach Government House, they
tended to arrive in the afterglow of highly successful campaigns, and
Wellesley felt safe in dismissing them as moot. With his brother Arthur — later created Duke of Wellington after commanding the armies
that defeated Napoleon at Waterloo in 1815 — he plotted the subjugation of the Maratha Confederacy, a network of Hindu chiefs who had
taken advantage of Mughal weakness to gain control of a wide swath
of central India, from near Goa, on the Arabian Sea, to Delhi, on the
Gangetic Plain. At the same time, in an end run around the Court of
Directors, he dispatched another brother, Henry, to London to explain
his policies and lobby Parliament for a free hand in pursuing them.

For the first time at Westminster, the British presence in India was
referred to as "the empire." Among those who liked the sound of it was
Prime Minister Pitt, who had come to power in the aftermath of the
American War of Independence and saw an opportunity to offset the
loss of the thirteen colonies. Lord Grenville, the foreign secretary, also
voiced support for Wellesley. But the Court of Directors had friends in
high places, too. One was the Prince of Wales, certain to be empowered
sooner or later as prince regent, owing to the mental incapacity of his
father, George III. He endorsed the Company's position that Wellesley's ambitions could not be realized without the astronomical expense
of maintaining what would necessarily constitute the world's largest
standing army. Given Bonaparte's seizure of power in France in November 1799, the future king located the more pressing need for military expenditure closer to home.

On paper, Henry Wellesley's mission failed. As a matter of form, it
was bound to — under the terms of the Company's charter, the governor general answered to the Court of Directors, not Parliament.
The directors dispatched to Calcutta what Richard Wellesley bitterly
termed "a peremptory order to reduce the military strength of the em-

pire." Complaining that he had authorized the buildup of the Company's army only "after consulting all the most experienced officers in India," he threatened to resign.

Pure bluster. He had made an empire; he had no intention of letting it go. His Indian campaigns ultimately would annex more territory than all of Napoleon's conquests in Europe. Wellesley was no merchant. He was an aristocrat, and money barely interested him at all. What he wanted was power—for himself and for Britain.

Acquiring and maintaining power over so many by so few required impressive shows of force. But Wellesley understood the need for effective civil administration as the everyday instrument of power's exercise. As long as the British saw themselves primarily as traders, they had little vested interest in the functioning of law courts or the assessment and collection of taxes or the suppression of religious practices that created unrest in a multi-ethnic society. Once they made the transition to rulers, those things mattered. After deeming "mercantile knowledge" an unnecessary qualification for Company service, Wellesley outlined the enormity of the task ahead:

"To dispense justice to millions of people of various languages, manners, usages, and religions; to administer a vast and complicated system of revenue throughout districts equal in extent to some of the most considerable kingdoms in Europe; to maintain civil order in one of the most populous and litigious regions of the world; to discharge the functions of magistrates, judges, ambassadors, and governors of provinces; these are now the duties of the larger proportion of the civil servants of the Company."

Wellesley despised Indians. At his direction, natives were excluded for the first time from all social occasions at Government House. But his ill favor extended beyond the color bar to encompass most of his own countrymen in India. In an era when the regular British army was aptly described by his brother Arthur as "the scum of the earth, enlisted for drink," the East India Company's army was even worse. Its motley ranks harbored criminals, deserters, and various other scoundrels who felt obliged to put Blighty behind them sooner rather than later, when they might well end up at the penal colony of Botany Bay, in Australia.

Though the Company's public servants cut more respectable figures, Wellesley found them wanting in both caliber and manners. To his wife, Hyacinthe, who remained in England, he wrote that "the men are stupid, are coxcombs, are uneducated; the women are bitches, are badly dressed, are dull." Their society, he complained, was so "vulgar, ignorant, rude, familiar, and stupid as to be disgusting and intolerable; especially the ladies, not one of whom, by-the-bye, is even decently good-looking."

Wellesley always had an eye for the ladies. He lived for years in Paris with Hyacinthe, an actress at the Palais Royal, with whom he fathered five children before they married in 1794. It was an indiscretion that his friends worried might ruin his career, and upon his appointment as governor they urged him to leave his family behind to spare himself embarrassment in Calcutta. To the dismay of his wife, who was scorned by London society, he took their advice. But he regretted his decision almost as soon as he arrived. Without the companionship of his beloved, he wrote, he feared he lacked the "fortitude to remain here long enough to accomplish all my grand financial, political, military, naval, commercial, architectural, [and] judicial reforms."

But Wellesley persevered, bucked up by the presence of his brothers and, in the matter of public administration, inspired by the example of Britain's greatest enemy. During his romantic idyll, he had acquainted himself with the French approach to conducting the nation's affairs abroad, which upheld fluency in foreign tongues as a qualification for diplomats and colonial officials. The "distinguished encouragement" of the French government to the study of Eastern languages in particular led one contemporary observer to note that Paris "abounds in proficiency in Persian, Arabic, Turkish and even Sanskrit," while London was said "not to contain an Englishman capable of carrying on conversation, much less correspondence, in Arabic or Turkish, and the Mameluke Chief, who was lately [t]here, sought in vain for an assistant to write his letters to the other chiefs."

Owing to his recent conquests, Wellesley felt the time was ripe for the British to emulate their rivals across the Channel. He announced that he meant to ensure a regular supply of qualified civil servants by training them at a residential college in Calcutta. Everyone nominated to the Company's service would spend three years there, completing a systematic course of studies in Indian languages, history, and law. The wheat would be winnowed from the chaff through rigorous examinations, administered twice yearly. At the end of the third year, successful candidates would be awarded degrees and certificates of proficiency. They would then be competitively assigned to positions on the basis of demonstrated merit.

It was a far cry from the status quo, under which novices appointed as "Writers"—Company parlance for clerks—took up their duties without undergoing a period of probation or training. Some were as young as fifteen when they arrived in India. Without informing the Company directors of his plans, Wellesley chartered the College of Fort William in July 1800. In a symbolic nod to the imperial responsibilities that compelled him to act, he backdated its establishment to May 4, the first anniversary of the Battle of Seringapatam, which had delivered the kingdom of Mysore into British hands after he took personal charge of planning a breach in the city's walls.

In a gesture that signaled a further change in the colonial mind-set, he appointed Anglican clergymen to oversee the college as provost and vice provost. Ability, he decreed, would not suffice to qualify candidates for official positions. The religious and moral character of every prospect would be ascertained before he could be declared eligible for service or fit for higher office.

The idea that the East India Company ought to involve itself in maintaining and upholding Christianity had never before gained traction among the men it sent to India. Piety was not their strong suit. In the "presidency" ports of Calcutta, Madras, and Bombay, they wandered the streets, from punch house—"punch," derived from the Urdu *panch* ("five"), referred to the concoction's number of ingredients— to whorehouse, drinking themselves silly in the former and contracting in the latter a severe venereal disease called *atashak*, which caused a monumental swelling of the scrotum and testicles. Job Charnock, the seventeenth-century trader who founded Calcutta, took a Hindu widow as his common-law wife; "but instead of converting her to Christianity," wrote an Englishman who knew him, "she made him a Proselyte to Paganism." After she died, Charnock "kept the anniversary Day of her Death by sacrificing a Cock on her Tomb, after the Pagan Manner." Then there was W. C. Blaquiere, the "startlingly effeminate" police magistrate of Calcutta in the late eighteenth century, a noted cross-dresser who took every opportunity to don female attire in public.

Wellesley's decision to call time on this rollicking state of affairs, though nominally based on reverence for the Anglican Communion, was compelled more than anything by his abiding fear of the Gallic menace. To counteract the corrosive concepts of *liberté, égalité, fraternité*, he prescribed for Company employees a strong dose of religion. All administrators, professors, and lecturers at the new college were required to swear an oath of allegiance to the king and declare that they would not "teach or maintain publicly or privately any doctrines or opinions contrary to the Christian religion, or the doctrine or discipline of the Church of England, as by law established." By functioning as a moral and spiritual bulwark as well as an educational institution, the College of Fort William would thus amount, wrote Wellesley, to "the best security" that could be provided for "the stability of the British power in India."

What Wellesley presented as founded upon duty and compelled by a sacred trust was recognized by the Court of Directors as a power grab. No governor general had ever had any say in appointments to the Company's service. The Indian patronage was the jealously guarded possession of the directors themselves, who nominated candidates from within their circle of acquaintance without regard to ability and placed them in positions as they saw fit. It was bad enough that Wellesley sought to reduce the directors' influence and authority by holding an effective veto over those they put forward for service. But in claiming for himself and his successors "the exclusive power of determining to what establishments of the service the students of the College should be finally appointed," Wellesley proposed a seismic shift in the locus of employee loyalty—from London to Calcutta.

By the time news of the college's founding reached London, it had already enrolled its first class of students. But the directors, who now regarded Wellesley as an uncontrollable despot, refused to fund it. It was one thing to accept territorial expansion, after the fact—they could scarcely act otherwise as politicians warmed to the imperial idea. It was quite another to accede to the wanton appropriation of their own perquisites and power. Though they paid lip service to the "liberal and enlightened" character of Wellesley's plan, they objected to its "considerable and unknown expense" and ordered the college's abolition in January 1802.

Wellesley backed down. But he took his time about it, and the College of Fort William continued to provide residential training for civil servants until 1805. By then his energies had returned to conquest. By then he commanded a private security force of British officers and locally recruited Indian soldiers that numbered 260,000 men—twice the size of the regular British army. By then the Mughal capital of Delhi had fallen, and Babur's descendant Bahadur Shah II ruled an "empire" that consisted of his household. On the marches of the subcontinent, the Sikhs of the Punjab and the Gurkhas of Nepal remained ensconced in their mysterious kingdoms. Most of the rest of India—from Cape Comorin to the Sutlej River—was British.

2

An Education

THIRTY-FIVE YEARS LATER, in January 1840, Nigel Halleck enrolled in the college that the Company's directors had decided
they wanted after all. But they also wanted to keep an eye on it, so they
located it on the site of a country house twenty miles north of London in Hertfordshire. The house was called Hailey Bury, and though
the school was officially established as East India College, it became
known as Haileybury soon after its buildings were completed and occupied in 1809.

Nigel was eighteen, the second son of Charles Valentine Halleck, a
barrister who was himself a second son, of a vicar. The Hallecks were
a venerable clan, an offshoot of the Holyoakes who had settled in the
Midlands prior to the Battle of Hastings. Recorded in Domesday Book
as the Haliachs, they once held a manor in Leicestershire, but they
had long since slipped from the provincial pantheon of landed gentry.
Apart from modest but comfortable houses in Coventry, they owned no
property, enjoyed no private income.

The best they could hope for, in class-conscious England, was to
maintain their status as gentlefolk. And the best way for Nigel to do
that, coming of age in a country then enduring what Jan Morris called
"the menopause between an agricultural and industrial society," was to
follow in the footsteps of his father and grandfather. Once he had secured himself a position where he interacted professionally or socially
with the nobility and the gentry, he was set for life, a gentleman among
gentlemen, his muted destiny fulfilled.

Instead, he wished to go to India. He harbored no creative ambitions of his own, but there was something of the artist about him, a
craving for connection with a heightened world. He had left England

for the first time the previous summer. His family lacked the resources to send him on the Grand Tour, the traditional trip to Europe, lasting months or even years, that served as a cultural and educational rite of passage for young Englishmen of privilege. But he visited Paris, Florence, Venice, and Rome. From Venice he wrote home wistfully of children at play, straddling the porphyry lions in the Piazzetta dei Leoncini, beside the Basilica of Saint Mark. They were the raggedest of urchins, on intimate terms with riches beyond price.

Standing watching in his white kid gloves and white silk hat, Nigel felt impoverished by comparison. With benefit of hindsight, it is tempting to imagine him a tortured romantic, and to attribute the allure of the East to an inchoate longing for Byronic exile. The truth is more prosaic. He saw India in practical terms, as a colorful and congenial setting for the sort of mundane career to which he had long resigned himself. As a pupil at King Henry VIII School in Coventry, he realized early on that his lack of interest in the law was surpassed only by his lack of aptitude for it. His father, while disappointed, assured him that as long as he applied himself to his studies, he could count on a place at a theological seminary in Durham, recently established by churchmen with ties to the family. Once he graduated and served three or four years as a curate, his grandfather's influence would be brought to bear in awarding him a "living" as a beneficed clergyman.

He need not be condemned, in other words, to the shabby parsimony of a country vicar in a Trollope novel. He might well live in something close to luxury, tending without haste or undue exertion to the spiritual needs of the Surrey aristocracy. A delightful rose garden, a mahogany-paneled study, and a supply of good claret, judiciously replenished. To envisage such comforts came naturally to Nigel; the one thing he possessed in abundance was imagination. But it failed him utterly when he tried to picture himself in a cassock and dog collar. Would it be possible, he wondered, for the family to marshal its influence elsewhere? With friends of friends who were known to be cordially acquainted with one of the directors of the East India Company?

Who might prevail upon that good gentleman to arrange his nomination for a place at Haileybury?

His father, at first, thought not.

Haileybury produced clerks. Haileybury produced managers. Haileybury produced civil servants. Haileybury produced what would come to be known and accorded respect as "white-collar workers," but in 1839 there was no such term and no such respect, not, at any rate, from the likes of Charles Valentine Halleck. Those positions were wholly unsuitable for gentlemen; ergo, gentlemen did not fill them. It was true that the earnings of men who did fill them qualified them for inclusion in the nascent middle class. It was also true that their income could exceed that of their genteel betters in the professional classes. That didn't matter, though. Gentlemen might make money, but money made no gentlemen.

"You were either a gentleman or not a gentleman, and if you were a gentleman you struggled to behave as such, whatever your income might be," wrote George Orwell, who took up a posting in the Indian Civil Service eighty years after Nigel and whose background in what he called "the lower-upper-middle class" was identical. Both were grandsons of clergymen; both came from families of diminished prosperity who clung to gentility as their birthright:

"Probably the distinguishing mark of the upper middle class was that its traditions were not to any extent commercial, but mainly military, official, and professional. People in this class owned no land, but they felt that they were landowners in the sight of God and kept up a semi-aristocratic outlook by going into the professions and the fighting services rather than into trade. Small boys used to count the plum stones on their plates and foretell their destiny by chanting 'Army, Navy, Church, Medicine, Law.'"

Few things were more abhorrent to Nigel's father than the prospect of his sons "going into trade." Over time, the Hallecks had lost their property, but they clung to their scruples about blotting the family copybook by profiting from commerce. They were forever bondholders, never stockholders. And now Nigel proposed to cast his lot with a company of traders?

Fortunately for Nigel, recent history provided a counterargument. On paper, the Company remained exactly what Charles Halleck said it was. But even as it accumulated ever more power and authority in India, its commercial standing was eroded at home by the increasing enthusiasm in Parliament for free trade. It had lost its monopoly on trade with India in 1813, due largely to lobbying by English manufacturers and provincial merchants but also with support from liberals, who argued that unrestricted trade would make essential products available to everyone and lead to a more equitable society. And the latest renewal of its charter by act of Parliament had forbidden it to trade at all.

The act, which granted the Company the administration of India for another twenty years, was defended in the House of Lords by Arthur Wellesley, Duke of Wellington. Without drawing attention to his own role in India's subjugation—he unblushingly blamed the Company's current deficit of £40 million on "all the wars in which that Empire has been engaged"—he dismissed opposition claims that an enterprise unsuited for trade could hardly be suited for governance. On the contrary, said the duke, the Company had proved a resounding success. It was responsible for the "proud situation" in which British India now stood, ready to assume the mantle of a higher calling.

Charles Halleck may have been a snob, but he was a high-minded snob, and the new rationale for imperial rule would have appealed to him. He was also a committed Christian, who would have approved of Haileybury's faculty—most were clergymen as well as academics. Taking their cue from Richard Wellesley's ill-fated College of Fort William, they saw to it that the curriculum placed as much emphasis on the teaching of religion and morality as on Eastern languages, literature, and history.

It was finally enough for Nigel's father. He would never have assisted his son in finding a niche for himself in the commercial class, but a role in the ruling class was something else again. It was a new sort of ruling class, to be sure, in a faraway place, and, like most British gentlemen of his age and station, he was deeply suspicious of anything new and everything foreign. In the end, he overcame his misgivings by weighing his duty in the balance of his conscience.

As a father, he yearned to say no.

As an Englishman and Christian, he felt bound to say yes.

Halleck duly secured the intercession of a local squire on his son's behalf, and, at the beginning of November 1839, Nigel received a letter from India House, the Company's headquarters on Leadenhall Street in the City of London. It informed him, without elaboration, that he had been nominated for an "Indian Writership" by one of the Company's directors.

Until recently, that would have sufficed to guarantee his admission to Haileybury. But the same legislation that ended the Company's commercial activities had also introduced the principle of competition into its hiring practices. Henceforth, nominees needed to pass a preliminary examination before admittance to the college.

Those who took the exam recalled it as an ordeal. It was administered in a large room at India House, typically to about forty young men, and lasted three days. Its components included Greek, Latin, English history, mathematics, and geography. But no one could complain that they were caught off-guard by the questions. The directors, noted one Company official, "were naturally interested in making the passage through Haileybury as easy as possible for their nominees." Details of the examination, "in all its particulars," were provided to candidates in advance by the college secretary. He was the same gentleman who stood before the assembled nominees a month or so after its administration and read out the names of those who had passed.

Most belonged to eighteen- and nineteen-year-olds like Nigel, second sons of families who could promise a patrimony only to their first-born. A disproportionate share were recognizably Scottish; a tradition of looking to India for a career among the surplus sons of the mercantile and professional classes there had taken hold with the Acts of

Union, and by 1771 almost half the Company's clerks were Scotsmen. Ulstermen were overrepresented, too. But the plurality of names intoned by the secretary were English, and in December 1839, Nigel's was one of them. With his intellectual and moral fitness proven (and no medical examination required, either before or after the College course, despite the hazards of the Indian climate), he was good to go.

At least as far as Hertfordshire.

Where he quickly learned that talking about India was considered poor form.

Haileybury proved as anomalous as the Indian Empire itself. Even the stately Grecian facade the college presented to the world was not what it seemed. No one ever drove up to it, and no one ever entered by it. An alumnus later recalled this "architectural fraud" as "a mere show-front—a sort of clever artistic sham," seemingly erected "with the sole aim and object of atoning for utter hideousness hidden away in its rear." The rest of the academic quadrangle consisted of charmless bare-brick buildings, pierced with small windows and roofed with cheap slates, "of a pattern which would scarcely have been tolerable in a barrack, a prison, or a workhouse." Its opposite sides housed two hundred students' rooms, all equally small, entered by doors opening out of narrow dark corridors. Each contained a recess for a bed and a curtain to draw across it, with a cupboard on one side. Light entered through a single window, guarded by iron bars that reinforced the impression of a prisoner's cell.

It was true that the qualifications of the faculty were above reproach. Most were recruited from Oxford and Cambridge, and very few were ever lured back; professor of modern history and economics Thomas Robert Malthus, who wrote his famous work on population at Haileybury, remained a professor until his death, thirty years after his appointment. It was also true that students were not allowed to proceed to India unless they passed examinations each term for four terms, in nine subjects, including Sanskrit, Persian, and Hindustani. And, finally, it was true that the Company directors were seldom disappointed when they came down in a body from Leadenhall Street twice each year to distribute prizes and learn of the success or failure of their nominees. With impressive ceremony, the Company chairman addressed fulsome congratulations on the state of the college to the assembled students and faculty, offering, in the words of one observer, "as rose-coloured a view as possible of its moral and intellectual condition."

The larger truth, however, was that Haileybury was notorious throughout England as a den of iniquity. "Drunkenness, lack of discipline, and wild local wenching" were cited by one historian as the "main charges" against the student body. George Canning, a Company director who was obliged to go down to the college to quell a riot, reported afterwards that, though he had faced bitter opposition in the House of Commons and encountered turbulent riots at Liverpool, "I was never floored and daunted till now, and that by a lot of Haileybury boys."

The daily routine began innocently enough, with a morning service in the chapel at eight o'clock. Except on Sunday, it lasted barely twenty minutes, and always included a special prayer for the college and the reading of a chapter from the Bible. The breakfast that followed was meant to be a humble repast of bread and butter with tea or coffee, served back in students' rooms by women—typically widows or spinsters—attached to each corridor as "bedmakers." In practice, it amounted to the onset of the day's revelry. Cleared of its bed recess and furnished with extra chairs or couches, a room became a "club" for eight to ten men, who pooled their resources to dine on meat and fish and pastries, washed down with beer or claret (thus flouting college regulations that prohibited consumption of alcohol except in "special cases").

When they'd had their fill, they sauntered down to the quadrangle to lounge about, smoking pipes, while tradesmen from Hertford touted their wares. Local medical men, holding themselves apart from the swarm of tailors, hairdressers, stationers, and booksellers, conducted a brisk business issuing "aegrotats" to students seeking exemption from chapel and lectures on grounds of ill health from ailments real (occasionally) and imaginary (mostly).

To acquire the only other acceptable excuses for absence, they were obliged to apply to the principal or dean for "exeats," which were granted for serious illness, deaths of near relations, and other urgent reasons. These passes empowered the holders to absent themselves from campus for two or three days or longer, and, like aegrotats, they were commonly obtained under false pretenses. Monier Williams, a classmate of Nigel's who went on to join the faculty as an instructor in Eastern languages after his health failed him in India, later described the genesis of what came to be known as "corn exeats":

"It was said of a dissipated and plausible youth in my time that having killed all his relations, he had to rack his brains for other expedients, till he happily hit upon the artifice of pretending that, as there was no Chiropodist in the neighbourhood, it was necessary to go to London to have certain painful excrescences removed from his feet, and so facilitate his walking with due punctuality to chapel and lectures."

Alas, this "master-stroke of invention" was taken up by others and tried once too often. The principal, after remarking that the current class was more painfully afflicted with corns than any other in his experience, enjoined the dean from granting further exeats on that plea.

When classes commenced, at 10:00 a.m., those lacking official excuses presented themselves for three hours of instruction in classics and mathematics (Mondays and Tuesdays), law, political economy, and history (Wednesdays and Thursdays), and Oriental languages (Fridays and Saturdays). Upon their dismissal, at 1:00 p.m., as recalled by another Old Haileyburian in recounting the riotous order of a typical day, they crowded into a large cellar storeroom for bread and cheese and beer, served by two "very pretty" girls. The ensuing horseplay and "coarse jesting" lasted until dinnertime, at six, followed by chapel, at eight, then "an indescribable hub-bub and uproar of oaths, songs, indecent jokes and horseplay as before," after everyone returned to the cellar. Though the "steady men" eventually retired to their rooms to hit the books, the "noisy ones" kept the party going, drinking and smoking, screaming and fighting and singing ribald songs until three or four in the morning, when "the inebriates would somehow be got to their rooms and silence would at last descend upon the Quad."

These were the men, then, whom the East India Company would shortly rely upon to uphold and reinforce what Richard Wellesley called "the stability of the British power in India." (Most of them, that is; one in five, on failing to pass their final exams, were instead offered an officer's commission in the less demanding Company cavalry.)

Men who would never be tolerated at the colleges of Oxford and Cambridge—at least not the blackest of the black sheep, known as the "Company's bad bargains." But at Haileybury they were treated with studied leniency, "for the obvious reason," wrote Monier Williams, "that every official in the College felt anxious to avoid ruining the prospects of the sons or relatives or nominees of the Court of Directors and Court of Proprietors."

Men who ended their studies as they began them, still relying upon "perusal of such stories as 'Hajji Baba' or 'Aladdin and His Wonderful Lamp'" for their ideas about the East.

Men who were advised in valedictory addresses that they would probably be sent to some remote province to function like a light set on a hill, so that "millions will watch your conduct and take their ideas of Christianity from your actions and words."

They were neither Britain's best nor Britain's brightest. But they were all of them meant for a kind of greatness, if only by association. Even as Nigel and his classmates crammed for the three-day exam that admitted them to the college, Queen Victoria—newly crowned and just out of her teens herself—took her first decisive step as sovereign and declared formally to the Privy Council her intention of marrying her first cousin, Prince Albert of Saxe-Coburg and Gotha. A reformer and innovator, Albert opposed slavery and child labor, championed free trade, education, and the improvement of working conditions, and had a particular interest in the application of science and technology to manufacturing. Their wedding, in February 1840, ushered in an era of accelerated change founded on industrial prowess and relentless imperial expansion, reaching its zenith in the only empire in history on which the sun never set. India, under Victoria, was transformed from a colonial possession into the driver of British destiny. It was up to the men from Haileybury to rise to the occasion.

Nigel's surviving correspondence mentions Haileybury only once, in passing. We have no way of knowing whether he ran with the "steady" men or the "noisy" ones. He seems, at any rate, to have acquired greater fluency in Persian than some of his classmates. Even if he amounted to one of the "bad bargains," though, it did not necessarily signify once he went East. There, noted Monier Williams approvingly, "these idle and stupid men" often proved themselves "men of great courage and pluck." Indeed, they sometimes provided better service than "their more intellectual fellows." No less a notable than John Lawrence, the Old Haileyburian (and future viceroy) under whom Nigel would serve as a tax assessor, went so far as to express his preference for weak-brained men, "provided they have a strong physique and a firm seat in the saddle."

Good bargains or bad, they all started on an equal footing once they got to India. None of them—not Nigel, not Monier Williams, the late-night readers no more than the late-night screamers and fighters— had the slightest idea what they were getting into.

3

Margalla Pass

1975

I PREPARED FOR MY own trip East by studying the language and
culture of Nepal for twelve weeks at The Evergreen State College,
in Olympia, Washington. My main instructor was Willi Unsoeld, one
of the first Americans to climb Mount Everest and the assistant director of the Peace Corps in Nepal for much of the 1960s. He often turned
over the classroom to his daughter, Devi, who at twenty-one was only
a year older than me. But she had grown up in Kathmandu and had returned several times on her own via the overland route from Europe.
It was a journey she recommended as the ideal introduction to Asia,
one that cost a fraction of the airfare from the United States — the
"Overland Guide to Nepal," in *The Last Whole Earth Catalog*, assured
travelers that a budget of no more than $100 would finance a trip from
Luxembourg to Kathmandu, meals and lodging included. It sounded
pretty good to me and several of my classmates, and in May 1975 I
joined two of them on a charter flight to Germany.

It was a decision we began to second-guess somewhere in Ana-
tolia, around three thousand miles short of our destination. Neither
Devi Unsoeld nor *The Last Whole Earth Catalog* had seen fit to address
the downside of living on greasy mutton rice for the better part of
six weeks and sharing third-class trains and cantankerous old school
buses with chickens and goats and children with fever. We persevered
because we had to, but not, ultimately, together; when we rendez-
voused in Iran with another group of students from the Nepal program, we discovered that we weren't the only ones whose camarade-

rie had eroded into conflict, and we each continued on with different companions. Mine was a woman from the San Francisco Bay area who coped with close-quarters tension by steering the conversation to pop culture trivia. It was a strategy, she confessed in Kabul, that had its drawbacks. No matter how hard she tried, she couldn't get the theme song from *The Patty Duke Show* out of her head.

Maybe it would take a change of scenery to change the channel.

It changed decisively a few days later, when the black licorice whip of asphalt unwinding ahead of the bus abruptly tunneled into the iron cagework of the fortified bridge at Attock. Far below, the full-throated torrent of the Indus churned wide and deep with snowmelt from the roof of the world.

India, at last.

Geographically, anyway. Partition had carved Pakistan out of this corner of the subcontinent in 1947. In those parts, there was no escaping history. Upstream lay Ohind, where the Macedonians under Alexander crossed into India on their bridge of boats. On the far side loomed the turrets and battlements of Attock Fort, built under instructions from the Emperor Akbar in 1583 and wrested by the Sikh emperor Ranjit Singh from the Sadozai Kingdom of Kabul in 1813. At the brink of the gorge rose the 40th Pathans War Memorial, a giant stone monolith in the shape of a .303 rifle cartridge, erected by a Punjab regiment raised by the British in the aftermath of the Indian Mutiny.

A frill of pleated tawny cliffs shimmered beyond the arch of the crenelated guardhouse that spanned the end of the bridge. The driver stopped and tried to bum a cigarette from one of the sentries. The sun beat down, and the sentry stayed put in the narrow band of shade cast by the catwalk above. If the driver wanted it, he could come and get it. The other sentry sat napping in a folding wooden chair with the barrel of his automatic nestled in the frayed canvas upper of a rubber-soled boot. A plaque affixed to a vertical girder beside him read:

WESTWOOD BAILLIE AND CO — ENGINEERS &
CONTRACTORS — LONDON — ENGLAND — 1880

I sat directly behind the driver. When he returned with his cigarette, he told me that the bridge had purposefully been built narrow, to
slow an invading army.

"Russian army," he said.

It was the first I had heard of Russian designs on India. (Rudyard
Kipling's *Kim* was on my reading list, but I had yet to crack my copy.)
Moscow seemed as far away as Timbuktu. But it was closer, after all,
than London, and the British in India had expected the Russians for
much of the nineteenth century. No army in the world was larger than
the East India Company's mercenary force of 250,000 men — except
Russia's. No empire in Asia had grown as fast as Britain's — except
Russia's. By the time the British signed a treaty with Ranjit Singh that
extended their influence northward to the line of the Indus, the Russians were probing southward to the khanates of Bukhara and Khiva.
Between the empires lay the wild mountain kingdom of Afghanistan,
its tribes and clans perpetually at one another's throats, an unnerving
realm of fratricide, patricide, and regicide, with eight changes of royal
dynasty in less than fifty years. Both powers overestimated its suscep-
tibility to foreign influence, but only the British played what came to
be known as the Great Game with the reckless abandon of a compul-
sive gambler.

The bus was still painted yellow. In make and model and probably
year, it was identical to the bus that picked me up across the street
from my house in a small town in the Pacific Northwest in the 1960s
and delivered me to elementary school. But there were two modifica-
tions for service in Pakistan. The first was a chain-link partition across
the width of the bus that divided the interior into two compartments.
The second was a working rear door that replaced the emergency exit.
Male passengers older than toddlers rode in front, females in back. Be-

fore we boarded in Peshawar, I had asked my classmate if she supposed that baby girls ever traveled in the arms of their fathers.

She gave me a look. We weren't in Afghanistan anymore, but the men around us seemed the same—ethnically Pashtun—and it was hard to tell the difference. In that country, the only thing a man ever carried in public was a rifle.

Or, sometimes, a rose. They carried red, long-stemmed roses and presented them to one another in the streets of Herat and Kandahar. There was no need to segregate the buses there. The only women out and about in Afghanistan were foreigners.

Half an hour past Attock, the driver turned off the pavement and announced a rest stop. The women stayed on the bus. The men smoked and stretched their legs. No one paid any attention to the granite obelisk that towered over us from a rocky knoll. It was the same vintage as the war memorial beside the Indus, but even taller and more commanding. I walked over to the stone steps that led up to an iron-bound door set into the base. I could make out a plaque beside the door. But it was a long, steep climb in blazing heat, and I stayed where I was.

One of the passengers joined me and introduced himself as a student at the Khyber College of Dentistry at the University of Peshawar. I'll call him Rasheed. He bent down and picked one of the wildflowers that grew on the slope beside the steps. Each of its five yellow petals was freckled with a spot of chocolate brown. These, he said, were the marks of the fingers and thumb of Muhammad.

"It is called the Prophet's Flower," he said, and handed it to me.

"You are Pashtun?" I asked, rhyming the word with "cotton."

"Pakh-toon."

He smiled as he corrected me, showing strong white teeth that must have been the envy of his classmates. A dentist with a smile like that would never need to advertise.

"Yes," he said.

Was this monument a tribute to his people, like the one at Attock? I asked.

He looked surprised.

"It is for Nicholson."

He spoke as if nothing more needed to be said, no more than Napoleon required a gloss at the Arc de Triomphe, or Lenin at Red Square.

"I'm American," I apologized.

Ahh.

Well, then.

Nicholson was a lawman, he said. Something like the sheriffs of the American West, around the same time. Except the British weren't settling the country themselves — they didn't want to live there. But they wanted peace on their borders. It was anarchy back then, every man for himself, the weak at the mercy of the strong, bandits everywhere. Anyone could see that peace depended on more civilized conditions for the native people. Laws and courts, punishment for crimes, things like that.

But the British knew they couldn't force it, not there on the North-West Frontier. No army was big enough to force it. So they decided to lead by example. They sent men like Nicholson to the lawless places. It was up to Nicholson to win the trust of the native chiefs. Then his job was to convince them to change their ways. And thereabouts, the only way to do that was to show that he was a better man than they were.

Which he had done quite famously at that very spot, soon after the Sikhs made war on the British by killing two of Nicholson's colleagues who were posted farther down the Indus. Nicholson knew it would be months before British troops reached the Punjab, so he called on hundreds of tribesmen from the adjacent hill country to join him in driving the Sikhs from a guard tower where the monument now stood, controlling the road through Margalla Pass. It was a drystone tower, built without mortar, and lacked a door. The only way to reach the top was by a ladder that the defenders pulled up behind them. There were only a few Sikhs inside, and Nicholson believed that a show of force by so many would make them surrender.

It was a gamble, though, one that depended on the staunchness of irregular native troops. And Nicholson lost. He thought that if he led the charge up the hill to the base of the tower, it would shame his men into following. The men, for their part, reasoned that if Nicholson was in front, he had no way of knowing who had stayed behind. Out of all those hundreds, only a handful of chiefs followed Nicholson. It was not until he reached the tower, under heavy matchlock fire by the Sikhs, that he realized they were on their own. They pressed themselves flat against the walls to dodge the bullets, but then the Sikhs changed tactics and hurled down heavy stones. Two of the chiefs died with their heads smashed open. Nicholson was badly hit. Finally they ran for their lives.

Reinforcements for the Sikhs were on the way. There was no time for angry words. Nicholson could barely stand. They helped him onto his horse, surrounded him in case he fell, and galloped away.

Rasheed gazed up at the monument, dark eyes shining. There were stairs inside, he told me. He had always wanted to climb them. On a clear day, one might see as far as Swat from the opening near the top. Or so it was said. Someone some years back had barred the door, saying there were bats.

Such caution in such a place! What were bats to Nicholson?

He sounded very brave, I said. But weren't structures like that usually raised to commemorate victories?

Rasheed stood silent for a long moment, perplexed.

Victories?

The British won the war, of course, and annexed the Punjab. It was theirs until Independence, then divided at Partition between India and Pakistan.

The monument was for Nicholson.

Not for what happened then and there.

It was afterwards that mattered.

As far as he knew, Margalla Pass was the last time natives failed to follow Nicholson into battle.

"There were many other incidents," he said. "He became a legend, you see. And here, I think, was the beginning of that."

And there, it seems to me forty years later, was the beginning of this. Standing there at Margalla Pass, I knew little about the British Empire, except that it was gone. But I took it for granted that its passing prompted unalloyed delight in the hearts and minds of its former subjects and their offspring. Whatever benefits they might enjoy from its material legacy—railways, irrigation schemes, the reconstruction and extension of the ancient Grand Trunk Road on which the school bus bobbed and weaved—were scant reward for all those years under the colonial thumb. I supposed that the British in that part of the world were miscreants to a man, all down the generations—in varying degrees, to be sure, but as monolithic in their essence as the obelisk looming overhead. They were the bad guys. Yet there beside me was a twentieth-century Pashtun implying the opposite, at least for a given man at a given time in given situations, someone my own age, someone educated, cheering on the cowboy instead of the Indian.

Until then I had given little thought to Nigel Halleck's life in India. Sure, before I left the States, I had promised my mother that I would look for his grave. But I knew next to nothing about him, or what sort of work he had done for what I assumed was the British government. Still, if there were good apples among the bad in those days, I rather hoped that he was one of them. And I soon found reason to think that Nigel might have been—at least by association.

Lahore was like most of the obligatory stops on the overland route to Nepal—a destination gained, only to be escaped as quickly as possible. It was too hot to move. Sightseeing was out of the question, so my classmate and I holed up in our two-rupee hotel room and watched geckos hunt cockroaches on the scarred and pitted stucco walls. Reaching for a clasp envelope to fan myself, I remembered its contents: photocopied pages from Nigel's letters home to England. In one of them, I dimly recalled, there was mention of Lahore, and I decided to see what my forebear had to say about the place. It wasn't long before I came across the first NICHOLSON, underlined twice in the margin in a bolder, darker hand than Nigel's. The second was in the Lahore letter, and there were half a dozen more in others, datelined Ambala and Bannu and Jullundur and Ludhiana, all annotating passages that referred to the officer—lieutenant in some, captain in others—by name. One of Nigel's relatives had taken pains to highlight his connection with a figure of importance, surely the Nicholson of the monument at Margalla Pass.

The Nicholson passages themselves were long on Victorian adjectives—noble, virtuous, strong, and true—but short on basic information. They revealed little about who Nicholson was or what he did. Nigel knew him and seemed to have worked with him, in more than one place, over the course of at least three years. It was clear that he thought the world of him. When I showed them to my companion, she called Nigel "besotted."

She said they sounded like love letters.

4

A Passage

December 1841

THE SUN WAS UP. Muddy waves slapped the steamer's hull. The river was wide as the Thames at Gravesend. The paddle wheel groaned against the crosscurrents of its confluence with the Bay of Bengal. The river, according to the *Hand Book for India and Egypt* that Nigel had purchased at Wm. H. Allen and Co. in London on the day he swore his covenant with the East India Company five months before, led to Calcutta.

It was supposed to be the Hooghly. But the native deckhands who had come aboard in Madras called it Ganga. They leaned over the gunwales, hands cupped to catch the splashing water. They drank and drank again. They wet their hair and washed their ears and eyes and nostrils.

The sun shone, the water ran.

"Oh, Ganga," sang the deckhands.

Saplings rose tentatively from the cheerless bank of the nearing shore. Few places in India were as holy as Sagar Island. Guano stained the pockmarked plaster of the ruined dome of the temple of Kapil Muni. On a plinth beside the entrance was an idol, thickly daubed with carmine. Its left hand held a small pot of water. In its right hand was a rosary.

Kapil Muni marked the site where Lord Vishnu had agreed to end a severe drought by permitting the waters of the celestial river Ganga to flow out of the heavens, issuing from his big toe. Since the force of the cascading waters would split the earth if left unchecked, Lord Shiva consented in turn to break their fall in the labyrinth of matted hair piled high atop his head.

On Sagar Island, too, were long enacted the rites of Ganga Sagar, intended to propitiate the forces of nature. Each January, when the sun made its transition from Capricorn to Sagittarius, as many as two hundred thousand pilgrims watched hundreds of mothers throw unconscious infants to the crocodiles and sharks lurking in the shallows. Thirty-eight years before Nigel's voyage upriver, the practice had been outlawed by the British. In a decree titled "A Regulation for Preventing the Sacrifice of Children at Saugur and other places," Governor General Richard Wellesley declared it to be murder, punishable by death. Never before had the East India Company interfered in the religious affairs of Indians.

The steamer breasted the current, barely progressing upstream. The slowness suited Nigel. He had never been nautically minded. He was Coventry-born and Coventry-bred, and no place in England was farther from tidewater than Coventry. En route to his tour of Europe before he entered Haileybury, he had been seasick before the Calais packet left the Pool of London, on the river Thames. As the river widened into its estuary, he felt better. He spent two shillings on a breakfast of cold meat, eggs, and coffee. He might as well have tossed the money into the Thames. If he successfully graduated from college, he would have to get to India, and the prospect filled him with dread. The Suez Canal was thirty years in the future. An iron vessel fitted with a screw propeller had yet to cross an ocean. The voyage by sail around the Cape of Good Hope lasted five months, sometimes six.

Seas were rough, cabins cramped and verminous. Crew members grew surly as the weeks wore on; officers responded with lashes of the cat. Much of the food was carried on the hoof, and none of it was suited to the conditions or the climate. In equatorial waters with air temperatures well above a hundred degrees, passengers in formal dress sat down nightly to roast beef, port wine, and plum pudding.

But by the time he graduated, it was possible to avoid the tedium and prolonged discomfort of the Atlantic passage. Beginning in 1835, mail for England was carried from Bombay to Suez on a small steamer built in India, then dispatched overland to ports on the Mediterranean. After coastal steamers extended the mail service to Calcutta, the next step was passenger service on the same route with a pair of paddle steamers. They rarely maintained their timetables, and the connection to Cairo involved a bone-shaking sixty-hour journey across the desert in horse-drawn wagons. Travelers continued on to Alexandria via the Nile and the Mahmoudieh Canal, on vessels that lacked the most basic amenities. In 1841, this new "steam route" was still in its infancy, and it cost more than the sea voyage. But it reduced the average travel time between India and Britain to two months, and Nigel persuaded his father to finance his fare on the packet boat operated by the Peninsular and Oriental Steam Navigation Company, from Portsmouth to Alexandria by way of Lisbon, Gibraltar, and Malta.

Like many passengers, he broke his journey in Egypt. But instead of visiting the Pyramids, he set his sights on a more exotic destination. Siwa, in the Western Desert, was a vast oasis 150 miles from Alexandria, site of a temple renowned in classical antiquity for the infallibility of the oracle within. In 334 B.C., Alexander of Macedon had crossed the slim blue mirror of the Nile and sought out the oracle to confirm his divinity and proclaim his destiny as master of the world.

It took Nigel three visits to the British legation at Alexandria to locate someone who even knew where Siwa was. He was finally referred to civil authorities at the labyrinthine Italianate palace of Muhammad Ali Pasha. There, at least, the oasis and its inhabitants enjoyed fair renown, though not for attributes that tended to encourage visitation. Debilitating fevers were mentioned, and religious fanaticism, and a wild, harlequin sort of people, immoderate in their habits. The Temple of Ammon, which housed the oracle itself, was thought to have been reduced to rubble by Bonaparte's French, expelled from Egypt forty years before by British and Ottoman forces. Another rumor held that it remained in use, the secret of its exact location guarded by its pagan keepers.

Nigel went away bemused. "So fantastic were the tales told," he wrote afterwards, that he suspected that the invention of responses to his questions had enlivened the tedium of a dull afternoon for the pasha's bureaucrats. But their well-intentioned warnings only piqued his curiosity:

"After so many stories about the place, I naturally wondered what the truth might be, and desired more than ever to see it for myself."

As far as anyone knew, the only Englishman to have visited Siwa was William George Browne. Fresh out of Oxford, he arrived in Egypt in 1792 and set out from Alexandria without asking advice or making any special preparation, apart from disguising himself as a Muslim. Though he survived the violent uproar that ensued when his imposture was discovered on the fringes of the oasis, he was sent packing without so much as having glimpsed the Temple of Ammon. Nigel nonetheless felt that he had found his cicerone when he located a copy of Browne's *Travels in Africa, Egypt, and Syria, from the Year 1792 to 1798*, published in London in 1799. He supposed that he might manage the same journey, and with a happier outcome, simply by learning from Browne's mistakes. (The sort of mistakes, sad to say, that Browne himself continued to make; he subsequently set off with similar abandon for the land of the Tartars and was murdered by robbers between Tabriz and Teheran.)

Above all, Nigel deemed it unwise to set out for Siwa until he could question someone who actually knew the place. His inquiries led him to a Frenchman who supervised irrigation projects for the Egyptian Ministry of Public Works. Louis Linant de Bellefonds told Nigel that Siwa had been safe for travel for the past five or six years. The oasis now contained a government office; archaeological work, he understood, was under way. Far from being ruined, the Temple of Ammon was relatively well preserved. As for the journey itself, date caravans left Memphis for Siwa at regular intervals. It was necessary only to secure a place in one, and hire a reliable interpreter. The expense, by English standards, was minuscule.

Linant offered his assistance in making the arrangements and procuring a firman, or passport. He advised Nigel to dress as a Bedouin —not as a disguise, but for comfort's sake, and to better blend in with his surroundings—and dictated a brief shopping list. It included fish-skin sandals, a striped brown woolen coat, a canvas shirt secured by a leather belt, and a kaffiyeh scarf, kept on by a cord of camel's hair. Sleeping arrangements were simplicity itself. There was no need for a tent, which was useful only in the rainy season. The sheepskin that covered the camel's saddle by day became a mattress at night. Food bags served as pillows, coats as a blanket. The journey might take ten days.

What happened next is unknown. A gap in Nigel's correspondence shrouds the rest of his stay in Egypt. No published works place him in Siwa. Nor do his surviving letters mention his presence there—though one, posted from India in 1846, compares a British official to "M. Linant, whose assistance proved so valuable in Egypt."

Whether he made it to the oasis or not, what really mattered was Nigel's decision to see it for himself. It transformed a gesture into a commitment, the romantic fantasy of following in Alexander's foot-steps into a shopping list for fish-skin sandals and a red-and-yellow-striped kaffiyeh. His decision was also a declaration, for a man who chose to see for himself was a man who meant to think for himself.

Such a man could look forward to a complicated career in British India.

SAGAR ISLAND WAS once the home of ten thousand people. In 1832, thirty years after Richard Wellesley put an end to the sacrifices that preserved it from the ravages of nature, the entire island was inundated by floodwaters twelve feet deep. Seven thousand people drowned. In the aftermath, crops failed in the salt-saturated soil. The starving survivors, many of whom contracted typhoid fever, crowded into Calcutta, where parents "were at last reduced to the necessity of supporting their lives by the sale of their children, the most emaciated of whom sold at last for one rupee only," according to a report in the London medical journal *The Lancet* on the epidemic that struck the city after the refugees arrived.

Even the tigers had abandoned the island, a crewman on the steamer told Nigel.

Even the snakes had slithered away.

He left it for Nigel to draw his own conclusions about cause and effect. The natives, plainly, had reached their own.

Nigel, for his part, thought it only natural that Indians would blame the actions of outsiders when misfortune struck the island. He saw the simple sense in it for superstitious minds, the day-and-night contrast of before and after.

The few died, so the many lived.

All died, and nothing lived.

The sun shone, the water ran.

"Oh, Ganga," sang the deckhands.

He imagined Shiva's tangled tresses. He pictured Vishnu's big toe. Two hours past Sagar Island, there was still no sign of Calcutta. As far as the eye could see, there was nothing to see, nothing but low flat leached-out lonely country that nothing but a fallen meteor would ever plow.

He wondered if the river was really the Hooghly.

He wondered if it really led anywhere.

Then the steamer rounded the great muddy bend called Garden Reach, and there it was.

Newer than New York, richer than Rome, more populous than either, revealing itself in a sweeping panorama that took your breath away.

There was Government House, with its dome and Palladian front. There were the pediments and colonnades of Town Hall, its noble complement. There was Bishop's College, with its pointed Gothic arches and slender, elegant clock tower. There were the houses like palaces, rising in their shining stucco masses from flowerbeds filled with imported English blooms on the undulating riverbank, their verandas spacious, their pillars lofty, their profiles Athenian.

There was broad Chowringhee Road, with its mansions on one side and the vast lawns of the Maidan on the other, and beyond the Maidan —large as Phoenix Park in Dublin—loomed the colossal brick octagon of the citadel, Fort William. Judged impregnable by engineers, it contained sufficient provisions and stores to withstand a siege as long as that of Troy. Beneath its ramparts, from quays jutting into the river, rose the stately masts of tall ships, crowded at their moorings by a thousand less imposing craft of every size and description, from the bulbous green *budgerow* barges to the delicate little *bauleahs*, pleasure boats for two, with private cabins discreetly screened by wooden blinds.

"There cannot be a scene more beautiful, connected with the bustle and business of life; and the heart of the traveller feels light within him as he views it," wrote Nigel's contemporary Joachim Stocqueler, in a passage that might serve as a prophecy for the wide-eyed young gentleman from Coventry:

"He experiences undefinable emotions of joy, and he imagines he is in a country in which he could dwell unrepiningly for ever, voluntarily debarred from the prospect of ever again beholding the gloomier shores of England."

5

A Griffin

Nigel took a deep breath and stepped onto the landing ghat, joining the pageant of jostling humanity.

Enrobed and beturbaned, barefoot and beseeching.

Umbrella bearers and parakeet vendors.

Tall, stern sentinels, black as midnight; spindle-shanked Brahmins, fair as Finns.

Slender, supple women, jars balanced on their heads, children astride their hips, swinging up the tide-washed steps past wizened water carriers in loincloths, filling goatskin bags with the turbid flow, seasoned with mango peels and coconut husks, fouled with bilge water and the carcasses of dogs.

The sun, the smoke, the laughter.

The chattering and salaaming.

"Sahib!"

"Sahib!"

"Sahib!"

It took a moment for him to realize that the clamor of the palanquin bearers competing for a fare was directed at him. As a foreigner, he existed in a state of ritual impurity, outside India's complex system of hereditary castes and subcastes. But his place in the social order was as fixed as any Hindu's. In a society based on knowing one's place, he could no more choose his own than the lowest sweeper could choose to be a Brahmin priest. A sahib—the respectful term used by natives to address Englishmen, corresponding to "sir" but more freighted with obeisance—was born, not made. And he was born, above all, to command natives. He was a ruler, but also a prisoner—of expectations, good and bad. A sahib had to act like a sahib. He was resolute in his actions, definite in his prejudices, dignified in his manner.

Gabbling unintelligible abuse to their competitors, the half-dozen bearers jostled before him, pushing one another on the slippery steps and banging their conveyances together in the struggle for his business. He wished that he might walk instead. He had ridden in a palanquin exactly once, on a stifling day in Aden, the British colony established in 1839 on the Arabian coast as a coaling station for vessels on the steam route. There he had been borne for two or three miles, lurching up and down steep slopes and peering out at the scenery through gaps in the dusty shutters that preserved his splendid isolation. After five days aboard the steamer out of Suez, he would have liked to stretch his legs. But one of the other passengers, a memsahib returning East with her husband after home leave, told him that such a thing simply "wasn't done." She clutched her parasol in the stiff, hot wind on the quay and told him that an Englishman never walked where he might be carried.

Dignity, she said, must never be sacrificed for comfort's sake.

The natives had a word for it: *pukka*, meaning genuine—absolutely genuine—and in India one ever strived to present oneself as a pukka sahib.

It was the pukka sahib, she said, whom natives trusted and respected most. Indians set great store by predictability. Any deviation from the standard risked exciting their liveliest suspicions, and imperiled the prospect of their immediate help.

Well, he would need a lot of help in India; that was plain enough. And he supposed that she knew what she was talking about. On the journey out, she was one of the only passengers who spoke of India at all, albeit mostly on the finer points of colonial housekeeping. (To be confident of snake-free bedding, he was advised, one put the legs of the bed into saucers filled with carbolic powder.)

He swept his eyes across the phalanx of beseeching bearers and nodded decisively at a muscular pair with glossy oiled hair and dust in the creases of their elbows. Framing his words carefully in Urdu, he said that they looked like brothers.

They eyed him blankly.

He tried again in Persian, the language of the law courts and imperial decrees, but an unlikely lingua franca on the rough-and-tumble waterfront of Bengal's first city.

Nothing.

"Brothers?" he said finally, in English.

"Yes, sahib," said one.

"Very good, sahib," said the other.

They bowed their heads respectfully, and he bent down to clamber inside.

He was a sahib, all right, but he was also a griffin.

No one seems to know how greenhorns in the East India Company's service came to be called after the majestic creatures with the body of a lion and the head and wings of an eagle. It was true that griffins appeared in Greek mythology as guardians of treasure and priceless possessions, and that India for the British represented both. It was true that the Persians regarded griffins as protectors of their bodily selves —from evil, witchcraft, and "secret slander"—and that the British prescribed their judicial system to cure identical Indian complaints.

It was also true that early Christians discerned in the union of a terrestrial beast and an aerial bird a symbol of Christ, who was both human and divine, and that British rule in India was routinely justified at home on religious grounds. But none of those noble associations fit the comical figure cut by the "griff" in his clumsy encounters with "the custom of the country." A typical portrait was sketched by Francis John Bellew, who was posted to Calcutta a few years after Nigel:

A Griffin is the Johnny Newcome of the East,—one whose European manners and ideas stand out in ludicrous relief when contrasted with those, so essentially different in most respects, which appertain to the new coun-

try of his sojourn. The ordinary period of Griffinhood is a year, by which time the novus homo, if apt, is supposed to have acquired a sufficient familiarity with the language, habits, customs, and manners of the country, both Anglo-Indian and Native, so as to preclude his making himself supremely ridiculous by blunders, gaucheries, and the indiscriminate application of English standards to states of things to which those rules are not always exactly adapted. To illustrate by example:— a good-natured Englishman, who should present a Brahmin who worships the cow with a bottle of beef-steak sauce, would be decidedly "griffinish," particularly if he could be made acquainted with the nature of the gift; nevertheless, beef-steak, per se, is an excellent thing in an Englishman's estimation, and a better still with the addition of the before-mentioned condiment.

The cluelessness of newcomers about everyday life in India was exacerbated by a tacit conspiracy of silence before they got there. The reluctance of those in the know to enlighten those outside it dated back to the freewheeling era of the buccaneers who had established the Company in India, when it was generally thought best that what happened in Calcutta should stay in Calcutta. In the days when nearly all of the city's British inhabitants had come East to amass a fortune as quickly as possible, few, wrote the social historian William Dalrymple, "had much interest in either the mores of the country they were engaged in plundering, or in the social niceties of that which they had left behind."

Nor did the nominal pillars of colonial morality go out of their way to set a higher tone. One curate was described as a "drunken tosspot." Another, an army chaplain in Calcutta called Mr. Blunt, was condemned as "an incomprehensible young man" by an attorney under the chief justice of Bengal, who reported that Blunt "got abominably drunk and in that disgraceful condition exposed himself to both soldiers and sailors, talking all sorts of bawdy and ribaldry, and singing scraps of the most blackguard and indecent songs, so as to render himself a common laughing stock."

Griffins—most of them freed from adult supervision for the first time in their lives—had long been regarded by common consent as the most debauched of a dissolute lot. Even on their best behavior, in what passed for polite society, they amused themselves at dinner by throwing half-eaten chickens across the table. (That Calcutta's Englishwomen tended to throw only bread and pastry—and then "only after a little cherry brandy," noted one observer—was judged "the highest refinement of wit and breeding.") Another traveler complained about the "difficulties and embarrassments" that "generally involve the young Writers," with special reference to "the keeping of race horses" and "extravagant parties and entertainments." Still another, more nostalgically, recalled that "the costly champagne suppers of the Writers Building were famous, and long did the old walls echo to the joyous songs and loud rehearsing tally-hoes."

By the time Nigel took up residence in Calcutta, new arrivals had more time on their hands than ever. Thanks to the continuing tension between the Court of Directors in London and its governors general on the other side of the world, all incoming civil servants found themselves in the same illogical boat—Company-certified in England as masters of three Asiatic languages, Company-compelled in India to demonstrate mastery of one in twelve months' time. Griffins were technically unemployed. During the year allotted them for attaining fluency in Bengali, Hindustani, or Persian, they received a monthly stipend of three hundred rupees—roughly £30 in the sterling of the day —and a small sum for a munshi, or tutor. They had no official duties, and could be assigned none.

There were, however, moderating influences. Stricter Victorian morality had begun to take hold. The governor general, Lord Ellenborough, was something of a new broom. A distant relative of George Washington, and no friend of the Company, he wanted the Crown to take over the administration of India for the Indians' own good. In the meantime, he meant to put the Company's own house in order from a moral standpoint, setting an example for impressionable natives. Acting on a matter that was painfully close to home—his wife had deserted him to live in a Bedouin harem—he subjected to stricture for the first time sexual liaisons with Indians, long tolerated on grounds that, as one army officer put it, "allowances are to be made for the ungovernable passions . . . which absolutely must have vent in this stimulating climate."

Among the more prodigious "venters" was Sir David Ochterlony, appointed British resident to the Mughal court at Delhi in 1803, who kept thirteen concubines. Another Company servant, mentioned in a popular guide to life in Calcutta in the early nineteenth century, showed less restraint and maintained sixteen. Provisions for native mistresses, or bibis, featured in at least one out of every four of the wills filed in India by European men until well into the nineteenth century, and many more Indian women were undoubtedly kept by sahibs who left no official paper trail behind them. Nor, in the aftermath of Ellenborough's condemnation of such attachments as "unnatural," did the bibis themselves disappear, though recorded bequests to them all but ceased by 1850.

Another long shadow over the tradition of unbridled revelry was cast by the Company's withdrawal from trade. The typical griffin no longer debarked in Calcutta with the expectation of riches to come. He simply expected to do better than he would have done at home, where the economy reeled from the movement of rural labor into towns. More than one in ten of the British people were paupers. Industrialization had so far created all manner of ill-paid factory jobs but little in the way of opportunities for educated young men. The siren song of India for most was security, not serendipity. Once they arrived, wrote Company historian Brian Gardner, life quickly became a "sapping battle against debt, gout, and the heat, with the prospect of the English counties and a pension far ahead."

This made for a new air of seriousness about the Writers Building, a three-story redbrick block of identical apartments near Government House. Each of its residents knew that he would face a board of examiners at the end of his freshman year in India. If he failed to display the requisite fluency in an Oriental language, he returned to his studies for six weeks. If he failed a second time, he was deprived of his appointment and shipped back to England.

Nigel's two rooms in the Writers Building led one into the other. The walls were painted white, with green-shuttered windows. A low bookcase divided the space. Pride of place in his library, he assured his parents, belonged to the Bible they had presented him as a parting gift on the quay at Southampton. More well-thumbed, perhaps, judging from the enthusiastic references in his correspondence, was *Les Six Voyages de Jean Baptiste Tavernier*, first published in 1676. Written by a goldsmith and dealer in precious gems, it riveted readers until the end of the nineteenth century with the sumptuousness of its narrative. Tavernier's India was a land of both fabulous riches—"We turn over in our hands Koh-i-Noors and play with trays full of rubies, emeralds, and sapphires"—and everyday plenty, where "even in the smallest villages rice, flour, butter, milk, beans and other vegetables, sugar and sweetmeats can be procured in abundance." It was a vision that whetted Nigel's appetite from the very beginning for what he imagined as the "real India."

His first order of business, though, was to establish himself in Calcutta society. Ideally, he would have possessed a letter of introduction to Lord Ellenborough, and his reception at Government House would certify his status as a young gentleman of promise and distinction. Afterwards, socially speaking, everything would fall into place—invitations to the best houses and early entrée into the sporting circles of the Bengal Jockey Club and the Calcutta Hunt. The letters he had managed to procure, however, were addressed to less grand households, none of them blood relations and only one with a connection to his family at all, through a distant relative of his father's partner in law. Deeply conscious that he was neither wealthy nor titled, he called on each in turn, expecting no better than a perfunctory welcome.

To his relief, he discovered that Calcutta was no London. The elasticity of its snobbery reflected the circumstances of what remained a commercially minded elite, enjoying a style of living that few could have managed in England. Outside of none-too-onerous working hours, which began after elevenses and ended at four or five in the afternoon, they were attended by retinues of servants — ten or twelve for bachelors, upwards of fifty for socially prominent families. Their beautiful detached houses, stuccoed on the outside to resemble stone and surrounded by gardens, earned Calcutta the sobriquet "City of Palaces." The rooms were large and windowed to the floors, with lofty ceilings, fine Persian carpets, marble tables, Venetian mirrors, luxurious couches. To every bedroom was attached a "bathing room," and French doors opened onto deep, columned verandas that ran the length of each floor and protected the interior from the heat of the sun.

Some kept racehorses. Many hunted: leopards, hyenas, hogs, antelope, deer of all descriptions, hares, partridges, snipe, quail. But for all their manner of privilege, they were most of them conscious they were not to it born. Nigel's origins in an old family of some provincial distinction served him well enough after all. Within a few weeks of his arrival, the honor of his presence was requested at two dinner parties. Those led in turn to the promise of mingling with "the beauty and fashion of Calcutta" at the weekly race meetings on the course beside Fort William.

Next on the agenda was hiring a munshi. Mindful of his embarrassment with the bearers on the quay, he decided that, since he was living in Bengal, he had better learn Bengali. He persisted in his decision even after discovering that nearly all fledgling civil servants received appointments in outlying areas where Urdu was more commonly spoken. He regarded it, he told his parents, as a challenge:

"I am advised that proficiency in Sanskrit is of great benefit in attempting mastery of the Bengali Language — you will remember that such proficiency as I can boast in Oriental Languages is limited to the Persian and to a lesser extent the Urdu, with my marks in Sanskrit only just barely 'up to snuff.' I should not be surprised that you wonder at my recklessness, but given this opportunity I think it is worthwhile to remediate a weakness if possible rather than accept it as a limiter on the course of my ambitions in the future."

Besides, he added, he was sure enough of his Persian that he was considering reading for an honor in languages in the subject at the College of Fort William, which survived from the Wellesley era as a small language school. Should he pass, he would receive a gold medal, a substantial cash gratuity (£160, more than five times the amount of his first-year stipend), and immediate qualification for an appointment, regardless of how well he took to Bengali.

Nigel's interview with a prospective tutor introduced him for the first time to an educated Indian. The munshi was fat and voluble, with eyes like pools of obsidian. He produced a letter of reference, furred at the edges and dated 1839. During the previous year, it stated, the writer had employed Mr. C——, a native of Howrah, as a tutor in the language and culture of Bengal. His performance was satisfactory and his habits were clean. At the conclusion of the writer's studies, he had paid Mr. C—— the customary bonus.

Nigel handed back the letter. He pointed out that the reference was more than two years old. Had the munshi tutored any pupils since?

Indeed he had.

Not, however, English pupils.

And not, he regretted to say, in Calcutta.

He had taken a position at Gopalganj, in Bihar, hundreds of miles to the northwest. His employer and pupil was the local squire of those parts, called a zamindar, a very rich man who wished to learn English in order to become even richer. But Gopalganj had proved intolerable. It lacked books and newspapers and coffeehouses. One felt in Gopalganj the loneliness of living too close to the land.

The conversation ended an hour later, after Nigel had satisfied the munshi's curiosity about the differences between Frenchmen and Englishmen, the physiognomy of Queen Victoria, and the status of the Indians and Persians who taught at Haileybury. He had thought that he was interviewing the munshi, he wrote afterwards, but the munshi had interviewed him. He had intended to sleep on any offer of employment —one could not be rushed into a decision to share the company of a native for two hours a day, six days a week. But it was the munshi who continued to pose the questions even as he took his leave.

Should they schedule their meeting time for eleven o'clock in the morning?

Or would earlier suit?

Half past ten perhaps?

It remained for Nigel to settle it, then—even as he understood that it was already settled, that the transaction between them was governed by what he vaguely recognized as the "custom of the country," that what finally settled the matter was the munshi's unaffected certitude that it was settled.

Loneliness, Nigel soon realized, was not limited to provincial towns like Gopalganj. For all Calcutta's bustle and self-conscious grandeur, the number of permanent white residents was minuscule, less than one-tenth the population of Coventry. With most of the civil servants of Nigel's generation stationed upcountry, and the young army officers in the vicinity isolated in the cantonments of Barrackpore and Dum Dum, some distance from the city, opportunities for friendship outside the circle of his fellow griffins at the Writers Building were limited to older Company officials and their wives. At times, he admitted to his parents, he suffered from the want of "congenial companionship."

Then there was the climate. "Two monsoons is the age of a man," ran the Anglo-Indian proverb, and a shocking number of Englishmen never lived to see a third. Calcutta's Park Street cemetery, which opened in 1809, was packed so tightly with monuments, columns, urns, and obelisks within a few years' time that one observer reported that "on both sides of the road . . . you see nothing beyond it."

Nigel felt fortunate to be settling in during the Cold Weather—the healthiest time of year. It gave him a chance to acclimatize before the onset, in March, of the dreaded Hot Weather. But there was no seasonal respite that year from thoughts of death. The news out of Afghanistan saw to that.

What came to be known as the First Anglo-Afghan War had been started by the British two years before, with the intent of installing a client prince, called Shah Shuja, on the Kabul throne. The Company's Army of the Indus had seen to Shuja's installation, but its troops proved unable to secure his reign. Word of an uprising in Kabul and the murder of the British political agent there reached Government House in mid-December 1841, about the same time that Nigel arrived in Calcutta. The end of January brought the first reports of the army's catastrophic retreat. Of the sixteen thousand troops and camp followers who left Kabul at the beginning of the year, only Dr. William Brydon survived the slaughter that ensued in the treacherous gorges and passes that led to the Afghan frontier. Grievously wounded, he appeared at the gates of the British fort outside Jalalabad on January 13, clinging to his exhausted, dying horse.

News of England's worst defeat since the Battle of Hastings shocked Calcutta profoundly. "No one talks of anything but Afghanistan," Nigel wrote to his parents. "All speak with great authority on what the new governor [Lord Ellenborough] must do, and the obscurity of what he can do in no way detracts from the mystery of what he will do."

They would all be deep into the Hot Weather before Ellenborough ended the suspense. He was not a modest man, and though he had never served under arms, he suspected in himself a genius for military command. (It was a suspicion that Prime Minister Robert Peel did not share; before Ellenborough left London, Peel turned down his request for the old courtesy title of captain general in addition to that of governor general.) From the moment he reached India, however, he found reason for prudence in exercising his martial authority. On February 21, as his ship hove in sight of the fort at Madras, the captain informed him of the tragic message conveyed by the signals on its flagstaff. The Army of the Indus was no more.

A fresh disaster occurred almost immediately. The garrison at the

fortified city of Ghazni, whose capture in 1839 had ended native resistance to the initial British invasion, surrendered to the Afghans.
Despite a guarantee of safe conduct, most of its Indian enlisted men
—called sepoys—were promptly massacred; the rest were sold into
slavery. Two large garrisons remained in Afghanistan. One held Kandahar, south of Ghazni. The other had fought off the besieging Afghans at Jalalabad, east of Kabul. Both commanders, whose dispatches
emphasized their desire to secure the release of British officers taken
prisoner at Ghazni, awaited instructions from the governor.

Fearing further losses, Ellenborough finally issued an order that
called for both forces to retreat to India. The prisoners, he implied,
would be abandoned. He changed his mind in late June, after receiving a rousing dispatch from Arthur Wellesley, Duke of Wellington
and a former Whig prime minister. Though the full extent of the loss
sustained on the Afghan frontier was not yet understood in England,
Wellesley began by observing that Britain would not recover "for some
time" from the blow to its moral authority, political power, and influence. It behooved Ellenborough, then, to seize the initiative:

"It is impossible to impress upon you too strongly the Notion of the
importance of the Restoration of Reputation in the East. Our enemies
in France, the United States, and wherever found are now rejoicing in
Triumph upon our Disasters and Degradation. You will teach them
that their triumph is premature."

The dispatch carried the imprimatur of Queen Victoria. It seems
likely that she personally prompted Wellesley to add, "There is not
a Moslem heart from Pekin to Constantinople which will not vibrate
when reflecting upon the fact that the European ladies and other females attached to the troops at Cabul were made over to the tender
mercies of the Moslem Chief who had murdered the representative of
the British Government at the Court of the Sovereign of Afghanistan."

Wellesley left it for Ellenborough to decide whether to act of-
fensively and invade Afghanistan again, or to "carry on our operations with more caution." Persuaded that he had underestimated the

strength of feeling at home, but unwilling to risk the danger of a prolonged reoccupation, the governor issued amended orders on July 4.
The garrisons would withdraw from Afghanistan by way of Kabul, in
a pincer movement on the city that would permit them to free British prisoners while inflicting "just, but not vindictive punishment" on
their tormentors.

With this "Army of Retribution" on the march at last, the long wait
for news of its exploits began. At the same time, to Nigel's relief, another wait ended. The hard winds blew from the Bay of Bengal, and
cloud castles loomed in the superheated sky. All Calcutta watched their
nearing, darkening, lowering ramparts.

"You can have no idea how the hotness strikes one like a blow," he
wrote home to Coventry. "There can be no honour in suffering the assault, only cowering before its awful brutality."

The parched, cracked earth itself seemed to hold its breath as the
clouds closed in on the merciless sun. Then, in a dreamlike moment of
arrested time, the Hot Weather kept its yearly promise, and culminated
in cataclysm.

Bṛṣṭi āsā.

The rains come.

He marveled at the economy of the native tongue, and approved of
it. What use was a word like "torrential" when it proved so inadequate
to its descriptive task? The rains fell with the force of projectiles, the
weight of heavy elements. The rains fell relentlessly, for several hours
each day; they fell noisily, clattering on the roof above and hissing in
the leaves outside. They fell, he was tempted to say, with a vengeance.

And yet.

The rains were the lifeblood of the paddy, the companion of the
plow. The rains fed India, and just a few days' delay in their onset
in any given province could mean famine there later, after they went
away.

And yet.

Like Lord Shiva, who embodied both creation and destruction, what the rains gave with the one hand they took with the other. The rains only quickened the frequency of the somber processions on Park Street. The Hot Weather assaulted the body, enervating and dehydrating; the rainy season invaded it, and proved deadlier still. It was in the stinking water tanks of Calcutta that Robert Koch would isolate the bacillus that causes cholera. It was during the rains in Calcutta that Ronald Ross would identify the mosquito as the vector for malaria.

Neither of these pioneers in bacteriology and pathology had yet been born when Nigel wrote home anxiously of cholera in Calcutta. He had reason to worry. Cholera, according to a report published earlier that year in *The Lancet,* had killed 18,115 people in Calcutta in the years 1832–1838. Options for treatment were limited. Bloodletting had fallen out of favor as "deadly." Patients at the city's General Hospital were subjected instead to "unceasing exhibition of ammonia," combined with doses of calomel and opium. But whether this "stimulating plan" qualified as a medical advance was debatable. "The majority of them die now," admitted one surgeon, "as they did in our earlier experience."

Smallpox was another serial killer. Tens of thousands had died in the epidemics of the 1830s, and the virus would return to Calcutta in 1843. Brucellosis, then called "gastric remittent fever," periodically reached epidemic proportions, as did bronchitis; both proved "extensively fatal." Amoebic and bacillary dysentery afflicted almost everyone at one time or another, weakening the young and strong and killing the old and weak.

"Two monsoons is the age of a man."

Nigel quoted the proverb to the munshi, who told him not to worry.

Those who succumbed so promptly were the married men, who brought out their wives and lived too softly.

"Too many servants, too much sickness coming into house."

What killed so many British, said the munshi, was not keeping to themselves.

6

Ghazipur

1975

IT TOOK MY classmate and me a week to get from Lahore to Benares, a distance of seven hundred miles. Just crossing into India from Pakistan consumed most of a day. There was no through bus service. Along the border was a no-man's-land a mile wide, which travelers were obliged to negotiate on foot. It was the height of the pre-monsoon Hot Weather. I shouldered my fifty-five-pound backpack and reflected on the absurdity of hauling a mountaineering ice axe and crampons across the featureless Punjab Plain, with the air temperature well above the century mark and the relative humidity just below it. Weedy marijuana plants lined the path to India. "Do you have any narcotics?" was the first thing we were asked when we staggered into Indian passport control.

Rudyard Kipling called the Grand Trunk Road that we followed to Benares "a river of life." But that was for natives. For sahibs and memsahibs, it was closer to a via dolorosa. Fatalities from heatstroke were so common when the British rebuilt and extended the road across the breadth of India that they constructed adjacent cemeteries for the interment of Europeans, at twelve-mile intervals for fifteen hundred miles. As we sweated our way eastward, it occurred to me that Nigel might conceivably be buried in any one of them. I did the math, and plumbed for the first time—but not the last—the depths of my regret for that easy promise to my mother.

At Benares, the old highway veered south, and our route to Nepal followed the course of the Ganges eastward to Patna. We decided to splurge on a few hours' relief from the heat and asked the clerk at the railway station if there were two seats available in air-conditioned class on the Vibhuti Express.

There were indeed, he beamed.

The problem was that only one compartment in air-conditioned class on the Vibhuti Express was, in fact, air-conditioned.

And it was fully booked. He had sold the tickets himself.

He picked up the rubber stamp resting on its ink pad beside him and wielded it like a gavel.

"Sold and stamped," he said, and suggested that we take a minibus.

The minibus, which turned out to be operated by his brother-in-law, made it fifty-odd miles to Ghazipur before it threw a rod. The driver assured us that we would reach our destination before dark; Patna was only a hundred miles farther down National Highways 19 and 84. Between ourselves we duly christened him Big Brother, and without much enthusiasm accepted his advice to make the most of the wait for a mechanic's ministrations and see the sights.

Of these there were two, on opposite banks of the Ganges. On the far side rose the redbrick facades of the Government Opium and Alkaloid Works, founded by the East India Company in 1820 and in continuously profitable operation ever since. Its grounds comprised more than forty acres; its employees numbered nearly a thousand. Its output served the global pharmaceutical industry and was whisked on special high-security trains to New Delhi and Bombay for export. According to the driver of the cycle rickshaw who conveyed us to the riverbank, it was the largest opium factory in the world.

No tours, though.

"No tastings?" I wondered.

The driver laughed.

No tastings for anyone but the monkeys who infested the grounds. They were all addicts, he said, from drinking the slurry that flowed from the factory in wastewater ditches.

Hundreds of monkeys, stoned out of their minds.

"Most comical," said the driver.

The attraction on our side of the river, decidedly more solemn, was open to the public. Sweeping immaculate lawns encircled an immense mausoleum, its heavy dome supported by a peristyle of twelve Doric columns. Flanking the sarcophagus within the rotunda stood generic figures of a Hindu, a Muslim, a British officer, and a native soldier, united in mourning the loss of the governor general interred there.

CHARLES CORNWALLIS, 1ST MARQUESS CORNWALLIS
1738–1805

I recognized the surname of the general whose capitulation to the combined French-American forces under General George Washington at Yorktown in 1781 had effectively decided the American War of Independence. I supposed that this Charles was a relative. But the English inscription beneath the statuary made it clear that he was one and the same.

"Great man," the rickshaw driver had intoned.

His regard was evidently shared by whoever replenished the bright fresh flowers that encircled the cenotaph. Natives, to be sure—sleepy, dusty Ghazipur seemed an unlikely locale for a colony of Cornwallis descendants.

Cornwallis, read the monument's inscription, had served two terms as governor general of India. He first took office in 1786, preceding Richard Wellesley. He returned in 1805, after the East India Company directors finally called time on Wellesley's expansionist activities. I knew next to nothing about Cornwallis. But there was no telling how much mischief he had gotten up to, having taken charge of India not once but twice. The meticulous maintenance of his tomb surprised me. Such a place ought by rights to have long since fallen into wrack and ruin. Even his epitaph anticipated its decay:

This monument, erected by the British inhabitants of Calcutta, attests their sense of those virtues which will live in the remembrance of grateful millions, long after it shall have mouldered into dust.

The virtues in question were enumerated by the monument's inscription, which also commemorated victories in battle against Americans in the Carolinas, Irish rebels in Connacht, and Indians under
Tipu Sultan, ruler of Mysore. Chief among them was Cornwallis' pro-
bity, which is conceded today by even the most censorious historians
of colonial rule. His first term of office followed the governorships of
Robert Clive and Warren Hastings, both of whom amassed fortunes in
India and returned home to face inquiries into the propriety of their
conduct. Unlike his predecessors, Cornwallis shrank from the prospect
of making money. He even declined to draw his full salary of £31,000,
worth the equivalent of $750,000 today. He moreover held underlings
to a standard that matched his own. For the first time, Company administrators were forbidden to engage in private trade or any other financial dealings. Transgressors were routinely sent home.

Cornwallis also acted to prohibit outright child slavery, introduced
legislation to protect native weavers from exploitation by Company
employees, and founded a mint in Calcutta that benefited the poor by
stabilizing Indian currency as cash replaced barter in the rural economy. Shortly after his return to India, he set out by barge up the Ganges to negotiate with chiefs of the Maratha Confederacy, who were as-
tonished to be offered agreements that restored to them huge swaths
of territory they had lost to the martial ardor of the Wellesley brothers. By the time Cornwallis reached Ghazipur, he had reduced British
holdings in northern India to Delhi, the upper Ganges, and the basin
of the Jumna. Calcutta still ruled more than half the subcontinent, and
the Company remained the major power. But retrenchment was clearly
the order of the day.

As fate would have it, though, the day was nearly done. When Cornwallis debarked in Calcutta that summer, he had struck the diarist William Hickey as "a wreck of what he had been when formerly in Bengal"; the voyage upriver at the height of the Hot Weather hastened his
decline. He was too ill to continue past Ghazipur. Letters posted there
in his name were written by his secretaries, and there was talk that he

had lost his mind before he finally succumbed to fever. He was a rather tubby fellow, with a pronounced squint, who wrote to a friend that he had accepted his appointment "much against my will, and with grief of heart." Above all else in life, he preferred the homely pleasures of an English country house. Yet there he finally rested in the lee of an opium factory, on the banks of a river that issued from Vishnu's big toe.

After I discovered the passages about John Nicholson in the fragments of Nigel's letters that I read in Lahore, I had made it a practice to scan them nightly for references to the locales we would pass through the following day. There weren't many. My most recent find was an amusing story about J——, a missionary he had met in 1843 who despaired of his posting to Benares, with its funeral pyres and its pilgrims and its chanting priests, the earthly abode of Lord Shiva and holiest city of the world's oldest religion. After failing to secure a single conversion there, J—— was struck with inspiration when he learned of the thriving community of Christians in the Portuguese colony of Goa, south of Bombay. It was in Goa that the Jesuits responded in 1542 to a royal call from Lisbon to evangelize the Indies, and it was in the environs of Goa that J—— hoped to found a new mission. There he would commence the harvesting of souls from a field plowed already by the Society of Jesus. Thousands of Indian Catholics had already taken the first step toward salvation. All that remained was to free them from the yoke of Rome.

Since Ghazipur was a detour from our intended route, it was not until I perused Nigel's letters again in Patna that I recognized it as a place where he had spent some time himself, conducting official business. The nature of the business seemed almost deliberately opaque, as if he was concealing it from his parents. I wondered if opium had anything to do with it.

7

A Safe and Prudent Distance

A TIGER DID THAT?"
Nigel stared at the enormous scar on the arm of a dockhand shouldering mailbags on a ramshackle wharf on a tidal waterway just west of the main outflow of the Ganges, Brahmaputra, and Meghna rivers. The dockhand repeated himself:

"*Shere*, sahib."

He had been in a boat with his cousin on one of the narrow streams that threaded through the mangrove thickets of the river deltas. The tiger sprang from the densely packed trees along the bank, knocking his cousin into the water. To save his cousin, he jumped onto the tiger, pushing its head underwater. In the struggle, its claws raked his arm. But then it started to swim away, and they clambered back into their boat.

The dockhand smiled. His teeth were stained a delicate pink from chewing betel leaf. Nigel had heard that there were Indian river dolphins of a similar color. He longed to see them.

It was February 1843. After fourteen months in India, Nigel was on his first foray outside Calcutta, en route to a temporary posting in the revenue office at Dacca, the great metropolis of Bengal before the British seized control from the Mughal nawab and shifted the capital to Calcutta. He had passed his language examination barely a year after his arrival, twelve weeks ahead of schedule. Though he came up short in his effort to obtain a degree of honor in Persian, with its handsome prize of £160, he managed one in Urdu and received £80 instead.

No one would call his future in Dacca an exciting one. Filling in for an assistant to the collector whose home leave had been extended, he would spend his days recalculating land tax rates based on reports from field inspectors. His impulse in volunteering to serve in Dacca was purely romantic. He had heard it described as the Venice of the East, and he wanted to see it for himself.

As the vessel bobbed alongside the wharf, he was eager to get under way. Apart from two officers in the Native Infantry of the Company army and a clergyman affiliated with the London Missionary Society, his fellow passengers on the four-hundred-mile voyage via paddle steamer were Bengalis. For months he had chafed at his cloistered life in Calcutta. Now he was out at last in Asiatic society, a companion of crocodiles, a confidant of men who brawled with tigers. The dockhand had casually conferred on him the connection that he craved.

Everything about the journey was intense. It was only February, but the air temperature reached ninety degrees by midmorning. They all stewed ceaselessly in a cauldron of heat, sweating by day beneath canvas awnings rigged on deck and tossing and turning in stifling cabins at night. The water itself was so hot that he marveled at the schools of slender, silver hilsa that shimmered in the steamer's wake: "I should think they would be cooked alive."

The meals matched the climate: fiery curries of mutton and fish that left him gasping for water after every mouthful. At sunset, the nightly bombardment of insects began—thousands of moths, beetles, and dragonflies, attracted by the vessel's lights. They flew unerringly into open mouths, making conversation impossible. It was no wonder, joked Nigel, that the voluble French had given up on colonizing India.

The route to Dacca followed the fringes of a vast virgin littoral mangrove forest, where the muddy Himalayan runoff from the north met the tidal waters of the Bay of Bengal to the south. For five thousand years this tangled floodplain, the Sundarbans, had resisted the civilizing impulses of the Indians themselves, never mind their would-be conquerors. No one lived there. But the Sundarbans teemed with life. Its inhabitants included spotted deer, crocodiles, wild boar, snakes, clawless otters, dolphins, some 315 species of waterfowl, raptors and forest birds, and a population of Bengal tigers that would continue to number in the several hundreds even as the species neared extinction in the twenty-first century. With shooting glasses borrowed from the Portuguese first mate, Nigel peered into the jungle, catching glimpses of deer, a rhinoceros, and a magnificent nesting sea eagle.

"Our noisy passage leaves them undisturbed, for these creatures have no fear of man," he wrote afterwards. "It is man who fears them, or rather the primeval state of their surroundings. They live in a vanished world whose dangers we have happily escaped, but which fascinates from a safe and prudent distance."

Talking with "J——," the missionary who shared his cabin, Nigel ventured a religious parallel. No Christian could contemplate the gaudy pantheon of the Hindus without revulsion for the "pagan rituals" that lowered their faith to the level of black magic. But leaving aside the error of their ways, there was "much to ponder in the infinite variety of their sacred practices."

J——, who had earlier regaled Nigel with his scheme to further Christianize the Roman Catholic converts of Goa, would have none of it. He replied sarcastically that few things seemed to serve the Company's men better in advancing their careers than a well-developed capacity for setting aside the error of native ways.

Had not Lord Ellenborough himself lately pledged to rebuild a heathen temple?

Were not objects of idolatry on parade in some remote province at that very moment, offered for public adoration on the governor's command and accompanied by a guard of honor selected from his personal bodyguard?

The objects in question were the Gates of Somnath, spoils of war plundered from the Afghan city of Ghazni by the army Ellenborough had dispatched the previous summer to free British prisoners in Kabul. Though its troops were instructed to refrain from "vindictive" punishment of the recalcitrant Afghans, any pretense of taking those orders at face value disappeared after British troops reached Jagdalak, site of the desperate last stand by the Army of the Indus. The hills there, wrote one officer, were "literally covered with skeletons, most of them blanched by exposure to the rain and the sun, but many of them having hair of a color which enabled us to recognise the remains of our own countrymen." Forced to trample the bones of the fallen for much of the difficult route, the men took revenge for the massacre on every Afghan they found.

One afternoon, after random shots were fired on a British cavalry column from a fortified village near Ghazni, on the road to Kabul, a company of foot soldiers was sent to investigate; as a result, noted one of them in his diary, about a hundred of the village's men were "butchered." Only the evacuation of Ghazni—Afghanistan's fourth-largest city—prevented the "Army of Retribution" from putting its population to the sword. Its commanding general, Brigadier William Nott, instead consulted his engineer officer and directed him to destroy "the city of Ghuznee with its citadel and the whole of its works."

Spared from the flames was a famous piece of loot. Eight hundred years before, an Afghan force led by Mahmud of Ghazni had plundered and desecrated the Hindu temple of Somnath, on the southwest coast of India. Tradition held that the invaders had removed the ornate sandalwood gates of the shrine and carried them back to Ghazni, where they were hung on Mahmud's tomb. Nott had recovered the gates, acting on orders from Ellenborough, who conceived of their triumphant return to India as a potent symbol for the Hindu majority of the defeat of the Afghan Muslims. When word reached the governor that they had been secured, he issued instructions that the gates be paraded through the cities of the Punjab in a special ceremonial car and brought by an honor guard to the old Mughal capital of Delhi. There, he announced in a proclamation to "all the Princes and Chiefs and the People of India," he would personally restore them to the keeping of the Indians themselves:

"My brethren and friends, our victorious army bears the gates of the temple of Somnath in triumph from Afghanistan, and the despoiled tomb of Mahmood looks on the ruins of Guzni. The insult of eight hundred years is avenged. To you . . . I shall commit this glorious trophy of successful warfare. You will yourselves, with all honour, transmit these gates of sandal wood to the restored temple of Somnath."

J—— could scarcely contain his fury. What was one to make of such a proclamation? Did it not elevate "Brahminical superstition" to a status denied time and again by the East India Company to the gospel of Jesus Christ?

Nigel knew that it was no use defending the Company's record in religious matters to someone like J——. Though the law forbidding missionary work had changed, the Court of Directors still believed that preaching to poor Indians that the meek should inherit the earth was tantamount to sedition. Missionaries were subject to onerous limits on the scope of their activities—religious discussions with native women, for example, were forbidden—and their freedom to travel was severely restricted. J—— had waited eighteen months for permission to visit Dacca, even though he had no plans to proselytize there.

"I could only convey to him that criticism of the Governor's regard for the relics retrieved from Afghanistan was general in Calcutta, where I heard it expressed in the strongest terms and lately with increasing frequency," Nigel wrote. "Residing in Benares himself, he was naturally ill-acquainted with the sentiments of the capital, and glad to know that they accorded with his own."

Half the truth, Nigel seems to have decided, was better than none. The East India Company's rank and file had indeed questioned the wisdom of Ellenborough's proclamation. What concerned them, though, was not his insult to Christianity but his disregard for the feelings of Muslims. Everyone knew that British control of the subcontinent depended on alliances with the Muslim princely states, whose rulers revered Mahmud of Ghazni as the founder of their power in India. They were bound to take offense at the affront to his memory. Among the Hindu princes, who were minor figures by comparison, there was general bewilderment. Almost to a man, they first learned of the "insult of eight hundred years" when the governor general proclaimed it avenged.

(The whole affair turned farcical when Hindu scholars called in to examine the gates rejected the idea that they were the originals taken from Somnath. As it turned out, they were not even made of sandalwood. It subsequently emerged that the mullahs of Ghazni had clung to the fiction as a means of extracting offerings from the faithful who visited the old conqueror's tomb. "The guardians of the tomb wept bitterly," wrote Major Henry Rawlinson, an Orientalist who had supervised the gates' removal in Afghanistan even as he concluded from their inscriptions that they were modern forgeries. "But the sensation was less than what might have been expected.")

Nigel, for his part, was less interested in the controversy than in the relics themselves, which he hoped to one day see for himself. He had never paid much attention to news of military adventure. But the uproar over the Gates of Somnath had drawn him into the reports filed by correspondents who met the avenging army on its triumphant return.

One was the saga of two hundred Europeans taken hostage at the outset of the fateful retreat from Kabul, who overthrew their captors in short order and turned their prison fortress in the mountain wilderness of the Hindu Kush into a defensive position. Within days the former prisoners had recruited an armed group of Afghans, run up a Union flag, and imposed a system of taxation on the local community. When they received word that a detachment of British troops had reached the vicinity, they marched out smartly to meet their would-be rescuers. All Calcutta delighted in the tale of their pluck, but what fascinated Nigel was passing mention of the backdrop to their valor: colossal stone Buddhas carved into alcoves in the mountainside.

Another was a darker story out of Kohistan, a district northwest of Kabul whose inhabitants were thought to have played a part in fomenting the uprising that forced the British to abandon the Afghan capital. Buried in the account of its righteous pillage was an aside about a scouting party who found themselves in a forested enclave of the Kafir, pagan tribesmen with European features. It seemed probable that their ancestors were deserters from another army that had once passed through those parts, led by Alexander.

The news did more than pique Nigel's curiosity about what lay beyond the boundaries of British jurisdiction: It also changed his thinking about the Company's army. To his surprise, there were learned men among the rough and ready soldiery. One was a player in the saga of the spurious gates, Henry Rawlinson. While helping reorganize the Persian army in the 1830s, he had located in the mountains between Hamadan and Baghdad ancient cuneiform inscriptions, which he went on to decipher after copying them at great risk to his life. It was a breakthrough that led to important insights into Babylonian and Assyrian languages and culture. Another officer, Lieutenant Robert Carey, was a botanist. Still another, Major Warwick Ball, was trained in archaeology.

It impressed Nigel that even as such men went about their military duties, they took scholarly stock of their exotic surroundings. War was destructive, he wrote. Yet warriors could also be agents for the advancement of knowledge: "Without war we should know almost nothing of Afghanistan, or suspect the existence there of that worth knowing."

The two army officers on board the mail boat were cut from different cloth than the likes of Henry Rawlinson. Though their regiment had seen action in Afghanistan, they had little to say about the country or its customs. They were en route to the princely state of Cooch Behar, an enclave south of the Himalayan kingdom of Bhutan. There they hoped to bag their share of big game while stepping up the pace of native recruitment.

Their principal contribution to Nigel's personal store of knowledge was the revelation that a group of tigers was called an "ambush." But he enjoyed their company, and relished the novelty of talking "mostly of India and Indians" with other Englishmen. It was a welcome change from Calcutta, where conversation revolved around England and the race meetings of the local Jockey Club, held at dawn to avoid the heat. Even the lectures and debates that Nigel attended were confined to such Occidental topics as iron suspension bridges, antique musketry, and the merits of meteorology — the last a protracted affair at Metcalfe Hall that left him wondering whether the venue had been selected on account of its architecture, borrowed from the Athenian Tower of the Winds.

On their third day out of Calcutta, they left the dark, primeval world of the Sundarbans behind. The jungle thinned into isolated stands of mangrove on sandbars surrounded by mud flats, and the first mate pointed out a species of smooth-coated otter domesticated by fishermen and used to drive fish into their nets.

Fishermen themselves were nowhere to be seen, even as signs of habitation appeared on lush Bhola Island, where the route veered northward up the Buriganga River. Dacca was just a hundred miles away. But crocodiles seemingly outnumbered people, and the island's paddy fields turned out to be abandoned.

Nigel remembered Sagar Island, at the mouth of the Hooghly, and asked if the islanders had been flooded out.

No, said the first mate.

They went away.

Went where? Nigel wondered. Most Indians lived out their lives within a few miles of their birthplace. The rigid social structure discouraged mobility of any sort.

To other lands, said the boatman.

All those lands were the zamindar's.

The zamindar decided.

The mail boat turned up the Buriganga. Dolphins leaped from the mottled brown water. They were not the storied pink variety of the Indus and the upper Ganges. But they were nacreous and lovely in the low-angle light of late afternoon.

In Nigel's letter home about hiring a munshi, he had explained to his parents that zamindars were the hereditary tax collectors of the Mughal Empire, "who have always held rank in society but have only come to prosper through acting in concert with our larger interests." But he failed to elaborate on how that prosperity had come about. Under the Permanent Settlement of 1793, promulgated by Charles Cornwallis, zamindars were transformed into British-style landlords, and the vast territories from which they collected revenue became their private estates. With a stroke of his pen, Cornwallis reduced the entire peasantry of Bengal to tenants with no enumerated rights, not even of occupancy to the land they cultivated.

Nor did Nigel specify just what those larger interests might be. The avowed purpose of the settlement was to fix land tax revenues in perpetuity. But its unspoken strategic object was the creation of a new propertied class that would be both loyal to and dependent on British rule.

The effect, for the dispossessed, was something close to slavery. Crop failures forced cultivators to borrow at usurious rates from moneylenders, often the zamindars themselves. When they failed to meet the terms of repayment, they became bonded laborers for the zamindars. Many proved unable to work off the compounding interest of their debt, let alone the principal, a circumstance that justified the servitude of their children to the zamindar after the death of the initial borrower.

It is unclear how much Nigel then understood about the effects of the Permanent Settlement. But a year had passed since he hired the munshi, and he would have known at least a little more about the zamindars. They were objects of ridicule in Calcutta society, which reserved its most withering scorn for the pretensions of the native parvenus. In the munshi himself he would have recognized another stereotype: the Bengali babu. The more powerful the British became, the more they relied upon the urbane, educated Indians of the emerging babu class. But the more the British relied upon the babu, the more they pretended that the babu was not to be relied upon at all.

All his knowledge of India was filtered through the conventional wisdom of Calcutta. It was a self-absorbed teenager of a city, obsessed with the dazzle of its own reflection in the gleaming windows of Chowringhee mansions. The zamindars were next to invisible; only their vulgar display was likely to intrude upon the field of view. Babus were seen for the most part as figures of fun. Even of the natives with the closest ties to the British, he knew almost nothing.

But that was about to change. Every churn of the paddle wheel closed the distance to a pair of Indias. One was the "real India" that Nigel longed to see. The other was the British India that he was forced to see, by the ghost city of Dacca.

8

A Mosque

WHEN NIGEL DEBARKED in Dacca in February 1843, its population numbered around thirty thousand. Less than a century before, after the British deposed the nawab of Bengal, as many as a million people lived there. A contemporary account described the city as "extensive, populous, and rich as the city of London." It owed its prosperity to India's status as the world's main producer of cotton textiles, with the export trade centered in Dacca. No printed cotton could compare to the poetically named textiles of the city, called *shabnam* and *abrawan*, after morning dew and flowing water. Those muslins, stretched on the grass and drenched with dew, become invisible due to their fragile transparency. Their perfection was prized by the Roman emperors, who paid fabulous sums to procure them. A millennium later, they were among the wares first brought to England by the East India Company. But by the 1840s it was Britain that dominated global textile production, exporting even to Dacca. The Company, through interference and regulation, had systematically destroyed Bengal's textile industry.

To observers in England, the need for such measures had been clear enough. Without them, wrote Horace Wilson in his *History of British India*, "the mills of Paisley and Manchester would have been stopped in their outset, and could scarcely have been again set in motion, even by the power of steam. They were created by the sacrifice of Indian manufacturers."

The extent of the sacrifice became evident to Nigel only gradually. At first he persisted in seeing Dacca through the romantic lens of its reputed likeness to Venice. The physical resemblance, he learned to his dismay, depended on the seasonal flooding of the principal streets, still months in the future. There was some consolation, though, in the city's frontage on the Buriganga. Stately buildings rose directly from its banks. The water reflected their picturesque decay in a manner he found "decidedly Venetian," at once melancholy and charming.

When he learned of a local ritual called *bera bhashan*, he discerned another parallel with the Most Serene Republic on the Adriatic. Every year after the rains, residents of Dacca sent rafts made with palm, plantain, and banana leaves out upon the Buriganga, to be carried out to sea and placate water spirits. It was comparable, enthused Nigel in a letter home, to the old Venetian ceremony on the feast day of the Ascension, when the doge embarked on his gilded *Bucintoro* galley to reaffirm the city's marriage with the sea by tossing a ring into the Adriatic.

It was an uncommon colonial who was capable of the imaginative leap that linked the humble rafts of the Buriganga with the majestic *Bucintoro*, processing down the Grand Canal. But in painting the larger picture, Nigel remained an Englishman of his time and place, supremely confident of the advantages of British rule:

"In Venice this colourful pageant of a thousand years' standing is now but a memory, lost to the strictures of Buonaparte. More happily for the populace of Bengal, their own rites of propitiation continue as before, with our full sanction in the lands under our control. Would be that the Corsican had extended to his foreign subjects the tolerance for tradition that we gladly show our own!"

Nigel's letters from Dacca say almost nothing about his professional or social life there. Unusually for an Englishman in the provinces, he lived and worked in the old central city. (To better ensure the separation of the rulers from the ruled, the British had taken to establishing civil and military cantonments on the periphery of urban areas.) His lodgings, which he expected to occupy for no more than six months before returning to Calcutta, were close to the quarter called Armanitola, which took its name from the Armenians who pioneered the jute trade, settled there now for a dozen generations. The commanding steeple of their Armenian Church of the Holy Resurrection punctuated a skyline that was famed throughout South Asia long before the first rude huts of Calcutta rose upon the malodorous banks of the Hooghly.

The most ancient landmark, a Hindu temple, Nigel found fascinating, if only for its ugliness. He thought it deserved the dilapidation into which it had fallen after India's conquest by Babur, founder of the Mughal Empire. To that "happy subjugation," he wrote, Dacca owed its legacy of splendid architecture, and much of its visible charm. The Mughal artisans, with their flair for proportion and line, transformed the city. The facades of their prayer walls, the domes of their prayer halls, the cool geometry of tile mosaic, and the rush and ripple of sinuous script—all brought serenity and order to the "fearful hotchpotch" of the full-throated, full-blooded East.

Probably because Nigel was based in Old Dacca, it took him longer to notice the effects of the more recent subjugation by his own countrymen. But as his tours of the Mughal monuments took him farther from the city center, he realized that Dacca's uncommon serenity owed less to architectural harmony than he had supposed. Entire quarters, he discovered, were overgrown and abandoned. Shocked by the silence, he traveled streets devoid of traffic, destitute of livestock, bereft of playing children. He passed deserted public fountains for bathing and laundering, slimed with algae.

When he wrote of Dacca's depopulation, he implied that the city had simply been eclipsed by Calcutta as the commercial and political capital of Bengal. Only in a passing reference to the decline of the beautiful Dacca muslins did he allude to the recent loss of the city's main industry. (Their very fineness worked against them, he lamented, "in our robust Mechanical Age.") But his detailed account of a visit to a mosque four months after he took up his post revealed that his understanding was deeper, and shadowed by a nascent unease.

With its three petite domes and thirty feet of frontage, the Tara Masjid was far from grandiose. Nor was it venerable—it was, in fact, the newest mosque in Dacca. The decor, however, was unique. Inlaid star patterns formed from broken pieces of china dappled the domes with a blue firmament, attracting those few Europeans who ventured out to "do the mosques." Foreign visitors typically arrived in groups of three or four, disgorged from horse-drawn carriages. They marched purposefully through the courtyard, cast sidelong glances at the shoe rack in the entrance arcade, and pressed coins upon the doorkeeper in extravagant *baksheesh* as they swept across the threshold.

The doorkeeper had noticed at once that Nigel was different.

To begin with, he arrived by himself, on foot. Then he took his time to reach the shaded portal of the prayer hall. For long minutes he surveyed the facade from different vantage points around the forecourt fountain, squinting in the sun. After that he wandered along the arcade, examining the mosaic tiles, with their motif of vases with flowers on the spandrels of the arches.

And then, finally standing at the entrance, he knelt to remove his shoes; in Egypt he had learned to mimic Muslim behavior. The doorkeeper stared:

> *He was much surprised that I followed the usage of the Mohammedans. Before entering the house of prayer it is usual for them to remove their shoes, for which a species of cupboard is provided for orderly storage and retrieval. This, despite the contrary appearance in our own eyes, has nought to do with religious observance . . . [T]heir own Prophet prayed with his shoes on, and even recommended the practice, as it set his adherents apart from the Jews. Nowadays, with the tradition of fine silk carpets having since been established within their prayer halls, the congregation naturally takes care not to soil them. For this reason, they consign their footwear to the door porter for safekeeping. It is no more than good manners for the Christian to follow suit.*

In his stocking feet, Nigel crossed the threshold. Conscious of the doorkeeper's gaze, he took care to enter with his right foot first. Again, it was only good manners — or so he supposed. He seems not to have known that it was etiquette recommended by the Prophet only to true believers. He was baffled by the sudden change in the demeanor of the taciturn porter, who leaped to his side with unsuspected grace, "giving voice to salutations in rapid local dialect."

When Nigel recognized his welcome as a coreligionist, he struggled to explain himself. But he lacked the vocabulary, and finally made the main point with earnest gestures. He drew a cross in the air, then made a "low salaam." The doorkeeper retreated to his post, stroking his hennaed beard reflectively.

From the outside, the Tara Masjid had summoned yet another memory of Venice. The bulb cupolas that surmounted its trio of domes faintly suggested the Byzantine roofline of the Basilica of Saint Mark. Padding into the prayer hall, he harbored no illusions that the interior would sustain the resemblance. Saint Mark's was the most opulent church in Christendom, golden with mosaics and gleaming with treasure. He held out hope, though, that the mosque might prove worthy of comparison with a lesser church he admired in Venice, Santa Maria dei Miracoli.

The Tara Masjid was no Miracoli. Inside the prayer hall, everything failed to impress. Instead of painstaking ceramic tile work, he found "broken bits of teacups, carelessly emplaced without symmetry or sense, as if their arrangement had depended on the whims of inattentive schoolboys." One wall, entirely devoid of embellishment (save a thin coat of whitewash, badly applied), was visibly out of plumb. He was no engineer, but he recognized the frailty of the squinches supporting the domes. He was no tile setter, but he knew the missed trick in the mosaic stars overhead — they would have caught the light and seemed to twinkle if only the planes of their pieces had been carefully offset.

Deeply disappointed, he pronounced himself surprised as well, "for the standard of Mohammedan structures is usually high." His expectations, admittedly, were probably "over-coloured" by the reputation of the zamindar who endowed the mosque, who was "very rich, of that type of Indian who spares no expense in erecting monuments to his own good fortune." Moreover, the Tara Masjid had been highly recommended to him by "two of our Native clerks, who are well educated by Asiatic standards and not, I should think, entirely without discernment."

He lingered inside, wondering. The place really was frightfully ill-made. Then it hit him: there were very good reasons—practical ones—for the sorry state of the Tara Masjid. Even in Dacca, depopulated as it was, laborers could always be found. The same could not be said for artisans, carpenters, and masons. Some, he presumed, had moved on to Calcutta, ever booming, ever building. Others would have grown old and died, without apprentices to follow in their trade. In a city with no buildings to erect, who would enter such a trade?

The mosque was exactly what it resembled: the project of amateurs. Its claim to fame was that it was built at all; what enthused his clerks was the simple fact of its existence. They were as proud of their city and the glories of its past as their contemporaries in Venice, impoverished by foreign rule after a millennium of freedom. Whatever the defects of the Tara Masjid, he wrote, for natives it could only seem precious indeed. Like a leafy shoot taking root in waste ground, it symbolized renewal.

He ought not to have sneered at the faulty stars in the vaults above. Viewed through the prism of Dacca's recent history, they twinkled after all.

"Crude as it was, the stellar canopy radiated Hope."

He stayed for a while, content with his surroundings, enjoying the "cool solemnity" that was typical of all the mosques he had visited. The same quality, he realized, characterized Santa Maria dei Miracoli, which pleased the eye with patterns of natural materials rather than figurative art.

So there was a connection after all. Perhaps such an environment was even better suited to "religious musing" in the hectic East. The Muslims did well, it seemed to him, to rely on abstract ornament and calligraphic script as focal points for the gathered faithful:

"In England, where life is good and the many prosper, no church is without its reminder of suffering in the form of the Cross, a reminder both necessary and beneficial. In India, where life is hard and the many starve, such are the circumstances of everyday life that suffering is not to be avoided. What is wanted is a refuge from its awful face."

Four months after his arrival in Dacca, Nigel stood in his stocking feet in the Tara Masjid, reborn as the rarest of his countrymen in India, a realist. Four months after he contrasted the downtrodden Venetians with the festive Bengalis, he could only lament their common poverty under foreign rule. Four months into his longed-for acquaintance with "the real India," he knew its essentials all too well.

Life was hard, and many starved.

It was no exaggeration. Annual reports by the East India Company estimated that two-thirds of the Indian population was undernourished, with the percentage in Bengal rising to four-fifths. Forty-odd years into the nineteenth century, seven famines had led to a million and a half deaths. (Readers who noticed that the Company's export of food grains from India to Britain continued even during famine years were left to draw their own conclusions about the practice.) It was commonly believed in England that Indians had lived in a state of perpetual want for millennia. But accounts by European travelers of Indian life prior to colonization suggested otherwise. J. B. Tavernier's *Les Six Voyages*—avidly read by Nigel—chronicled the abundance of foodstuffs found in even the smallest villages during the mid-seventeenth century. Tavernier's contemporary Niccolò Manucci, a Venetian, reported of Bengal that "all things are in great plenty here, fruits, pulse, grain, muslins, cloths of gold and silk," and declared it the equal of Egypt—a judgment later disputed by a Frenchman, François Bernier:

"The knowledge I have acquired of Bengal in two visits inclines me to believe that it is richer than Egypt. It exports in abundance cottons and silks, rice, sugar, and butter. It produces amply for its own consumption of wheat, vegetables, grains, fowls, ducks and geese. It has immense herds of pigs and flocks of sheep and goats. Fish of every kind it has in profusion."

Times had changed. With its peasantry enslaved by the zamindars and its economy destroyed so that Lancashire's might thrive, Bengal was a tragedy.

Nigel didn't say so, not in so many words, not to his family. The truth he shared with them was sunny, even though it shone upon a devastated land. Hope was the beauty in the imperfect mosaics of the Tara Masjid, and hope sprang eternal.

The truth he spared them was a wintry one. He could see for himself that British "help" in Bengal had succeeded only in making most people poorer.

He took off his shoes, he started looking around, and entered uncharted territory for a sahib. Not for the last time in India, he stepped entirely out of his sturdy English self and saw the opposite of what was there before he set his Englishness aside.

9

An Asiatic Rome

NIGEL RETURNED TO Calcutta two months later, in September 1843. He expected to be posted shortly to a humbler locale. Nearly all fledgling civil servants received appointments to the hinterlands of British territory, where they served as underlings to collectors, judges, and magistrates. Settled at remote stations with only a handful of European colleagues, under skies too hot to be blue, they saw to the payments of taxes and land rents and administered justice, exercising authority over districts that in size and population dwarfed the largest English counties. For the most part, they followed an effortless path to promotion as their superiors retired. (Or succumbed —by the end of British rule, two million Europeans lay buried on the subcontinent, in more than thirteen hundred cemeteries.) The more they distinguished themselves—by resisting, principally, the temptation to ease their exile with drink and dissipation—the likelier the trajectory of their careers would one day return them to the concentrated wealth and power of the capital.

When he learned of his assignment instead to a plum job at Government House, in the Accountant General's Office, he wrote to his parents that he could scarcely believe his good fortune. He assured them that "many" benefits would accrue to him by remaining in "the Asiatic Rome," without elaborating on what they were. But one of his contemporaries, Fanny Parkes, the wife of a junior official in charge of ice making in Allahabad, would sum them up in her *Wanderings of a Pilgrim in Search of the Picturesque*, published in 1850:

"The advantages of a residence in Calcutta are these: you are under the eye of the Government, not likely to be overlooked, and are ready for any appointment falling vacant; you get the latest news from England, and have the best medical attendance."

In the stratified society of colonial India, the unlikelihood of being overlooked was a pearl without price. The European population was divided into three classes. The first, covenanted servants, comprised the civil and military officers, typically graduates of Haileybury or its sister college, Addiscombe Military Seminary, for candidates seeking commissions in the Company army. In the second, commonly called "commercial men," were the managers of the large trading houses and financial agencies established by British merchants and banks in the aftermath of the Company's withdrawal from trade. Members of the third (and, by 1840, the most numerous) class, the uncovenanted, included clerks in the private agency houses, assistants to the clerks in government offices, tradesmen, and various others, ranging from itinerant merchant seamen to missionaries.

With rare exceptions, uncovenanted Europeans were denied entrée to functions at Government House, which set the controlling precedent for all British India. This effectively placed them on the same social footing as natives. For the others, society revolved around activities and organizations that demarcated the ruling elite and fostered a sense of community within it. It was a closed society, in which everybody knew everybody else and all were conscious that making the right impression constituted an investment in one's future prospects in India. And no stage on the subcontinent came close to Calcutta's as a showcase for a turn in the spotlight.

As in England, blood sports were the first resort of young gentlemen with an eye on impressing their elders. Nigel found little to recommend in the popular pursuit of "pig sticking." But he shot snipe in the bush across the Hooghly, and parrots in the jungle that crowded its waters farther upstream. Upon first payment of his salary, he subscribed to the Calcutta Hunt, founded in 1774, whose kennels were replenished annually with thirty pairs of hounds imported from England. Standing in for the English fox as the object of the chase was the native jackal, larger in size but equally speedy. And, despite initial doubts about his dexterity with a five-iron, Nigel began to patronize the Royal Calcutta Golf Club, the world's oldest outside Britain. Since its members were notorious for spending more time over drinks at the "19th hole" than on the links themselves, it was probably no exaggeration when he assured his parents that his outings there were "always jolly."

About his attention to the non-sporting side of the colonial social calendar—the balls and fancy-dress parties of the Calcutta "season" —he had less to say. For many they were occasions to be endured, not enjoyed. These insular affairs were little more than ill-disguised auctions of what a subaltern in the Company army called the "marketable commodity" of matrimony, where a young officer might "pick up as partner some artless creature . . . who at the conclusion of the dance receive[d] from her haughty maternal" the stern admonition that the poor fellow was only an ensign, not yet even passed in the languages.

"The young man gets a withering scowl from a yellow-faced, overdressed, spiteful, dowager," reported the subaltern, "and, rushing out of the first door, registers a hasty vow never to enter into female society again—a vow too frequently kept."

Nigel—passed in the languages and appointed to Government House—was a better catch. He dutifully presented himself that fall at the round of balls that commenced with the arrival of the "Fishing Fleet," the influx of unmarried daughters who joined their families in India for the Calcutta "season" in hopes of finding a husband. (At season's end, those who met with disappointment went back to England, where they were unkindly known as the "Returned Empties.") But his letters hinted that he was simply putting in appearances. His tenancy at the Writers Building was coming to an end, and he seemed to be too worried about the cost of setting up a household to even contemplate marriage. Rents in Calcutta compared unfavorably with those in most parts of England, and the likely annual outlay for something suitable to his position, without a stick of furniture, was considerable.

Then there were the premiums to be paid for such necessities as glassware, imported from England at a markup of two or three hundred percent, and candles. The price of beeswax — scarce because Indians harbored ethical scruples about ending so many lives for the purpose of robbing honeycombs — was the despair of even the wealthiest households, but cheaper tallow tapers were too odoriferous for all but the poorest Europeans to abide.

Even if Nigel could afford to take a wife, he was unimpressed by the spectacle of institutionalized spouse hunting. At best, it struck him as rather comical. In November, after accepting an invitation to the station ball at Dum Dum, a cantonment for the artillery corps eight miles outside Calcutta, he fled the ballroom for the adjacent library within minutes. The proceedings, which he later recalled as "frantic," were worthy of a Restoration playwright. For all that, though, it was too "close and hot" to properly enjoy the show. His description jibed with Miss Emma Roberts' account of a ball there that fall — possibly the same one. Thirty or forty young ladies, thronged by "all the beaux who have any hope of being noticed by them," were obliged by custom to dance with each and every one of them.

Nigel discovered that he was not the first wallflower to desert the ballroom for the reading room that evening. Lieutenant M—— and Captain Lieutenant C—— were both stationed at Barrackpore, another eight miles upriver, awaiting staff appointments after completing two years of service with their regiments of the Bengal Native Infantry. In the meantime, they were "chumming it," sharing a bungalow and household expenses. When C—— rose from his armchair to shake Nigel's hand, he laid aside a volume of Persian poetry. M——, it turned out, was keen on Mughal architecture. Their shared interests overwhelmed their habitual English reserve, and the three men chatted like old friends for hours. When they parted, Nigel promised to call on the officers at Barrackpore, where the governor general kept a country residence with a fine park and a famous menagerie, noted for its tigers and cheetahs.

Though no record survives of that visit, it must have gone well. Nigel returned to Barrackpore several times afterwards, riding with M—— and C—— in the broken wooded country beyond the cantonment boundaries and joining them for meals at their bungalow or the officers' mess. Their friendship cut across the prevailing Company grain, which separated British civilians from British troops as a matter of policy. Fort William, in Calcutta proper, was garrisoned by a single regiment, with the forces actually considered necessary for the city's defense stationed well outside its boundaries.

It wasn't long, however, before Nigel found himself wishing M—— and C—— Godspeed on their posting to Ferozepore, a thousand miles distant on the far western frontier of British India. Ferozepore, where Lord Ellenborough had personally greeted the returning "Army of Retribution" after its rampage through Afghanistan with an honor guard of 250 decorated elephants, was everything Calcutta was not. Rustic, tribal, and practically lawless, it was situated, as the young John Nicholson wrote home upon his posting there in 1840, in "a perfect wilderness: there is not a tree or a blade of grass within miles of us; and as to the tigers, there are two or three killed in the neighbouring jungle every day."

M—— and C—— were thrilled. Action in the field was the surest means of advancement in their military careers, and they had yet to see any. The previous fall, Ellenborough had promised that henceforth the government of India would devote all its efforts to "the establishment and maintenance of general peace." In a magniloquent proclamation, he ordered a commemorative medal struck with the legend PAX ASIAE RESTITUTA ("Peace Restored to Asia"), and ambitious officers like M—— and C—— had to wonder if commands under fire might ever come their way.

Less than six months later, the governor lifted their spirits with another proclamation, annexing the province of Sindh. A prosperous country south of Ferozepore, Sindh was ruled by independent emirs who cherished their control of the Indus River, the main artery to the Sikh kingdom of the Punjab. Ellenborough's proclamation meant war, and M—— and C—— were off to fight it.

Nigel, for his part, was right where he needed to be to make his own career: ensconced in the Asiatic Rome. At the beginning of 1844, about the same time he said his goodbyes in Barrackpore, he received the surest confirmation possible that his star was on the rise. Bastions of the colonial elite though they were, Calcutta's Hunt Club, Golf Club, and Jockey Club lacked the cachet of the gentlemen's social clubs that were emerging as the pinnacle of refinement in the empire's first cities. Patterned after the venerable upper-class institutions of White's and Boodle's, in the City of London, they aimed to reproduce the comfort and ambience of "home" in an alien land. Preeminent in Calcutta was the Bengal Club, founded in 1827 and well on its way to securing the reputation it would enjoy until the end of British rule as the premier haunt of the most pukka of India's sahibs.

Exclusivity, needless to say, was the watchword. When one of Nigel's superiors offered to sponsor his candidacy for election, he rushed to put pen to paper, detailing for his parents the charms of the Hepplewhite, Chippendale, and Louis Quinze that graced the handsome rooms on Chowringhee Road. There was no finer setting in Calcutta, he wrote, for taking meals, reading newspapers, and playing cards or billiards. What appealed to him most about the Bengal Club, though, was the serviced apartments made available to members. Nearly as worrisome to him as the expense of renting and furnishing a house of his own, he confided, was the prospect of hiring and managing the necessary retinue of servants:

I shall have to have a khansama, or butler, who does the marketing and supervises the kitchen, holding first precedence above the others, whose company is astonishingly numerous. To begin with there is the cook. Secondly, the khidmutgar, the boy who lays the table and waits upon it during meals. Thirdly, the musalchee, corresponding to the scullion of an English pantry. Having seen to the culinary necessaries, I must then employ a principal house servant or bearer, the sirdar, who acts as valet and prepares the evening lights, among other household duties. Since there cannot be a principal in this country without a subordinate, the sirdar naturally requires a bearer's mate to assist him. Next must be engaged the essential trio of bheesty, or water bearer, mihtur, or sweeper, and dhobee, or washerman. Owing to the strenuous exertions of the latter, and the damages occasioned by his zeal, it is necessary to maintain a durzee or tailor on the premises as well, although I am assured that a half-time appointment should suffice in service to a bachelor. In this census I omit the outdoor servants . . . Does it surprise that one of my age and inexperience in all things domestic should be daunted by the prospect of administering such a surfeit of Native labour, cheap though it may be?

In the long term, he calculated, he would save on living expenses by residing at the Bengal Club, where all customary services were included in the rent. The short term was complicated by the club's requirement that its annual subscription fee be paid in one lump sum. Fortunately, he had saved enough during his sojourn in Dacca that he could just scrape by.

"I am inclined to suffer the leanness of two or three months as the price of resolving my future in a manner that frees me from further anxiety about the arrangements of everyday life—anxiety which I fear would only assume another form upon establishment of an independent household."

His relief was palpable, and so, unusually for Nigel, was a note of self-satisfaction. "My thoughts, when I am sitting alone here in the evening," he concluded, "now turn to the diversions of life, a pleasing realm to contemplate."

The message to Coventry was clear: The uncertainties and awkwardness of griffinhood were behind him. Now in the full tide of his life in India, he was swimming well.

Three months later, however, seemingly out of the blue and much to the bemusement of his parents, he requested and received a transfer to Patna. Three hundred miles up the Ganges from Calcutta, it offered none of the capital's advantages. But it was thought to be the oldest continuously inhabited city in the world.

10

Patna

1975

THE HUMIDITY IN Patna rose from the plain in extravagant whiffs, binding the damp gray ground to the billowing clouds that smothered the sky. The driver of the minibus who dropped us off at the Ganges Guest House didn't know if Patna was the hottest place in India, but he was sure that it was one of the wettest. The abundance of moisture was a terrifying thing. It drenched you from within and deceived you from without, suppressing the spectrum and dissolving all you saw into a uniform, enigmatic gray. It might have been the color of the Ganges, which was more like a sea than a river there — three miles wide, swift and deep and dense with silt. But what was the color of the Ganges but the color of the mud-hut villages that ranged to the horizon, villages in their turn the color of the footpaths that linked them, and the fields that fed them, and the canals that watered the fields, opening into buffalo ponds with their sheen of tarnished pewter in the saturated light?

The monotony seemed infinite. It almost was. There was drier country upstream. There was lusher country down. But the differences were as subtle as the rise of the Delhi Ridge that divides the basins of the Indus and the Ganges, without visible interruption of the one great plain. For the schoolgirl transported by tornado to its western marches in Pakistan, there would be no Dorothy moment, no not-in-Bihar-anymore. There would be the same heat, oppressive to the point of prostration, the same turbid water flowing everywhere, and the air would sweat and weep upon the rice fields and canals and villages and shriveled trees, endlessly repeating in their sameness and tameness.

A wilder prospect greeted Gautama Buddha when he passed through Patna on his way to Kusinara in the last year of his life. Nigel Halleck saw it in the twenty-third year of his, before the internal combustion engine added its fumes to the sepia shroud of the atmosphere. In 1845, he wrote home to Coventry of crystalline fall mornings when the mist burned off the fields and the air turned holy blue, like the Virgin's cloak in Titian's *Annunciation*, and the only clouds were high and distant, knife-prowed and noble, a great white fleet afloat upon the northern sky.

But those were no clouds. Those were the earthly abodes of the gods. Those were the Great Himalaya Range.

Two months out of Istanbul, we were finally nearing Nepal. The distance by road to Kathmandu was less than 250 miles. If we were lucky, we would be there in a couple of days. Patna was actually a bit out of our way. But it was Nigel's last address in India, and my mother thought it was one of the places where he might have been buried. Perhaps the Nepalese authorities had shipped his remains back to British territory; he was, after all, an Englishman. I had talked my classmate into making the detour with the promise of paying a visit to a local landmark, described by the contemporary British writer and diplomat Compton Mackenzie in a memoir of his postwar visit to India, just prior to Independence:

"Just before we reached Patna, General Stable pointed out Mahatma Gandhi's little house beside the river, that little house from which such an influence upon the course of history had emanated. The Mahatma himself was not there at the time."

"Gandhi's house?" repeated the desk clerk when I asked for directions the next morning. "She lives in Delhi, you know."

Within a fortnight, Prime Minister Indira Gandhi would suspend civil liberties, then rule by decree for the next twenty-one months.

"Mahatma Gandhi," I said.

"Ah, Gandhi*ji!*" he said. "Of course."

About the house, though, he knew nothing. In fact, he had never heard of it. Gandhi had visited Patna during the campaign for independence, there was an ashram where he rallied his followers, there might be one of his spinning wheels in the museum . . .

Perhaps there had been such a house, he said. But he thought it was probably gone.

I showed him the passage in Mackenzie's *My Life and Times*. He pondered it.

Finally he asked when the author had visited the city.

"Nineteen forty-seven."

He nodded.

That would explain it.

It was the time of Partition, he said gravely.

A time of much confusion.

And violence, he might have added. A million people dead. Millions more homeless. The British quit India, and acceded to the creation of Pakistan, with what came to be seen by many as indecent haste, almost criminal carelessness.

"About Gandhiji's house I think these Englishmen were mistaken."

There was, at any rate, a European cemetery. The desk clerk was delighted to tell me how to get there. He was genuinely sorry about the apocryphal abode of the mahatma.

I went alone. A Toyota taxi took me to a quarter called Gulzarbagh. The driver stopped where a lofty dome rose above the Ionic portico of a Roman Catholic church. He directed my attention to a pair of iron gates, double-padlocked, and the thicket of tapering obelisks within.

Two boys materialized beside me as I paid the fare. They gave me to understand that I must summon the chowkidar, or gatekeeper. I paid them half a rupee apiece to find him, and they ran off giggling. The driver told me not to worry.

"They are good boys."

It was a long wait. I leaned against the gates and tried to sketch the scene in my notebook. Compton Mackenzie described Patna as "seething." If there was a better word for the enervating heat, I couldn't think of it. No more than a minute passed before my clothes were drenched with sweat. The point of my pen started going through the paper.

What a place to live, I thought.

What a place to die.

The chowkidar was old and bent. He snapped open the padlocks, and I followed him through the gates. The grounds were the size of a softball diamond, surrounded by a lichen-stained wall topped with fangs of broken bottle glass. There might have been fifty monuments and markers, a dozen-odd tombs.

They were not maintained to the standard of the Cornwallis memorial in Ghazipur. The inscriptions wanted cleaning. But I could read them.

There was Thomas Amphlet and William Eaton and Marmaduke Collins.

John Kinch, John Howit, John Johnston.

Henry Harling, Henry Hutchinson, William Crawford.

The sun beat down. Every name on every gravestone was that of an adult male who died in October 1763.

Epidemic?

Massacre?

The chowkidar spoke no English.

Nigel wasn't there.

11

A Folly

PERHAPS IT WAS Barrackpore that changed Nigel's mind about casting his lot with the colonial elite in Calcutta. Perhaps the craving for adventure of the young officers he befriended there proved contagious. Like their counterparts in the U.S. Cavalry during the same era, they were called to the taming of a Wild West. Once they brought Sindh to heel, they were sure to march on to the princely state of Gwalior, where a mutinous army, an eight-year-old maharaja, and factions in the Council of Ministers combined to make the country ripe for British intervention. Perhaps he could not resist the temptation to be three hundred miles closer to the action.

Or perhaps he simply remained a creature of romantic impulse, beguiled by the charm of points unknown—the oasis of Siwa, the Venice of the East, the oldest inhabited city in the world. Perhaps the Nigel who set out by barge up the Ganges for Patna in April 1844 was consciously turning his back on the Nigel who was wont to satisfy his appetite for the "diversions of life" by rising at dawn for horse races on the Maidan and running down jackals with pedigreed hounds. Patna, he wrote in one of his last letters from Calcutta, was a rare and special place.

Its history was glorious—Gautama Buddha himself had prophesied the city's great future, even as he predicted its eventual ruin. When the Greek ambassador to the court of the emperor Chandragupta Maurya arrived there in the fourth century B.C., he was amazed. Even the splendor of the Persian capital at Susa, wrote Megasthenes, did not compare with Patna. The city stretched nine or ten miles along the banks of the Ganges. Palaces and pleasure gardens lined the river frontage. Under Maurya's command were more than four hundred thousand men, with three thousand war elephants, and His Imperial Majesty traveled in state with a bodyguard of female warriors, Indian Amazons loyal only to him.

If Megasthenes is to be trusted, Patna—then called Pataliputra—was the greatest city in the world, capital of an empire stretching from the Bay of Bengal to Afghanistan. For a millennium it held sway over South Asia. After the Maurya kings came the Shungas, after the Shungas the Guptas, after the Guptas the Palas. And then came the ruin foreseen by the Buddha, again and again and again.

Ruin by flood. Ruin by fire. Ruin by feud. Ruin so complete, Nigel discovered to his dismay after he arrived, that it left no ruins. All that survived of imperial Patna, he learned, was "a pillar somewhere."

There were no temples or mosques of any importance.

No splendid Mughal monuments.

He was told that the want of stone in the vicinity prevented their construction. He was told that the only building material thereabouts was earth, so impregnated with saltpeter that bricks began to crumble as soon as they were formed. And he was told that Patna proper was so unsuited for habitation—so filthy and disorderly—that no Europeans had lived there for at least a generation.

They lived, exclusively, in the outlying civil station, with its oval parade ground and leafy, reverential hush. In leaving Calcutta, Nigel discovered, he had traded the insular for the hermetic.

"The new arrival in the capital is pressed for a personal accounting of the various affairs of the day, and must respond as best he can to feminine curiosity about the latest in fashionable attire," he wrote in what was probably his first letter from Patna. "The new man here is subject to no such interrogation. The world outside the Station seems so distant as to be unworthy of sustained attention, or at any rate the appearance of energetic interest."

Any undue expenditure of energy amounted to a local taboo. Card parties—nightly amusements for his set in Calcutta—were maligned for running too long and too late to be countenanced by the man who valued his health. Upon dining at the home of the collector, he found that even after-dinner conversation was judged too taxing for prolonged indulgence. The company rose as one as the table was cleared, repaired to the cool air of a terrace to smoke in silence, and departed for their bungalows soon afterwards, with perfunctory expressions of gratitude. Host and guests were home in bed before eleven o'clock, he marveled, and that on a Saturday!

For several weeks after his arrival, he tried to enlist one of his colleagues in the audit division of the revenue office to join him in ascending the beehive-shaped structure that loomed above the treetops on the edge of the station. It was only a short walk, and the view from the top was said to be the best in the district. On the clearest days could be seen the icy heights of the Himalayas, two hundred miles distant. But nobody wanted to go. Finally, on a sultry Sunday morning in May, he set out by himself, shielded from the sun by a *sola topee*, the cloth-covered helmet that was destined to be immortalized by Hollywood heroes from Errol Flynn to Harrison Ford.

For ten or fifteen minutes he strolled past whitewashed bungalows housing civil servants like himself, shaded by toddy palms and neem trees. Each had its lush back garden and its broad veranda, furnished with reclining chairs whose arms extended to provide a footrest. Bent over one of these "planter's long-sleevers" stood a turbaned manservant, shaving a sleepy Englishman. Even enlisted men in the Company army employed Indians to shave them in their barracks bunks. Nigel, however, preferred solitude during his morning toilet, and shaved himself.

The Golghar was four hundred feet around and a hundred feet high. Its design was patterned after the mound-like structures raised by Buddhists to house relics of the Enlightened One. Four portals at the base of the dome marked the cardinal directions. Passageways tunneled from each, through walls twelve feet thick, to massive doors that opened on the granary chamber. Affixed to the doors were commemorative plaques that recounted the story of the granary's construction.

The unlikely architect was Captain John Garstin, an engineer with the East India Company. He was sent to Patna in the aftermath of a famine that lasted from 1769 to 1773 and killed nearly ten million people in the lower Gangetic Plain. He conceived and built the Golghar to store 140,000 tons of grain — not for the local populace, but for the Company army. For efficiency in filling it, he designed two spiral staircases that climbed opposite sides of the dome and converged at the opening on top. Porters would carry grain bags up the shallow steps of one flight, empty them, then descend the steeper steps of the other to collect their next load.

Nigel started up. Adjoining the ascending stairs at regular intervals were broad resting platforms. He ignored the first, stopped briefly at the second, and lingered at the third, panting in the oven-like heat reflected off the stucco and brick. A hundred yards away churned the Ganges. He wondered if there might be a breeze off the water when he reached the top.

No such luck. Nor were the mountains visible in the haze. Thirsty and a little dizzy, hand cupped over the brim of his headwear to cut the glare, he searched out the local landmarks — such as they were, for the only imposing structure anywhere near Patna was the Golghar itself. Close by to the west, the square house built by Captain Garstin turned its back to the river. To the north there was nothing but the water's muddy margin, which lacked even bathing steps; certain stretches of the Ganges, he was given to understand, were less copiously endowed with sanctity than others. Eastward, tangential to the parade ground, ranged the neat grid of bungalows, overlooked from a slight, almost imperceptible rise by the collectorate and the two- and three-story houses of government officials — the commercial resident, the district judge, the various revenue officers, the civil surgeon.

None qualified as mansions. Only the surgeon's, with its pocket portico and tall arched windows, pretended to grandness. But its distinction had nothing to do with the status of the medical profession. Divided into apartments, it had formerly housed the agents who carried on the largest part of the Company's trade in India. That business, as at Ghazipur, was opium.

Production of the narcotic had begun under the Mughals, who were fond of it themselves. Unlike alcohol, opium was not proscribed by Islam, and its production and sale became a state monopoly. With the decline of the Mughal Empire, control of the trade passed first to the merchants of Patna and then to the British. By the end of the eighteenth century, after the Company turned to opium to erase its trade deficit with China, East Indiamen laden with half a million pounds of opium each departed almost daily for Canton, returning months later with cargoes of tea.

Few Indians used the drug themselves. Warren Hastings, the first de facto governor general, had decided shortly after his appointment in 1773 to spare natives its temptation:

"Opium is not a necessity of life, but a pernicious article of luxury, which ought not to be permitted but for the purpose of foreign commerce only, and which the wisdom of the Government should carefully restrain from internal consumption."

The welfare of the Chinese, in other words, was someone else's problem. (Which it rapidly became: the tenfold increase in the amount of opium exported to China by the Company between 1790 and 1836 resulted, by one estimate, in a fiftyfold increase in the number of addicts there.)

Despite the Company's withdrawal from trade, it retained a monopoly on granting licenses for opium production and sale. Revenue from such licenses, which totaled £729,000 in 1834–35, would reach £3.3 million in 1849–50. The drug still accounted for a fifth of its revenues in India, with the percentage in Bihar as high as four-fifths. The opium agents stricken from the Company's payroll in Patna a few years before Nigel arrived were busier than ever. Some had gone into business for themselves. Others worked for private firms. They resided now in the Company Bagh, the Eurasian neighborhood sandwiched between Patna and the low rise at the edge of the civil station.

Even at that distance from the Golghar, a half mile or so, the Company Bagh could be recognized for what it was: a bastard child of East and West, unplanned and unloved. Mean, meandering streets, flat-roofed tenements, a colorless bazaar. Here and there, fine houses of a certain age, oddly placed and haphazardly maintained. Most belonged to the class of "commercial men." A few housed well-to-do natives of the zamindar class. There were two or three churches, and the District Court House. Overhanging all was a sallow pall of dust that merged in the distance with the undulating smudge of the old city wall. Beyond, through its western gate, lay what the British called the Black Town.

One of its last European residents was Francis Buchanan, a surveyor whose journal of life there in 1811–12 reads like an indictment. To his mystification, natives often spoke of their fondness for Patna. As far as he was concerned, "it would be difficult to imagine a more disgusting place." Amenities such as paving, cleaning, and lighting, considered essential in any European town of similar size and prominence, were "totally out of the question." The principal street, though "tolerably wide," was "by no means straight or regularly built."

The only thing Buchanan found to praise about the city was the "great number of fine-formed women" who frequented the riverbank, fetching water. But their burdens roused him to further indignation. Unlike most of the larger Indian cities, Patna lacked any waterworks. Thus, he wrote, "the capital of Behar continues to stand parched and dusty by the river's brink. The Ganges is at her feet and offers her its treasures, but her arm seems palsied, for she does not stretch it down to receive them."

Even wells were poorly utilized. Those near the river were inconveniently deep, and liable to contain water too saline for drinking. Better wells could be found farther inland, but no one had ever attempted to distribute their supply to the city.

About the Golghar, Buchanan struggled to contain his exasperation. He noted that the structure was "intended" as a granary. But it had never been filled. Captain Garstin, so diligent in perfecting arrangements for depositing the grain, neglected to provide for dispensing it: the four sets of doors opened inward. Even a small amount of grain inside would prevent them from opening at all.

There was no reversing the doors on their hinges without enlarging the access tunnels, no enlarging the tunnels without running the risk of bringing down the dome.

It was irremediable.

There stood the handiwork of the engineer John Garstin, by profession an apostle of the "regularly built." How then had it risen so hugely and absurdly on that graceless shore of ocher clay, as illogical and irregular as anything conceived or concocted by the wild, unknown men in the Black Town, that warren of chaos beyond the Company Bagh?

If only it was made by the natives, then that would explain it.

But it was not.

12

A Policeman

Nɪɢᴇʟ'ѕ ʟᴇᴛᴛᴇʀѕ ʜᴏᴍᴇ from Patna sketched his life in broad, sunny strokes. He reported that his job was auditing the tax receipts of the zamindars who controlled the district's extensive croplands. He said nothing about the predominant crop, *Papaver somniferum,* the opium poppy. (After he finally visited the Black Town, he included the East India Company's original factory in a list of the principal buildings there, noting its cavernous dimensions but omitting mention of its conversion to an opium warehouse.) Yet opium, without a doubt, was the central sun around which his work at the Patna Collectorate revolved. It was the principal source of the taxes whose assessment he calculated and whose collection he certified.

He was silent, too, about the outbreak of cholera in Patna in 1845, and insisted with some energy on his own good health, which he credited to a daily regimen of exercise in the cool of the morning, followed by a cold bath and a hearty breakfast of eggs, ham, and "fruit of all descriptions." Mindful, perhaps, that he was already on record about the dullness of station society, he never hinted that he missed Calcutta or regretted his decision to leave.

The plain truth, though, was that he had effectively killed his chances of climbing high on the Company career ladder when he put in for his transfer to Patna. There he earned an annual salary of £500 as an assistant to the collector, who in turn earned £2,000 and reported to a district collector making £3,000. As long as his health held out, Nigel could count on a collectorship coming his way in a few years' time. The odds of his taking charge of a district after that were better than even, especially if the pace of territorial expansion kept up. But that would have been the extent of his prospects. If he had remained at Government House, he might have aspired to an income of £7,000 a year, sitting among the heads of the service as secretary to government. The price of leaving Calcutta—and spurning the Bengal Club—was visibility. Without it he was just another young Englishman doing his duty, in a place where no one who was anyone wanted to be.

Patna did have a certain homely appeal, in its informality and its gentler connection between the rulers and the ruled. Gentlemen paying their evening calls forsook jackets, wearing instead two-layered waistcoats of white linen, with the outer garment sleeved. A sensible adaptation to the climate, it amounted to unthinkable freedom by the standards of Calcutta. The standard conveyance of the capital—a palanquin borne by natives—was shunned by most Europeans for the tonga, a light horse-drawn carriage that was faster and more comfortable but decidedly less imperial. (Highborn Indians and arriviste natives of the zamindar class, Nigel noted, stuck to palanquins.)

The official intolerance for Indians and their culture that was codified by Richard Wellesley had by then taken firm hold in Calcutta, Madras, and Bombay. There, as well as in some of the larger Bengal cantonments, an Englishman's exposure to Indian customs had become limited indeed. But the old ways died hard in the provinces. And part and parcel of the old ways for the British in India was what Salman Rushdie, talking of modern multiculturalism, would term "chutnification." They came, they saw, and in one way or another their imaginations were conquered.

Nigel arrived a generation too late to see any overt signs of Indianization among his colleagues in Patna. With its orderly ranks of bungalows and antipathy for the Black Town, the station had swung into step with the march of empire from its coastal strongholds into the bewitching mosaic of the Indian heartland. Compared with the rate of change in Calcutta, though, the cadence was a trifle off—just enough to whet his appetite anew for the "real India." When he learned he would be leaving Patna for a fortnight after Christmas to conduct a field audit in Ghazipur, he was eager to go:

"I should not want to live and work in the riotous surroundings fa-
voured by Indians everywhere, irrespective of their class or creed. Yet
one feels troubled at times by a sense of missing out on the good as
well as the bad. I do look forward to being reminded once again of the
colour and novelty of what is after all an exotic place to practise even
the most mundane of professions!"

The 150-mile journey to Ghazipur took six days. En route, he slept
in shabby dak bungalows, government guesthouses situated twelve to
fifteen miles apart that provided free accommodation to traveling officials and welcomed others for a small fee when space was available.
They were places, wrote Kipling in *My Own True Ghost Story*, where
one was apt to meet "all sorts of men, from sober traveling missionaries and deserters flying from British Regiments, to drunken loafers
who threw whisky bottles at all who passed."

"Daks" were tended sometimes by families but more often by elderly
khansamahs, male cooks and house stewards who could be counted on
to remember the idiosyncrasies of every sahib they had served. The
khansamah of the bungalow on the last stage to Ghazipur was a Rajput
from western India. He sat on his haunches in a gray-washed kitchen,
where gobbets of curing goat flesh hung from the rafters and chile
peppers spilled from an overturned wicker basket. He told Nigel that
he admired the British. To their lasting credit, they did not take bribes.
This was a novel development in the governance of India and a welcome departure from the ways of the past, which denied justice to the
poor.

The khansamah stirred the embers in a cooking hearth made out
of mud and finished with a wash of cow dung. He recited for Nigel
the names of the warrior kings of the Rajput clans, who fought off the
Greeks and bore the brunt of the invasions by Turkic and Afghan war-
lords. He spoke of the three sieges of Chittorgarh, each with its own
jauhar—the mass self-immolation of the female population to avoid
capture. He missed the kite-flying festival of his native Ahmedabad
and the fat, sweet pineapples that perfumed the bazaar. Rooted in the

hard-packed earth beside the kitchen doorway was a stunted mango tree. It never bore fruit. He supposed that he would die in that dusty bungalow on the road from Patna.

The sky outside turned orange, melting upward into violet. A fretful rooster announced a new arrival. The khansamah gave out a chuckle. He had promised Nigel a supper of spinach and hard-boiled eggs. Now there was another mouth to feed. That, he said, called for something heartier. He reached for a whetstone.

The latecomer, whom Nigel identified as H——, was a moustached policeman from Ulster with eleven years' service in India. Over chicken curry he regaled Nigel with his adventures as part of a task force established to suppress a murderous cult of highway robbers. Lurid accounts of the campaign against the Thugs had been a staple of colonial journalism since the 1830s. But Nigel was fascinated to meet someone with firsthand knowledge of the killers.

Thuggee, which dated back to the twelfth century, was a hereditary brotherhood whose scouts infiltrated groups of travelers and lured them to encampment sites where their confederates lay in wait. They strangled their victims with a rumal, the strong cloth noose that every Thug wore knotted around his waist.

Initiates subscribed to a strange code of ethics. They were taught from childhood that the Tantric goddess Kali had personally instructed the fathers of thuggery to kill without permitting bloodshed. Kali had also forbidden indiscriminate killing. Among those not to be harmed were the maimed and the leprous, fakirs and Ganges water carriers, musicians and dancers, sweepers, oil vendors, carpenters, and blacksmiths. (Women also constituted a protected class, but wives traveling with their husbands were routinely strangled in order to preserve the brotherhood's secrecy.)

Nor did Thuggee target Europeans. That probably explains why the British had long turned a blind eye to a cult that first came to their attention in the late seventeenth century. Until the abolition of ritual infanticide at Sagar Island in 1802, there was also a tradition of noninterference with Indian religious customs, however wicked they seemed to Christian sensibilities. The rise of evangelism changed all that, and East India Company chairman Charles Grant cited reports of mass murders committed by bands of stranglers roving the countryside of central India as evidence of the "darkness, vice, and misery" that ought to compel more strenuous efforts to "Christianize" the population.

Though such reports began reaching Calcutta in 1812, the government had no way of connecting the killings for several years, until the bodies of fifty victims were found in a series of wells along the Ganges. Close examination of the corpses convinced the authorities that a single secret society was responsible.

At a time when the methodology of detective work was in its infancy even in England, the British acted decisively to crush Thuggee. Profiling was employed to differentiate suspected Thugs from dacoits —garden-variety highwaymen who roughed up their victims but rarely killed except in self-defense. Data from each discovered attack site was collected, analyzed, and shared, eventually enabling police to predict the times and locations of future attacks. Agents disguised as merchants and pilgrims staged meticulously planned ambushes, surprising large bands of Thugs who believed they were attacking harmless travelers.

H—— had specialized in intelligence gathering, primarily through informants recruited from captured Thugs. About fifty, he said, had chosen to save themselves by turning King's evidence. Thousands more were imprisoned or transported to penal colonies in the Andaman Islands. Of the five hundred executed, many asked permission to place the hangman's noose around their own necks.

(A witness to the execution of eleven Thugs convicted of murdering thirty-five travelers in 1830 reported that "one of the youngest, a Mohammedan, impatient of the delay, stooped down so as to tighten the rope, and, stepping deliberately over the platform, hanged himself as coolly as one would step over a rock to take a swim in the sea!")

Few in Calcutta ever guessed how many active Thugs there were, said the policeman.

He was thirty-four, exhausted and overdue for home leave. He hated ships and life at sea. He meant to recover his health en route by breaking his journey for six months at the Cape of Good Hope. The climate there was said to be delightful. If the colony suited him, he might well stay. Police work was challenging anywhere. But in India there were ever more obstacles to getting it done.

"He reflected that the Government, confident in the superior wisdom of the Capital, makes scant allowance for the exercise of discretion by its agents in the provinces," wrote Nigel. "They are thus enjoined to act with reference neither to their knowledge of local conditions in the first place, nor their gauge of Native Feeling in the second."

Working relationships between Englishmen and Indians naturally suffered. They were, in fact, officially discouraged. Yet what was the suppression of Thuggee if not proof that close cooperation between the races could accomplish great things? Natives, of course, had good reason to work with the British — as couriers, informants, and trusted intelligence agents. Their people were the ones at risk, just as their ancestors had been at risk, just as their children would remain at risk until the cult was broken. (The fanciful notion that it survived covertly into the twentieth century would serve as the premise of the film *Indiana Jones and the Temple of Doom*.)

The British, on the face of it, had acted out of noblesse oblige. Unthreatened themselves, they spared no effort or expense in fighting the menace to those they ruled — a menace that modern historians contend was exaggerated by the Company but at the time was held to be responsible for as many as thirty thousand deaths in the 1830s alone. When you thought about it, though, Calcutta had a vested interest in the outcome. Thuggee was ecumenical. Though initiates regarded their victims as sacrifices to their patron deity Kali, the cult was open to Muslims and Sikhs as well as Hindus. Any secret organization that united Indians across the barriers of religion and caste—let alone one whose members were ruthless killers—posed a threat to the established order. And any threat to the established order was a threat to British rule.

The campaign against the Thugs, to borrow from the lexicon of another century, was a surgical strike.

Surgery is a delicate art. H—— feared that the British in India were losing their touch. He blamed it on the end of the Company's trading privileges. You could not trade with people unless you got to know them, over time. How many Englishmen had any contact with Indians at all anymore, apart from their servants and employees?

Listening to the policeman, it occurred to Nigel that there might be something ominous about the ever-widening gulf between the races, something more consequential than his melancholy sense of missing out on local color. In matters of human relations, of course, there was no one so predisposed to pessimism as a policeman. But the man had a point. The subjection of the subcontinent depended on mutual accommodation more than military power. Most of what the British had in India they owed in the first place to alliances and arrangements, to compromise and contracts. They had not so much conquered the country as cajoled it.

It was an approach, to be sure, that had lately been strained to the breaking point on the western frontier of British India. Less than a month had passed since forty thousand Sikhs crossed into Company territory on December 11, 1845. Trained by French and Italian generals, they constituted the only rival military power that remained on the subcontinent to challenge the British. Their kingdom of the Punjab, up to three hundred miles across, lay between the Sutlej and the Indus, rising from dusty alluvial plains to the forested hills and mountains of Kashmir. It was a rich and populous country, but its ongoing state, six years after the death of Ranjit Singh, the "Lion of the Punjab," was one of anarchy.

Enthroned in Lahore was a boy king with a conniving queen

mother, in league with a treacherous prime minister and at odds with a large, turbulent army, run by committees addicted to intrigue. Some senior officers played at kingmaking; others talked treason with the British. Following the demise of her elderly husband, Rani Jindan Kaur schemed to protect the birthright of her son Duleep, whose legitimacy as Ranjit Singh's heir was doubted by most of the population and, more worryingly, by powerful factions in the army. A foreign war, she decided, would best relieve the pressure.

A case could certainly be made for a preemptive assault on the British. The number of Company troops on the Sutlej frontier had shot up from twenty-five hundred men in 1838 to fourteen thousand in 1845. Most were added by Lord Ellenborough. After the annexations of Sindh and Gwalior to the south and east, his assurances to the Sikh administration of peaceful intentions were naturally received with skepticism.

"We have no right to seize Sind," said Charles Napier, the general sent to quell the insurrection there, "yet we shall do so, and a very advantageous, useful and humane piece of rascality it will be."

Suspicion only increased when word reached Lahore that Henry Hardinge, Ellenborough's brother-in-law and successor as governor general, was en route with his staff to the frontier outpost of Ferozepore, less than fifty miles from the Sikh capital. Unlike Ellenborough, Hardinge was a professional soldier—he had lost a hand while serving under Wellington in the Waterloo campaign—and thus a plausible commander in chief of an invasion force.

The rani, in concert with her prime minister and lover Lal Singh, had persuaded the army that it was better to seize the initiative and invade first. Even as Nigel sat talking with H—— in the dak bungalow, Henry Hardinge was reeling at Ferozepore from a pair of battles that had either killed or severely wounded a thousand troops and all but two officers of the general staff. At the second, one of the hardest-fought in the history of British arms, only the mysterious failure of Sikh reinforcements to attack the weakened Company army prevented its annihilation. Told on the battlefield that the Sikhs were withdrawing, Hardinge replied, "Another such victory and we are undone!"

Ignorant of the present crisis, Nigel saw the subjugation of the Sikhs as a foregone conclusion. The momentum that unrolled the carpet of colonial control across the entire Punjab Plain was regarded by the Company rank and file as an unstoppable force of history, the British equivalent of the American doctrine proclaimed in a New York newspaper on December 27, 1845, a day or two before he left Patna for Ghazipur: "the right of our manifest destiny to overspread and to possess the whole of the continent."

But what happened next?

Would they readily accept "the superior wisdom of the Capital"?

Or would they want to talk about it?

And if Calcutta refused to talk about it, what then?

If you couldn't trade with people until you got to know them, how then might you rule them, through one-size-fits-all decisions made a thousand miles away?

The difficulty seemed plain enough to Nigel in the mellow circle of lamplight in the homely lodge on the road to Ghazipur. But in his letter home, he supposed rather forlornly that everyone at Government House would dismiss it as claptrap and nonsense. The idea that the fate of the empire depended on paying close attention to the welfare and wishes of its inhabitants was as out of date as a tricorn hat. He doubted that anyone of importance had espoused such a policy in India for at least fifty years.

In this, he was about to discover, he was very much mistaken.

13

A Christian Soldier

SOON AFTER MAJOR Henry Montgomery Lawrence rode into Ghazipur on January 10, 1846, Nigel joined the civilians who gathered round him at the home of the local collector. Some would dine out for years on the story of their evening in the presence of a legend. Lawrence is regarded today as one of the heroes of empire. An island in the Indian Ocean and a town in New Zealand are named after him, as are the prestigious Lawrence Schools in Himachal Pradesh, Tamil Nadu, and the Punjab, which he founded for the education of the children of European soldiers serving in India. But when Nigel first met him at Ghazipur, his star burned no brighter than a score of others in the colonial firmament. Lawrence drew a crowd not because of who he was, but because of where he came from. He had served since 1843 as British resident in the mountain kingdom of Nepal, homeland of the Gurkhas, the stalwart soldiers now famed for their mercenary service in conflicts all around the world. With thousands of those reputedly ferocious fighters in worrying proximity to Ghazipur, just a few days' march from Nepalese territory, everyone wanted to know if they would take their cue from the Sikhs and cross the border.

Lawrence, a thirty-nine-year-old cavalry officer who had made a name for himself in forcing the Khyber Pass with the Army of Retribution, told his listeners that he saw the Gurkhas as a formidable defensive force in their own country, but insignificant invaders. "The danger of the Ghorka troops he thought much exaggerated by people in the plains," Nigel wrote in a reassuring letter to his parents, adding that in any case he would shortly return to Patna, where the garrison was "large and very staunch."

About the likelihood of a Gurkha offensive, however, Lawrence held his tongue. A letter written a few days earlier by his wife and posted from Segowlee, on the Nepalese frontier, revealed his concern about "disaffection to a large extent" among certain regiments of Company troops, with "presents" known to be reaching Nepal from the mutinous units. But he probably saw no point in alarming the small clutch of civil servants based in Ghazipur.

He surprised them nonetheless with his views on the future of the Punjab. Once the Sikhs were subdued, he said, they would not be punished. Annexation of their territory, contrary to expectations of the Company rank and file, was not on the cards.

"He maintained, to some astonishment, that such a course was unnecessary and unwise," wrote Nigel afterwards. "He thought it better to re-order the Sikh government and emplace a resident in Lahore, under whose guidance the energies of the people might be turned towards improvement of their welfare, rather than provoking hostilities whose certain outcome would be their further suffering, and greater ruin."

Lawrence was en route to the camp outside Ferozepore where Governor General Henry Hardinge was reorganizing his command in the aftermath of the Pyrrhic victory over the Sikhs, which had killed most of his officers. Among the fallen was Major George Broadfoot, political agent for the Punjab, and Hardinge had summoned Lawrence to take his place. Three years before, to Lawrence's consternation, he had been passed over for the same position by Hardinge's predecessor, Lord Ellenborough. Though his qualifications and his valor as an officer were beyond dispute, Lawrence's conduct as civil administrator of Ferozepore district had raised eyebrows in Calcutta. Upon taking office, he had immediately challenged the status quo. High-handedness might have served in the past, he informed his subordinates, but it had got to stop:

"More mischief has been done through the overbearing demeanour, the rude language, the haughty bearing, of many of the functionaries of India towards the natives than from almost any other cause."

Lawrence, who was born in Ceylon and had lived among Indians for most of his life, likewise wasted no time in deploring application of the term "niggers" to natives; his refusal to tolerate its use in his presence would cause bemusement in high places for the rest of his life. But his greatest quarrel concerned the very nature of the revenue officer's work in India. "At least nine tenths of his time," Lawrence wrote, ought to be given over not to the collection of taxes but to "measures which may raise the status and add to the happiness of the people."

Such a pronouncement could only antagonize Ellenborough, who had never factored "the happiness of the people" into the equation of governance at all. He not only vetoed Lawrence's promotion but overlooked him in distributing military honors for the Afghan War. Though his service entitled him to the distinction of Companion of the Bath, Lawrence failed to receive it, adding insult to his sense of injury. Ellenborough regretfully wrote to inform him that the matter was out of his hands. But he offered what he called "ample proof" of his estimation for Lawrence with a new appointment, as British resident at the court of Nepal.

The position was well salaried. It carried with it plenipotentiary powers. But it required no great inductive leap for Lawrence to recognize the position for what it really was. The public work of the resident there, wrote his biographer, consisted of "studiously doing nothing." He was ordered by Ellenborough to "abstain absolutely" from any interference in the kingdom's internal affairs. The Kathmandu residency was exile, pure and simple.

Just three Europeans — the resident, a surgeon, and an officer commanding their escort — were permitted entry to the kingdom. In the beginning, at least, Lawrence would be deprived even of the company of his wife. Nepal, he was warned, was "a country where no white-faced woman had ever been seen." Its rulers, moreover, were thought to believe that "the introduction of a foreign woman would be the downfall of their empire." When Honoria Lawrence's husband departed for Nepal, she remained behind in Lucknow with their five-year-old son, "awaiting the ultimate decision with no little trepidation."

She was devout but down-to-earth, a cousin of Henry's from Ulster. He had courted her for nine years—mostly via correspondence—before pressing his suit at the age of thirty-one. On the eve of their wedding, she solemnly promised his sister Letitia that she would make it her mission to look after his soul. Wherever Henry went, she meant to follow.

And so she did. Her grand-niece Maud Diver wrote that Honoria and her children—she would bear four, of whom two sons and one daughter survived—became "camp equipment, jolted in bullock carts and on the backs of camels, exposed to dust, sun, heat, cholera and malaria, moving always from tent to bungalow and back again, gypsies without a home, hearth beneath the stars." Conditions improved when they settled into a fixed abode after Henry's posting to Ferozepore, but not by much. There they lived in two "little pigeon holes" in a crumbling mud-and-brick fort, itself the only pukka building on a forbidding plain that Mrs. Lawrence described as "a wilderness of cacti, prickly scrub, sandy hillocks and the bleached bones of camels and bullocks."

She was a remarkable woman, independent of spirit and far less mindful of her exalted status as a memsahib than her contemporaries. (Most of whom, she privately maintained, were better off keeping to the larger civil stations; the Indian countryside was no place for "a lady who has nerves, a lady who shrinks from driving over rough and smooth, or riding through a jungle.") Though "not beautiful in the ordinary acceptance of the term," wrote one of her husband's assistants, "a harmony, fervour, and intelligence breathed in her expression."

Accustomed to circumstances that no gentlewoman of the day was expected to endure, Honoria left it to functionaries in Calcutta to fret over the difficulties that awaited her if the Nepalese authorities chose to let down their guard. She felt certain that their "fears and misgivings" were exaggerated. None of them, after all, had firsthand knowledge of the country or its customs. If anything, she supposed that the leisurely pace of life in Kathmandu would prove something of a tonic, especially for her hardworking husband, who still suffered from the effects of cerebral malaria contracted during his service as an artillery officer in Burma. When he wrote that there would be no objection to her coming, she rejoiced in the onset of a heaven-sent holiday:

"How delightfully snug we shall be! How much we shall read, and write, and talk, and think!" she responded from Lucknow. Soon enough, her husband confided in a letter to a friend that Honoria was right. What he still called his "exile" was turning out to be a blessing in disguise, so much of one that he would choose it over the job denied him by Lord Ellenborough.

Nonetheless, he hastened to add, it was "not unpleasant to think that some people fancy I ought to have got charge of the Sikh duties." Nor did his contentment prevent him from working diligently to reinforce their opinions. He had long harbored literary aspirations, and he soon learned of the founding of a review devoted entirely to Indian subjects by John William Kaye, a brother officer in the Bengal Artillery. Its target audience was the emerging English-educated Bengali middle class; its purpose, defined by Kaye in the Editor's Statement, "simply to bring together such useful information, and propagate such sound opinions, relating to Indian affairs, as will, it is hoped, conduce, in some small measure, directly or indirectly, to the amelioration of the condition of the people."

Kaye himself called the *Calcutta Review* "a bold and seemingly a hopeless experiment," one that he expected would "last out a few numbers and then die." But it proved a success, one that he later credited "in no small measure" to the contributions of Henry Lawrence. "It was precisely the organ," wrote Kaye, "for which he had long been wishing as a vehicle for the expression of his thoughts."

Lawrence promised to contribute to every number. His wife served as his editor. He never wrote well, but buried in the turgid prose of his lengthy papers on such topics as "The Sikhs and Their Country," "Military Defence of our Indian Empire," and "History of the Punjab" were cogent insights and provocative parallels:

"The same causes operated for our first success in both India and Afghanistan; and the errors by which we lost the latter may any day deprive us of the former."

Gravest of all those errors, Lawrence argued, was the "Forward Policy," which called for further expansion of British India to its "natural boundaries" to prevent Russia's dominance of Western Asia from spreading to the subcontinent.

In truth, he wrote, the chief danger to British rule was from within, not without. The enemy who could not reach them with his bayonets could touch them more fatally by rousing the distrust of their subjects. Earning and keeping the trust of the native population required treating them as partners, not subordinates. Their well-being ought to be the principal objective of the Government of India.

His views naturally found favor with the Bengali intelligentsia, whose support made the *Calcutta Review* a going concern. After Ellenborough returned to England, they also caught the attention of his successor at Government House. Henry Hardinge opposed any further annexation of territory, which he believed could not be held by force of arms without dangerously weakening the British position elsewhere in India. In this he saw eye to eye with Lawrence; after reading his articles, he concluded that no one in India was as wise and well informed about the Sikhs of the Punjab, who constituted the biggest threat to his policy of peace. The death of Broadfoot—whose arrogance is cited by many as a factor in the Sikhs' decision to go to war—probably hastened a change that Hardinge had already decided on.

Lawrence told his listeners at Ghazipur that his articles made a detailed case for repudiating the Forward Policy and forgoing annexation of the Punjab, based on his own experience and observations while serving there. But he neglected to specify where they were published, and as he prepared to retire for the night, Nigel asked him.

Their brief conversation set Nigel on the path he would follow for the rest of his career. Lawrence questioned him about his education, saying that there was no better preparation than Haileybury for meeting the challenges that the British now faced in administering India. Both Henry and his older brother George were Addiscombe men, graduates of the Company's military academy who began their service as cadets in the Bengal Army. Their younger brother John had intended to follow their example, but was sent against his wishes to Haileybury and, like Nigel, came East as a "Writer."

It was John, Henry said presciently of the future 1st Baron Lawrence and viceroy of India, who was best positioned to achieve great things in India. Soldiering was a noble occupation, and a necessary one, but henceforth progress would depend on curbing its role in the arrangement of affairs between the races:

"He said that the object of Government is peace, and must be so at all times, for does not Scripture tell us that its makers are blessed? He means to show in the Punjaub that peace may be achieved by earning the respect of Natives through words and deeds instead of arms, and indeed by acknowledging all that is respectable and good in the Natives themselves. He is soft-spoken and seems at times almost shy, but there is an Irish fire burning deep within, and after he said his good-byes the room seemed a little colder in his absence—a most remarkable man."

Before Lawrence left, he asked Nigel how his Persian was. Nigel replied that he had just missed out on a degree in honor at the College of Fort William, and Henry recorded his name in a small notebook that he carried in his pocket.

14

Gulzarbagh

1975

WHEN I RETURNED to the Ganges Guest House after visiting the European cemetery in Patna, I asked the desk clerk if he knew of any other places thereabouts where an Englishman might have been buried.

He frowned.

I had not found the gravestone I was seeking?

I told him that everyone interred there had died in 1763, long before the man I was looking for was born.

Not only that, I added, but they had all died in the same month, October.

That was odd, he said.

He wondered why that would be.

There were famines in the old days, but of course not among the English.

Cholera, perhaps, though that tended not to kill everyone in short order; such epidemics might last years.

He couldn't think of any rebellions, either.

Not that far back.

The Mutiny was more recent.

"Eighteen-fifties."

I nodded. For once I felt knowledgeable about Indian history. Rasheed, the Pashtun who befriended me at Margalla Pass, had mentioned that John Nicholson was killed at Delhi, leading a charge against the mutineers.

Well, said the desk clerk, it only stood to reason that there must be another cemetery. Unfortunately, he had no idea where it might be. He suggested that I inquire at the British Council library, located on Bank Road.

In Gulzarbagh.

Quite near the cemetery I had just visited.

There was no concealing my dismay. He gave me a knowing look.

"You will like it," he said. "It is air-conditioned."

India is full of surprises. The air conditioning at the British Council library in Gulzarbagh turned out to be functional. The tables were filled with neatly dressed Indians poring over recent numbers of *The Economist*, *Nature*, and *New Scientist*. A bulletin board promoted an impressive schedule of English Learning Programmes. Everything was very clean. Slinking up to the help desk in my sweat-stained bush shirt, I felt like an intruder.

A pleasant young woman in a patterned silk sari welcomed me and listened sympathetically as I recounted my fruitless search of the graveyard by the Catholic church. She said that it was the oldest local Christian cemetery, but by no means the largest. That would be the burial ground at Danapur Cantonment, a few miles to the west. She had not visited it herself, but Danapur had been the second cantonment established by the British in India, after Barrackpore, and she was sure there were hundreds of officers interred there, if not a thousand or more.

I asked if it was limited to army officers. She said she believed so. I told her what my mother had told me: that Nigel had worked for the government. I hadn't yet learned that he was actually employed by the East India Company.

She said that someone who died while in the civil service was likely to be buried in the churchyard where he worshiped. Such a grave could be difficult to find, because most of the churches from that era had lost their congregations when the British left India. There would be a care-taker, but without knowing the location of the church itself . . .

"He quit his job before he died," I said. "He probably stopped going to church. He was supposed to have gone native. He lost touch with his family."

In that case, she said, there would be no grave to find.

He would have been cremated. That was the custom, if he had truly gone native and was living among Hindus.

That he was, I said to myself. At the time of his death, he was liv-ing in Nepal, where the king himself was revered as an incarnation of Lord Vishnu.

To the woman at the library desk I said, "Oh."

I said I guessed that Nigel's family had never thought things through.

Then I added that I was grateful to be spared the swelter of an out-ing to Danapur.

She smiled. She called it a "challenging" time of year. She asked if there was anything else.

I told her that I couldn't help wondering about the cemetery that morning. How was it that those fifty-odd Christians had all died at the same time?

"They were the victims of a massacre," she said. "Would you like to read about it?"

She said nothing more as she steered me to the history shelf. I found myself admiring her tact even as I regretted my own gaucherie. I imag-ined another kind of "Indian" in another part of the world, asked by the descendant of a cavalryman how General Custer and his men had come to meet their maker.

Then I opened the account of the Patna Massacre. Its perpetrator was a European, a German butcher's son named Walter Reinhardt, who "dressed in Moghul dress, kept a zenana" — a harem — "and had gone native." After serving with the East India Company's army in the

1750s, he attached himself to the cause of Mir Quasim, the nawab of Bengal, and led the assault in Patna that resulted in the deaths of the Englishmen buried together at Gulzarbagh. He then ordered the dismemberment of their bodies, and had the parts thrown in a well.

India is full of surprises.

15

A Conquest

THE ENTRY OF Nigel's name in Henry Lawrence's notebook proved to be his ticket out of Patna. In August 1846, after seven hundred miles of dusty travel by stagecoach on the Grand Trunk Road, he arrived at the cantonment of Ambala, just a few days' journey from the Punjab frontier. The Anglo-Sikh War was over, won by the British in the decisive Battle of Sobraon that February. Henry Lawrence, now appointed resident at Lahore and raised to the rank of colonel, had installed his brother John to serve as commissioner of Trans-Sutlej Jullundur Doab, a territory between the Sutlej and Beas rivers ceded by the Sikhs to British India under the terms of the treaty that ended the fighting. Nigel was one of the Company civilians whom John Lawrence had employed on Henry's recommendation, to work on the settlement of tax revenues in two of the outlying districts he administered, Kapurthala and Hoshiarpur.

Under Sikh rule, the revenue system in the Punjab had evolved into a species of organized plunder. The policy in Bannu district, for example, was to allow taxes to fall into arrears for two or three seasons, then send to Lahore for an army to confiscate all the crops and whatever material goods the troops could get their hands on. These exactions, seldom collected without a fight, often led to the destruction of whole villages. Henry, charged by Calcutta with holding "peaceful viceregal authority" over the province and "assisting" the Sikh administration in matters of revenue, decided to make tax reform the linchpin of British efforts to pacify the Punjab without resort to arms. He began by calling a halt to taxing entirely, pending the painstaking process known as "settlement." To ensure that taxes were collected on the basis of objective criteria, every patch of cultivated land in an area was walked and assessed for its worth, and a rate of land tax "settled" on it. Given the state of the Punjab, Lawrence believed, the rate itself ought to be low:

"Our assessment should be so light as to require no compulsion in the collection, and we should rather be protectors in the land than tax-masters."

The first phase of a district settlement involved securing the cooperation of tribal elders, and most of the army officers seconded by Lawrence to positions as civil administrators enjoyed it. They rode from village to village, seeing the countryside and enjoying the hospitality of clan leaders and village chiefs. It made for a welcome change from paperwork.

"Office work and confinement within doors is not my speciality," wrote Harry Lumsden, an officer around Nigel's age. "I would always rather ride twenty miles than write a note."

The routine of assessment, though tedious, was all right, too. Revenue parties were accompanied by small military escorts, and Lawrence's men valued the companionship of the English officers in command. The Punjab in 1846 was a wild and lonely place compared with the vast ordered grid of cropland it later became with the construction of irrigation canals under British administration. Much of it remained untouched jungle, interrupted by a serpentine web of cultivation along the courses of its five great rivers and their tributaries. Crocodiles swarmed their waters; panthers prowled their banks. Crossings — at deep and treacherous fords or by ramshackle ferries — were laborious and time-consuming at the best at times, dangerous at the worst. But the adventure relieved the monotony of the fieldwork itself, and natives warmed quickly to the new regime.

It was only back at headquarters that the settlement process turned onerous. Documenting rates, assessments, and payments required thousands of entries in cross-referenced ledgers, and native clerks proved slow to get the hang of it. Checking and rechecking their record keeping became the principal occupation of such unlikely over-seers as Harry Lumsden, who had first come to Lawrence's attention when he led a bayonet charge into enemy trenches at the Battle of So-braon, "killing all the gunners on the spot, and driving the whole line of the Seikh infantry from the right of their entrenchment into the river, where they were shot down like so many ducks."

Though Calcutta had promised Henry Lawrence a supply of Eng-lish clerks to relieve these men of action, they proved slow in arriving. He took matters into his own hands, "borrowing" civilians whom he had encountered on his travels. Though Nigel remained on the books at the Patna Collectorate, he would spend most of the next three years working out of Jullundur, a hundred miles up the Grand Trunk Road from Ambala.

Newly established as the administrative center of the Trans-Sut-lej districts, Jullundur was thought to be the Punjab's oldest city. Like Patna, it was mentioned in the Mahabharata, and among the ruins in the adjacent countryside along the Beas River were a dozen colos-sal altars to the gods of the Greek pantheon, erected by Alexander the Great to mark the easternmost extent of his empire. It was on the banks of the Beas—the ancient Hyphasis—that his Macedonian troops mutinied in the monsoon rain in 326 B.C. and refused to go far-ther, after eight years on the march. And it was in Alexandria on the Hyphasis, founded nearby, that many of them chose to remain, rather than risk the hardships of the return.

But it was a story out of recent history that captivated Nigel when he called on the political agent at Ambala, a cantonment laid out by the British three years before to replace an installation abandoned during the malaria epidemic of 1841–42. Though actually farther from Sikh territory than the Ludhiana Cantonment, Ambala more closely resem-bled a frontier outpost. It was raw and relatively unkempt, the pace of life quickened by proximity to Simla, the hill station twenty miles away where Governor General Hardinge had chosen to reside in the war's aftermath rather than return to Calcutta, just to keep an eye on things. That proved to be a wise decision, because a band of renegade Sikhs at a mountain stronghold had threatened Hardinge's "policy of peace" almost as soon as he proclaimed it.

By far the largest fort in the Himalayas, the citadel of Kangra was also one of the oldest in India, first cited in the war records of Alexander. It stood atop a rocky crag at the confluence of two rivers, surrounded on three sides by water. Another steep hill, called Jayanti Mata, rose from a wide, deep valley on the fourth side. Over the centuries, its formidable defenses had repelled all but the greatest of the warriors whose armies swept up from the plain.

On March 9, 1846, with the mark of the eight-year-old boy king Duleep Singh on the Treaty of Lahore, Kangra had passed with the rest of the Jullundur Doab into the hands of the British. But they had yet to take possession when Henry Lawrence learned, a month later, that the Sikh garrison there was bricking up the gateway. The troops insisted that they would not surrender the fort until Duleep Singh appeared in the flesh and asked them to do so.

Kangra's garrison was small, about three hundred men. In strictly military terms, it posed little threat to British interests. The danger lay in the example of defiance. The hill tribes of the district held forts of their own, which, under the terms of the treaty, now belonged to the Government of India. Kangra was a test case for British control of them all. The insurrection, Henry advised his brother John, would have to be put down immediately. John, the civil official immediately responsible, would organize a siege train in Jullundur and advance toward Kangra.

Henry, for his part, would intercede with the Sikh administration —known colloquially as the Durbar—in Lahore. He warned Prime Minister Lal Singh of grave consequences for the Sikhs of even the slightest delay in surrendering the fortress to the British officer sent to take its command. Lal Singh promised to obtain the surrender, without making any conspicuous effort afterwards to do so. Due to "the evident hesitation of our reluctant allies," Lawrence counseled Hardinge, his own presence at Kangra was clearly required.

Once there, he meant to resolve the matter without resort to force. A siege was certain to be prolonged and bloody. "Kangra is a Gibraltar," he explained. "It is five miles round, and has one accessible point, which is defended by thirteen gates, one within the other."

He worried, too, about making martyrs of the defenders, and Hardinge agreed.

"A gallant resistance by the Sikh garrison," replied the governor, "is a very undesirable result."

Lawrence hoped to reach Kangra by the end of the month. When he was delayed, Lal Singh belatedly dispatched emissaries who were authorized to offer a bribe of twenty-five thousand rupees to the garrison in exchange for their surrender—not to the British, but to their coreligionists, before John Lawrence and the accompanying force under Brigadier Hugh Wheeler arrived on the scene. Though Henry welcomed this strategy to settle the matter without loss of life or face on either side, he refused to assume that the bribe would be accepted, and prepared to depart from Lahore.

Before he left, he paid a call on the bane of his existence, Rani Jindan Kaur. The queen mother was the daughter of an officer in charge of the royal kennels, and had married Ranjit Singh four years before his death. Henry Lawrence would later describe her as "the only active enemy to our policy," and though her political activity was his principal grievance, he also took exception to her sexual liaison with Lal Singh and the power and privileges she conferred on her maidservant, a slave girl who was also the mistress of Jindan's brother. All in all, he thought it a pity that the rani had disregarded the example of several of Ranjit Singh's older wives, who immolated themselves on his funeral pyre.

Lawrence wrote of Rani Jindan and her lover only in terms of moral

outrage. Another British officer, who was presented at court in Lahore
that September, sketched a fuller portrait:

> *I was initiated into the mysteries of Grand Durbars and the like, intro-*
> *duced to Lal Singh, the Prime Minister, young Dulip Singh, and a large*
> *bundle of clothes, placed on a chair and called the [Rani], out of which,*
> *now and then, might be seen a pair of feet and a remarkably pretty little*
> *hand. When the bundle was addressed, even in the most flowery Persian,*
> *the reply was always in a grinding sort of sound, strongly resembling that*
> *produced in the process of grinding coffee. However, the bundle, although*
> *she will not show her eyes, evidently has good ones, and shows her taste in*
> *the choice of her wazir [prime minister], Lal Singh. I have seldom seen a*
> *better looking man than Lal Singh. He is, I should say, about thirty years*
> *of age, strongly built, tall and very soldier-like, though as cunning as a fox;*
> *talks in a bland, kind tone, which could not hurt a fly, though he would just*
> *as soon cut a man's windpipe as look at him.*

When the rani received Lawrence, she deigned not to show herself
at all. She spoke to him from behind a screen in the Palace of Mirrors,
inside the great fort. Why was it, she asked, that Lawrence needed to
go to Kangra in person? Lal Singh had sent agents to make his wishes
known. Was it not fitting for a man in his position to remain aloof in
his power and majesty?

Lawrence replied that British troops had been ordered against the
garrison, and as the official agent for foreign relations and agent for
the Punjab, he needed to be there when they arrived. He had other
reasons, too, left unspoken. His brother John had shown an aptitude
for logistics but had no experience managing fighting men, and remained untried at diplomacy and making hard decisions. Kangra also
presented Henry with an opportunity to visibly assert his supreme authority over the affairs of the province.

Nearing the fortress on May 2, he noted the terrible condition of
the road that led to within gunnery range of its four-foot-thick walls.

Bringing up the wheeled carriages of artillery en route from Jullundur would take some doing—and could not be done at all without a leveling operation by thousands of laborers, working full-time for months. Guns borne by elephants, he advised Hardinge, were a proven alternative, "employed in these very parts by Maharajah Ranjit Singh," who had captured the fort from a local raja in 1809.

Lawrence's strategy, inspired by Ranjit Singh's, depended on intimidating the Kangra garrison into surrender with a show of firepower they could not long withstand. He immediately sent to Lal Singh, asking for as many elephants as he could spare. The following day, after Lawrence learned that the emissaries sent by Lal Singh had yet to approach the garrison with an offer to purchase their cooperation, he shamed them into calling at the fort "to make at least a show of fulfilling their mission."

Late that evening, they returned with two men, who were brought into Lawrence's tent to explain their refusal to accept such a bargain. In the flickering candlelight, they repeated what Lawrence called "the old excuse": that "Maharajah Ranjit Singh, of blessed memory, had enjoined them never to give up their post, even though many messages should come to order them. When he shewed his own face, it would be time enough for them to open the gates of Kangra."

Lawrence replied that Ranjit Singh, had he still been alive, would have journeyed to Kangra to release them from their obligation. The new maharaja, unfortunately, was too young to leave his capital. The garrison ought to have accepted the terms offered by the officers he had sent in his place, but they had not. Their fate was now in his own hands, and the only condition he could offer was to spare their lives if they surrendered.

They promised to return by noon the next day with an answer. But the messenger sent to fetch them was greeted by a gunshot, followed by cries that the garrison "would listen to no terms." To dramatize their resolve, riflemen began a campaign of sporadic sniper fire, aimed in the direction of Lawrence's camp.

There was nothing to do but wait for the guns—of a size, he knew, as yet unseen in those parts—and the elephants. The latter began arriving around the middle of May, accompanied by a notable of the Durbar who proposed that the garrison be allowed to leave with their luggage and arms. Lawrence refused, explaining in a letter to Hardinge that he could not permit men "who have been gratuitously firing on us for twenty days, to retire with the honours of war."

When the garrison itself made the same request, to march out bearing arms, Lawrence stood firm. On May 19, with the artillery a week away, he delivered an ultimatum. Heavy guns were nearing Kangra, he warned, and when the batteries were opened, "you need expect no mercy but you will be treated as Rebels and as Robbers."

His recalcitrance alarmed the governor and his staff in Simla. Hardinge worried that Lawrence was sabotaging the prospect of a negotiated settlement. This he deemed more important than ever, after receiving high praise from Prime Minister Robert Peel in the aftermath of the Sikh war. Peel judged Hardinge's policy of restraint "ten times more gratifying to the public mind" than the annexation of the Punjab would have been, and his colleagues in government were just as enthusiastic:

"They consider that [annexation] would have been a source of weakness and not of strength, that it would have extended our frontier at the greatest distance from our resources and on the weakest points."

And there was more to it than that. Even as Peel wrote, Britain was preparing for war with the United States over the Oregon Country, in the drainage of the Columbia River. The Americans, despite the dubious nature of their claim to territory north of the river's mouth, at the forty-sixth parallel, wanted the boundary fixed at 54°40'. The British government, much against the wishes of the Hudson's Bay Company, had offered to split the difference, proposing the forty-ninth parallel as the dividing line. The American president, James Polk, who had campaigned for office with the slogan "Fifty-four Forty or Fight!," rejected the compromise. But Peel believed—rightly, as it turned out—that the news out of the Punjab might make Polk think twice:

> *These are Indian considerations; but there are higher considerations still nearer home, affecting still more vital interests, that are decisive in favour of your policy. There is not a country in Europe or America that does not do us justice, that does not admire the signal proof of bravery and military skill ten times the more, because it was called forth in a righteous cause and because it has been followed by dignified forbearance and moderation in the hour of strength. I believe that what has taken place on the banks of the Sutlej will have its influence on the banks of the Oregon; that there is not an American who will not feel that if England follows the example you have set of moderation and justice in her negotiations, and is compelled to vindicate her rights or her honour by an appeal to arms, she will also follow on the St. Lawrence or the Hudson the example of disciplined valour and heroic devotion.*

With Hardinge basking in official favor for hewing to a course of "forbearance and moderation," he felt abashed by Lawrence's talk of merciless treatment for "Rebels" and "Robbers." He could live with the damage to his own reputation if the Sikhs refused to back down. But the consequent injury to larger British interests might prove grievous —even catastrophic if it soured the last hope of keeping the peace in North America. Was it worth the risk?

Lawrence stubbornly defended his tactics. By May 27 the big guns were only one hill away from Kangra. That evening, a deputation was summoned from the fort to meet with Lawrence and his brother John, who had arrived in advance of the guns. Both repeated the demand for unconditional surrender, and engaged the Sikh elders in discussion that lasted long into the night. When they finally prepared to leave, John invited them to remain in camp to watch the guns ascend the hill of Jayanti Mata at dawn. Such a feat they considered inconceivable, he wrote afterwards, but for all their skepticism they agreed to stay:

"At four a.m. they were awakened by vociferous cheering. They started from their rough beds and rushed out, believing that it was a sally from the garrison. They were soon deceived; for a few moments later, there appeared a couple of large elephants slowly and majestically pulling an eighteen-pounder, tandem fashion, with a third pushing behind. In this manner, gun after gun would make its way along the narrow pathway, and by the help of hundreds of sepoys, safely rounded the sharp corners which seemed to make further progress impossible."

The Sikhs watched until the last gun reached the plateau, saying nothing. Less than an hour after their return to the fort, a white flag fluttered from its ramparts. "The garrison defiled out man by man, and throwing down their arms, quietly took their way to the plains," wrote John. "Thus passed what might have developed into a very serious affair."

Henry Lawrence, like Ranjit Singh before him, had achieved the bloodless conquest of India's Gibraltar.

16

A Peace

AFTER REPORTING TO LAHORE, where Henry Lawrence had established his headquarters at a disused Mughal tomb in the suburbs, Nigel backtracked out of Jullundur to Hoshiarpur district, seventy-five miles to the northeast. As he set to work sorting out the tax assessments in the fall of 1846, he was conscious of playing a supporting role in a larger drama. Henry Lawrence had charged his brother John with winning over natives who were skeptical about the latest in a long line of outsiders who came from somewhere far away and insisted they were there to help. Officially, the Trans-Sutlej districts were wanted as a "buffer zone," an equilateral triangle of real estate some seventy-five miles to a side, its apex aimed like the point of an arrow toward the mountain passes leading into Kashmir. But Lawrence also saw the region as a potential showpiece of British good works for the benefit of an audience beyond its boundaries. No less than with the spectacle of the enormous guns borne by elephants to the mountain citadel of Kangra, he wanted word of the new government's integrity to spread throughout the Punjab.

"The conditions of daily living will be as rustic as any I have known," wrote Nigel in a letter to his parents. "But I relish the opportunity to bring timely relief to Natives who have long been afflicted with Robbers in the guise of Revenue Officers."

As he expected, his accommodations at Hoshiarpur were on the rough side, in a house where the racket of rats inside the walls subsided only in the small hours of morning. But it was situated on a quiet lane lined with jacaranda trees, and he delighted in the prospect of the forested Siwalik Hills nearby. The local household fuel was aromatic

pinewood, a welcome change from the dried cow patties burned elsewhere in India.

Above all, Hoshiarpur was "reliably safe," despite its recent status
as enemy territory. The closest hostilities during the war were a hundred miles away. Two or three thousand Company troops were stationed nearby at Jullundur, fulfilling Henry Lawrence's vision of the
Punjab's future: a sovereign Sikh kingdom, "fenced in and fortified by
British bayonets." The Sikhs moreover were now allies, not enemies,
having proven themselves under British officers on a military expedition sent by Lawrence to install a Hindu ruler in predominantly Muslim Kashmir. (A success at the time, it proved to be the worst decision
Lawrence ever made, and led to religious conflict that persists today,
with nuclear weapons replacing matchlocks in the arsenals of the ag-
grieved.)

So there was really nothing much for an Englishman to worry
about in Hoshiarpur, apart from malaria and snakebite and the con-
stancy of house servants in matters of hygiene. From some of the pe-
rennial banes of colonial existence there was no escaping, anywhere
in India. But the difficulties that Nigel feared might impede his work
there—anti-British feeling, principally, and resistance to change—
had so far failed to show themselves when he wrote home after a few
months in his new position. Most of the people were Hindus or Muslims who cared too little for the Sikh administration to regret its departure. Instead of resenting the Englishmen who had taken charge,
many seemed to welcome them. Cultivators were surprised and delighted by the promise of lower taxes. Once the British proved themselves as good as their word, the initial battle for the hearts and minds
of the populace would be won.

For the first time in years—perhaps for the first time ever—Nigel
believed in what he was doing. He wrote with evident pride of his own
part in "gaining the favour of the inhabitants through fulfilling their
desire for fair treatment," and lauded Lawrence for his wisdom:

"I am sure that he is the man to keep the peace, if the peace is to be kept."

On the other side of the Punjab, however, were the wilder Trans-Indus districts where the lieutenants who came to be known as "Henry Lawrence's Young Men" had a tougher challenge. There, between the Indus River and the mountains of Afghanistan, such officers as Harry Lumsden, John Nicholson, James Abbott, and Herbert Edwardes were obliged to reckon with warriors, not farmers. Their daunting brief was to apply Lawrence's humanitarian principles to Muslim tribes who were accustomed to governing themselves by Pashtunwali, an unwritten social code dating back to pre-Islamic times.

Most of its precepts were directly tied to notions of honor. The law of *tureh*, or bravery, required Pashtuns to defend their property, families, and women against all incursions. The law of *sabat*, or loyalty, insisted upon unconditional loyalty to friends, family, and tribe members. By the law of *nanawati* the Pashtun was expected to shelter and protect anyone who sought asylum under his roof, even one of his enemies and even at the sacrifice of his own life and property. Less onerous hospitality—food and accommodation—could be demanded under the law of *melmastia* by any traveler who appeared at his house and demanded it, with no expectation of favor or remuneration.

Paramount above all was the law of *badal*, which could be translated with equal accuracy as either "justice" or "revenge." The concepts, under Pashtunwali, were identical. Even a taunt was regarded as an insult that could be redressed only by bloodshed. Nor was there a statute of limitations. *Badal* applied to the wrongs of the past as well as of the present. If the original wrongdoer was dead—even a thousand years dead—his descendants might still be held to account for his misdeeds.

In consequence, the Trans-Indus country was a land of unending violence fueled by ancient vendettas. In 1849–50, the first year in which statistics were kept at Peshawar, murders or crimes accompanied by murder occurred at a rate of one per day. On public roads, as on private property, fear reigned supreme.

"The men, although wearing arms as regularly as others do clothes, seldom or never move beyond the limits of their own lands except disguised as beggars or priests," noted Henry Bellew, a surgeon who served under Harry Lumsden. "Feuds are settled and truces patched up but they break out afresh at the smallest provocation."

The situation faced by Herbert Edwardes, charged by Lawrence in March 1847 with "starting fair on an era of law and order" in Bannu, was typical. The country itself—an oval basin irrigated by two rivers and bounded on three sides by mountains—was the picture of an Eastern Arcadia, a "smiling vale," fecund and lovely. In Bannu, wrote Edwardes in his memoir *A Year on the Punjab Frontier, in 1848–49*, crops never failed:

> *The rudest and idlest agriculture is overpaid with corn, sugar, turmeric, and almost all the Indian grains in abundance. In spring it is a vegetable emerald; and in winter its many-coloured harvests look as if Ceres had stumbled against the great Salt Range, and spilt half her cornucopia in this favoured vale. As if to make the landscape perfect, a graceful variety of the shee-shum tree, whose boughs droop like the willow, is found here, and here alone; while along streams, and round the villages, the thick mulberry, festooned with the wild vine, throws a fragrant shade, beneath which well-fed Sayuds [holy men] look exquisitely happy, sleeping midway through their beads. Roses, too, without which Englishmen have learnt from the East to think no scenery complete, abound in the upper parts, at the close of spring.*

Alas, the promise of this land of plenty was betrayed by the malevolence of its inhabitants:

"Altogether, nature has so smiled on Bunnoo, that the stranger thinks it a paradise; and when he turns to the people, wonders how such spirits of evil ever found admittance."

There were the Bannuchi peasants, riven with faction and addicted to assassination. There were the *sayuds* and other "religious mendicants," who held mortgages on two-thirds of the land, "sucking the blood of the superstitious people." There were "the mean Hindu traders, enduring a life of degradation, that they may cheat their Muhommudan employers." Finally there were the Waziris, the only group in which Edwardes discerned qualities to admire, "half pastoral, half agricultural, wholly without law, but neither destitute of honour or virtue." By far the most feared of the Pashtun tribes, the Waziris lived in the mountains surrounding Bannu and descended to the plain every winter to graze their livestock and plunder the Bannuchis.

Such was the land; such were its holders. And there was one more thing: before departing for Bannu, Edwardes sent a native spy ahead to draw up a rough map. "He returned with a sheet of paper completely covered over with little squares and lozenges, and a name written in each, with no space between," recalled Edwardes afterwards.

> *"Why, Nizamooddeen," I said, "what is this?"*
> *"That," he replied triumphantly, "why that's Bunnoo!"*
> *"And what are all these squares?"*
> *"Oh! those are the forts."*

At the lowest estimate, they numbered no fewer than four hundred. It was, he noted sardonically, "a pleasing prospect" for one entrusted with the district's subjugation.

Edwardes arrived in Bannu on March 15, accompanied by a force of five hundred Sikh troops. He was twenty-nine years old, a clergyman's son with a strong evangelical bent. He believed that his ultimate mission in India was nothing short of divine. He had never commanded troops in the field, or distinguished himself in any way during his career in India as a field officer with the 1st Bengal Fusiliers, a European regiment manned mostly by Irishmen. He had come to the attention of both Henry Lawrence and General Hugh Gough, commander in chief of the British forces in India, as the anonymous author of a series of essays devoted to the military and political questions of the day that appeared in the *Delhi Gazette* in 1845.

Both men agreed with Edwardes' assessment of the mistakes made in prosecuting the Afghan War. Gough, upon ascertaining the writer's identity, invited him to join the general staff. Shortly after Edwardes arrived in Delhi, the Sikhs crossed the Sutlej. Edwardes, like most of Gough's aides, was wounded by gunfire in the war's opening engagement. He went on to become Henry Lawrence's personal assistant in Lahore.

With no reputation as a fighting man, Edwardes endeavored on the march to Bannu to secure his fame as a just one. En route from Lahore, he took a hard line against misbehavior by the Sikh troops under his command, who were accustomed to treating such expeditions as ongoing opportunities for plunder. With great ceremony, one of the worst offenders was publicly flogged; Edwardes then assembled the officers and said that the lives of their men depended on the maintenance of discipline, and he would "never overlook" further breaches of it. If the Sikhs refrained from plunder, the force would be received "as friends." If not, he warned, the "fanatic Bunnoochees" would resort to their "old system" of night attacks, "rushing in on the horror-stricken sentries with *juzail* [cutlass] and knife, and running amuck among the sleepless Sikh soldiery in the lines."

Afterwards, noted Edwardes with satisfaction, the "news of the anti-plunder regulations in our camp, spread through the country." The Bannuchis "flocked into our camp, and bought and sold with our soldiers, and sat and talked in our assemblies, as friends instead of enemies."

That "the small end of the wedge of civilized intercourse had at last been introduced," Edwardes wrote in his report to Henry Lawrence, was the "one great object gained" by a six-week expedition that was otherwise a failure. The fractious populace of Bannu refused to pay their taxes or, indeed, any heed at all to the wishes of Lahore. In November, Edwardes returned with instructions from Lawrence to subdue them "by a peaceful and just treaty; and reduce the nominal revenue, which was never paid, to a moderate tribute in acknowledgement of sovereignty."

After summoning the Bannuchi and Waziri chiefs and elders to a public council at his camp beside the Kurram River, Edwardes moved first to win over the Bannuchis. He meant, he said, to collect the arrears of revenue, build a fort, establish a Sikh garrison, and put their fertile land under a tax collector, "like any part of the Punjab kingdom." If they assisted him, ten percent of the Bannuchis' assessments would be divided each year among their chiefs assembled there. "If you do not," he warned, "I shall depose you and confiscate your estates."

The majority saw the advantages of coming under the protection of the new regime, and readily agreed. But the Waziris, offered the same terms, proved recalcitrant. Their leader, Sawan Khan, informed Edwardes that Waziris did not pay taxes as a matter of principle.

Without their acquiescence, Edwardes knew, his mission was doomed. The Waziris—who could muster an army of at least fifty thousand men in the vicinity and perhaps three times that many from their tribal territories as a whole—held the balance of power not only in Bannu but across the entire Trans-Indus region. With "peace or war depending on the issue," he drew a deep breath and proceeded to lecture them in Persian, which was translated into Pashto by an interpreter.

Over the course of twenty-five or thirty years, he began, the Waziris had taken advantage of divisions within the Bannuchis to invade their fertile valley and possess themselves little by little of extensive tracts of land. This occurred at a time of "no law" in Bannu, during which the Bannuchis themselves respected no man's rights, and acted on the principle that land belonged to whoever was strong enough to seize it. "They cannot complain if you followed their example," he declared, to warm approval. "Foreigners are always expected to adopt the customs of the country."

That time, however, was past. Maharaja Duleep Singh had determined to occupy Bannu, and the laws of his kingdom had come into force. Whoever held land in Bannu would have to pay taxes. No favor would be shown to any tribe, great or small, strong or weak. The Waziris, so argued Sawan Khan, had never paid revenue to any king, an argument that held good in their own country, which was still independent.

"If you do not like laws, and paying revenue," said Edwardes, "you are quite at liberty to give up your lands to the Bunnoochees, from whom you took them, and return to those happy hills where there is no revenue to give and no corn to eat."

He concluded by assuring the Waziris that he would either make them pay revenue like the Bannuchis or expel them from Bannu. He did not believe that they were fools enough "to forsake in a day the lands which you have been thirty years in conquering, or forego the whole of your rich harvests rather than pay a part." But the choice was theirs:

"Think over these things deliberately, and then give me a decisive answer, Yes or No."

After taking their leave from Edwardes, the Waziris met through the night, during which his spies provided updates on the stormy deliberations. Words at all times "ran very high," and Sawan Khan was accused of selling himself and his tribe to the East India Company. Some called for a local jihad against the infidel Sikhs and their British allies, but most considered the Bannuchis unreliable allies in a holy war. The tension finally broke at midday on December 17, when the chiefs and elders "sternly" returned to make "an unconditional surrender."

Edwardes wasted no time in producing a copy of his ultimatum and securing signatures from the bemused, illiterate Waziris. Work began the following day on a fortress, located on a plot of high ground overlooking the Bannu bazaar and called Duleepghar, after Duleep Singh. The next order of business was a legal code, promulgated on December 21. In criminal matters, the tenets of Pashtunwali were implicitly rejected. When a murder or a robbery was committed near a village, its inhabitants were held responsible for either producing the culprit or assisting in his apprehension. Suttee, infanticide, and slave dealing were henceforth regarded as crimes, subject to severe penalties. The system of *begdree*—forced labor—was no longer allowed, and "[n]either may either Hindoo or Muhommudan buy girls any longer by the pound; nor those sacred races who cannot degrade themselves by giving their daughters in marriage to meaner men, be permitted any more to strangle them."

On January 4, when the walls of the fort's inner citadel reached "such a height as to form a complete and almost impregnable intrenched position," Edwardes decided it was time to commence with the leveling of Bannu's four hundred forts, which he judged "the only really hazardous part of our enterprise." How to go about it was the question. Henry Lawrence had recommended that they be razed by the occupying troops. But Edwardes felt that their destruction should be carried out by the Bannuchis themselves. Their irritable tempers, he reasoned, were sure to be inflamed by the intrusion of Sikh soldiers into their villages and among their women. After sitting up "hour after hour" that night, trying to decide what to do, he drafted the proclamation that would make him a legend.

Now that just laws were in force, he wrote, it was no longer necessary that each village should be a fort. Every man's hut was a castle, because no one dared enter it to injure him.

"You are hereby ordered, therefore, to throw down to the ground the walls of every fort and enclosed village within the boundaries of Bunnoo; and I hold the Mullicks [chiefs] responsible for the carrying out of this order within fifteen days.

"At the end of fifteen days I will move against the first fort I see standing, considering the inhabitants as enemies."

For the first few days after the proclamation was posted, all of Bannu thought Edwardes was joking. Unease followed as his "serious manner" convinced the inhabitants he was in earnest, and everyone waited for their neighbor to make the first move. Reluctance began to ebb after Edwardes sent parties out to report back to him on where demolition work was proceeding and where it was not. As Edwardes followed up with personal inspections, Bannuchis and Waziris alike took up the task with increasing enthusiasm, and local chiefs rushed out to greet him with offerings of fat sheep. By the end of the month, the only fort standing in Bannu bore the name of Duleep Singh.

It was a triumph without parallel in the lawless lands beyond the Indus. In less than three months, without recourse to shot or shell, a lackluster junior officer had succeeded in a conquest "that the fanatic Sikh nation had vainly attempted, with fire and sword, for five-and-twenty years." In his preface to *A Year on the Punjab Frontier*, Edwardes explained that his feat had been accomplished "simply," by means of a balancing act:

"For fear of a Sikh Balancing army, two warlike and independent Mohammedan tribes levelled to the ground, at my bidding, the four hundred forts which constituted the strength of their country, and, for fear of those same Mohammedan tribes, the same Sikh army, at my bidding, constructed a fortress for the Crown, which completed the subjugation of the valley."

But there was more to it than that. The likes of Sawan Khan would never have persuaded their proud, unruly tribesmen to do Edwardes' bidding had they not recognized in him a new type of Englishman — as wily in his own way as they were in theirs, but for all that a man who respected them as men and admired their code of honor even as he hewed to the course set by his own. He was, in short, someone they could trust.

The same could be said for the impression made that winter by Lawrence's other lieutenants. "What days those were!" one of them later remembered. "How Henry Lawrence would send us off to great distances; Edwardes to Bannu, Nicholson to Peshawar, Abbott to Hazara, Lumsden somewhere else . . . giving us a tract of country as big as half of England, and giving us no more helpful directions than these: 'Settle the country, make the people happy; and take care there are no rows!'"

With minimal armed support, each relied on his personal influence to turn the local tide of anarchy and violence. The tranquility prevailing throughout the Trans-Indus districts by mid-January 1847 was so profound that Henry Lawrence's brother George brought his wife and children out to live with him in Peshawar, and Henry himself temporarily vacated his post in Lahore to take his first home leave in fifteen years.

17

Bankipore

1975

AFTER I READ about the history of the Patna Massacre at the British Council library in Gulzarbagh, I took my leave by thanking the woman at the help desk. She said it was her pleasure, and asked how long I would be stopping in Patna.

Not long, I said. I expected to be leaving for Kathmandu with my companion the following day. I told her that we had been studying Nepal at our college in the United States and were anxious to get there and see what it was like.

"It is cooler!" she said.

Then she said there was a nearby landmark with a connection to Nepal, an enormous granary built by the British almost two hundred years earlier. There was a fine view from the top, and at one time it was possible to see as far as the Himalayas. When the maharaja of Nepal was told this when he passed through Patna in the 1850s, he insisted on paying a visit. The maharaja, who was called Jang Bahadur, was on his way to England and wanted a last glimpse of his homeland. The difficulty was that the steep staircase that spiraled up the granary could not be negotiated by bearers with a palanquin, and it was beneath Jang Bahadur's status to climb the stairs on foot. To general amazement, he and his brother rode their horses to the top, which had never been done before.

Or since, as far as she knew.

The granary, known as the Golghar, was really quite famous, she said, one of the principal historical attractions in Bihar state. It was less than a five-minute walk.

"Shaded walk," she added.

She said that if Nigel had been stationed in Patna, he would have lived in the vicinity of the landmark himself, since the neighborhood surrounding it had originally been developed as an enclave for the British, who called it Bankipore.

"What is now the Gandhi Maidan was their polo field."

Following Bank Street to the entrance of the park surrounding the Golghar, it pleased me to imagine Nigel playing polo. It was nice to think about his life instead of his death. But not for long. Because it was impossible, outdoors in Patna in the Hot Weather, not to think about the climate. And now that I was acquainted with it, my mother's theory that the Nepalese might have shipped Nigel's body back to British territory for burial seemed ludicrous. There weren't any refrigerator cars in those days.

I walked on, conscious for the first time in India of following in Nigel's actual footsteps, beneath the very trees that would have shaded him as he went about his business. Years would pass before I read the letter that recounted his ascent of the Golghar; it was missing from the sheaf of correspondence that my mother had given me before I went East. But among those fragmentary pages were several written at his bungalow in Bankipore, and there I was. Such of the vintage bungalows that still stood were hidden, set well back from the pavement behind walls and dense hedges, but the grid of roads intersecting at right angles gave the game away. Unlike the rest of Patna, this district was planned.

And yet.

So, too, was the Golghar, gleaming whitely. It resembled the upper half of a colossal Easter egg, ornamented by the sweeping spirals of its staircases. A plaque at the base dating to the colonial era identified the structure as the world's largest silo, "part of a general Plan" ordered

by East India Company officials in Calcutta "for the perpetual prevention of Famine in these Provinces."

Without mentioning that the grain meant to be stored there was reserved for consumption by the Company army.

Without mentioning that the granary was never filled in any case,
since its inwardly opening doors would have blocked access to the
grain if it had been.

Of these omissions, as of Nigel's visit to the Golghar in 1844, I only
learned much later. I trudged up the narrow stairway, looked out over
the treetops and rooftops to the Ganges on the one hand and the old
city on the other, and tried to put myself in Nigel's place there.

I could not, and it was more than just the heat and humidity and
absence of conditioned air. I still had only vague ideas about the role
of the British in India, and most of what I thought I knew came from
a novel, E. M. Forster's *A Passage to India*. It was the sole work of fiction assigned as required reading in the college class I took to pre-
pare me for a year in Nepal. The story was set in a civil station called
Chandrapore. The English in Chandrapore despised India and Indians.
They conceived of themselves as bearers of the white man's burden, in
service — albeit grudgingly — to a higher calling. That calling, principally, was justice, yet what Forster chronicled was their deliberate injustice, visited cruelly and relentlessly upon a native falsely accused of
criminally assaulting an Englishwoman.

They were horrible people, those English in Chandrapore. And
though they were fictional, it seemed to me that Forster's depiction
rang terribly true, of a certain type at a given place in time. But even if
the time and place were right for Nigel, the type was all wrong.

From reading his letters, I knew he wasn't like that. He was too sensitive, too idealistic, too conscious of imposture as a pukka sahib.

And maybe that was it.

Maybe Nigel himself couldn't occupy his place there, not finally.

Maybe the motivation for his exile was identical to that of Forster's innocent native, who forsook his home and profession even after his accuser recanted and he was freed:

"His impulse to escape from the English was sound. They had frightened him permanently, and there are only two reactions against fright: to kick and scream on committees, or to retreat to a remote jungle, where the sahib seldom comes."

Of Chandrapore, too, there was something I only learned later, long after I stood atop the Golghar and looked down upon Bankipore.

The civil station of Chandrapore was fictional, but Forster based it on a real place, and that place was Bankipore.

18

A War

WHEN HENRY LAWRENCE went on leave at the beginning of 1847, he left his duties as resident in the hands of his brother John. He instructed his subordinates to hew strictly to his proven policy of "indirect rule" and insisted upon finesse rather than force as the solution to any problems that might arise.

One locus of potential trouble was Multan, a city-state on the western edge of the Punjab, two hundred miles south of Lahore. The Sikh emperor Ranjit Singh had captured Multan from the Afghan Durrani Empire in 1818. To rule it, he appointed a Hindu governor, Sawan Mal. In return for a hefty tribute, paid annually to Lahore, first Sawan and then his son Mulraj were given a free hand. The problem, from the standpoint of the Lahore Durbar in 1848, was that Mulraj had seized the occasion of Ranjit Singh's death, nine years before, as a pretext for withholding tribute.

Before Henry's departure, he had dispatched an emissary, charged with pressing Mulraj to pay the arrears. All John needed to do in his absence was to think of himself as a carpet dealer in the bazaar, with Mulraj his prospective customer. There would be haggling and bluff calling and indignant professions of wounded pride, but ultimately Lahore would get some of what it wanted without forcing Multan into a public loss of face. That would be the most dangerous outcome in that part of the world and one to be avoided even at the cost of getting rather (but not incontestably) the worst of the bargain.

The Durbar, after all, was not without fault in the matter. The Sikhs had ignored their accounts receivable for almost a decade. The role, then, of the British, having taken charge of Sikh foreign policy with the Treaty of Lahore, was to mediate, not dictate.

When John heard back from Multan in March, he received the expected parry to his brother's opening thrust. Ignoring the demand for payment, Mulraj informed Lawrence that he wished to resign as governor; his son would take his place. It was clearly a gambit to confuse the issue, one that John doubted he was meant to take at face value. A healthy man in the prime of life ruling a city of several hundred thousand people as he saw fit was an unlikely candidate for retirement.

By that time, however, John Lawrence had himself been forcibly retired from acting on Henry's behalf. Back in England, the incoming Whig prime minister had nominated Lord Dalhousie to replace Conservative appointee Henry Hardinge as governor general. The change of the party in power at home heralded a return to expansionist policies abroad, which Dalhousie strongly favored. He was also a staunch advocate of centralized authority who distrusted the freewheeling Lawrence brothers. After learning from Dalhousie that he was being replaced as acting resident by Frederick Currie, a bureaucrat from Calcutta, John Lawrence was obliged to ask Mulraj to postpone his decision, pending Currie's arrival.

Currie, who knew nothing of the Punjab, swept into Lahore determined to enforce the imperial discipline of Government House. He abandoned the open-door policy for natives established by the Lawrences, who made a point of hearing out anyone who called on them with a grievance or a question.

"With you we contest and badger and dispute," one Sikh noble told John Lawrence before he left to resume his duties at Jullundur. "You are one of our own. But what can we do with Currie sahib?"

Mulraj found himself asking the same question in Multan. Currie accepted his resignation without further ado and ignored his request that his son succeed him. Instead he appointed Khan Singh, a Sikh from the Durbar. Without consulting Mulraj, Currie also decided to disband some of the local troops in Multan and replace them with new regiments from Lahore. William Hodson, one of Lawrence's "Young Men" who had expected to take up the post of political agent at Multan, lost out to the far less experienced Patrick Vans Agnew, probably because Currie suspected that Hodson was cut from the same unorthodox cloth as Henry Lawrence.

Currie also named Lieutenant William Anderson, a young infantry officer, as British military commander there. Rather than join Khan Singh on the march to Multan — and get to know the seven hundred troops of the Sikh army who escorted him — Vans Agnew and Anderson sailed down the Ravi River. Oblivious to Currie's high-handedness in dealing with Mulraj, they had a comfortable, pleasant voyage; in a letter to a friend, Anderson exulted in what a "lucky fellow" he was.

Both men's luck ran out on April 19, the day after their rendezvous with the military force. Following a tour of Multan's fort, the Englishmen were attacked with spears and swords by Multani troops as they crossed the bridge over its moat. Khan Singh saved their lives by rallying the party's mounted escort, which carried the wounded men to the sanctuary of a prayer pavilion outside the city walls. But it soon emerged that even the Sikh troops under Khan Singh could not be relied upon. All but a few disappeared that night, abandoning the Englishmen to their fate. On the morning of the 20th, a mob rushed in. Vans Agnew died first, beheaded by blows from a saber as he sat comforting Anderson, who was then hacked to pieces in the bed where he lay. The following day, Mulraj presented Khan Singh with a blood-drenched cotton sack and contemptuously bade him return to Lahore with "the head of the youth he had brought down to govern at Mooltan."

Having thrown down the gauntlet, Mulraj appealed to disaffected Sikh officers throughout the Punjab, imploring them to widen his revolt into a full-scale rebellion that would force the British back across the Sutlej. At first they demurred, and an irregular army of three thousand "bold villains," raised by Herbert Edwardes from the tribes of

Bannu, captured a strategic fort held by troops loyal to Mulraj. They went on to besiege Multan itself, where Edwardes waited for assistance from Lahore.

Ignoring warnings from John Lawrence and Henry's political officers that time was of the essence, Currie temporized. A month after the murders of Anderson and Vans Agnew, he finally informed Edwardes that the rebellion would be crushed, but not "until the close of the Summer and Rainy seasons."

The news that no army would advance from Lahore for five or six months was all it took to set the Punjab ablaze. On June 8, a regiment of Sikh cavalry mutinied and joined the Multan rebels. When Sikhs garrisoned at Bannu followed suit, Fort Duleepghar was lost. Rebel troops then rose in Peshawar. By the time General Hugh Gough took to the field that fall, the mutineers from Multan were on the march toward a rendezvous in the central Punjab with a large rebel army, raised in the northern Hazara district after its Sikh governor declared war on the East India Company.

Delaying that convergence became the principal objective of Gough and his sixteen thousand men for the duration of the Second Anglo-Sikh War, one of the bloodiest ever fought anywhere. In battle after battle, the British suffered grievous losses under leadership so disgraceful that there was talk of a drumhead court-martial for Gough — even his execution. (Commander in more general actions than any British officer of the nineteenth century except the Duke of Wellington, he had a penchant for softening up enemy defenses with waves of charges by infantry.)

But delay it they did, until the decisive Battle of Gujrat, on February 21, 1849. Gough, who had just received orders recalling him to London, knew it would be his final engagement, and he rose to the opportunity to save his reputation by embracing the tactical use of artillery for the first time in his career. After a bombardment so intense that the opposing Sikh gunners abandoned their weapons and fled, the

British suffered the loss of only ninety-six men, compared with more than two thousand Sikh fatalities. Eleven days later, the rebel commander agreed to terms for surrender. His army—reduced by mass desertions to ten thousand men and ten guns—handed over its arms and disbanded.

Almost alone in pronouncing himself immune to "the hot fit of annexation" that broke out afterwards was Henry Lawrence, who had returned to India as Sir Henry following his investment in England as a Knight Commander of the Order of the Bath and resumed his duties at the residency in Lahore on February 1. He blamed the war on Frederick Currie and the military. Had Multan been captured in early September, he argued, there would have been no larger insurrection. He continued to believe that "indirect rule" was the best option for the British in the Punjab, and better served the long-term interests of the country's inhabitants. But his opinions were dismissed by Lord Dalhousie, who also rejected Lawrence's advice that the Company army be transformed by admitting natives to the officer corps.

"Lawrence has been greatly praised and rewarded and petted," Dalhousie wrote to Sir George Couper, "and no doubt naturally supposes himself a king of the Punjab." But his sovereign reign, as far as the governor was concerned, had reached its end:

> *[Lawrence] took charge three days ago from Sir F. Currie, and commenced his career by proposing a Proclamation which I have forbidden and shaken him for it. It began by saying that he was anxious it should be generally known that he had returned to Lahore, desirous of bringing peace to the Punjab, and then promising all sorts of things. I told him this sort of thing would not do at all; that I had great confidence in him, but that I could not permit him to substitute himself for the Government, whose servant he was, or permit a word to be said or an act done which should raise the notion that the policy of the Government depended in any degree on the agent who represented it; or that my measures and intentions would be the least affected by the fact of his being the Resident.*

The message was clear: there would be no more Kangras. The era of romantic individualism in conducting the Company's affairs of state had passed. Calcutta was in charge.

Lawrence was so shocked by the terms of the annexation proclamation that he refused at first to sign it. He preferred to resign, he told Dalhousie's chief secretary, Henry Elliot; clearly he had "no sort of influence" with the governor. Dalhousie, for his part, wished to avoid an open rupture with a well-known public figure whom Queen Victoria had lately received as an overnight guest at Windsor Castle. According to Herbert Edwardes, who was acting as Lawrence's personal assistant, Dalhousie charged Elliot with persuading Lawrence to change his mind. Elliot, wisely, appealed to Henry's idealism:

"He succeeded, mainly by the very just argument that the Resident's own favourite objects — the treatment of the vanquished with fair and even indulgent consideration, the smoothing down the inevitable pang of subjugation to those proud and brave enemies, with whose chieftains no man was so familiar as he, or could so fully appreciate what there was of noble in their character — were in imminent danger of being thwarted, if his moderating presence were removed between conqueror and conquered."

On March 29, the British flag was raised over the citadel of Lahore, and the following day Maharaja Duleep Singh sat for the last time on the golden throne of his father. On behalf of himself, his heirs, and his successors, the twelve-year-old monarch renounced all claims to the sovereignty of the Punjab. The Kingdom of the Sikhs was no more.

19

A Giant

NIGEL WAS ENTERING his eighth year in India when the Second Anglo-Sikh War ended, in March 1849. He was based in Kapurthala, where he had been transferred after completing work on the revenue settlement books at Hoshiarpur. Less than fifty miles away was a cantonment called Ludhiana. Though displaced by Lahore as the principal British outpost in western India, it remained the closest regional approximation of an English market town. There were books to buy in Ludhiana, and sweets, and tins of "hermetically sealed" provisions from England. There were also European doctors and dentists. Nigel would have paid a visit from time to time, and he probably had social connections there — friends of friends or colleagues.

Ludhiana also had its Little Kabul, where a clutch of Afghans lived under British protection. Most belonged to the clan that had ruled Afghanistan, the Sadozais. It was a Sadozai, Shah Shuja, whom the British had restored to the Kabul throne in their doomed attempt to subjugate his countrymen. And it was a Sadozai whom Nigel met and befriended in Ludhiana in the spring of 1849, though how they became acquainted is anyone's guess. Mentioned in passing by Nigel as "S——" in a letter written that June, he joined him on a road trip in September, traveling westward across the Punjab. It was their first immersion together in the "river of life" of the Grand Trunk Road; it would not be their last.

The official reason for the journey seems to have been Nigel's assignment to assist in the training of native revenue clerks in the Yousafzai district, outside Peshawar. The mysterious S—— went along to conduct some unspecified business of his own in Peshawar proper. On their way, they paid a visit to the most famous of "Henry Lawrence's Young Men," John Nicholson.

The same age as Nigel, but with two years on him in India, Nicholson was the nephew of a director of the East India Company. He had relied on his uncle's influence to secure a direct appointment to the Bengal Infantry without completing the mandatory two years of training at Addiscombe, and sailed for Calcutta a few weeks after his seventeenth birthday. He was a quiet boy but tall and strong, fast on his feet and free with his fists—"just a great big bully" according to his older sister Mary. His education was limited to the Royal School Dungannon, founded by James I for the sons of local merchants and farmers in Ulster, and he struggled for five years to master Urdu. He was neither a reader nor much of a writer; he so detested filing official reports that he sometimes condensed them into a single sentence. One dispatch to John Lawrence read, in full, "Sir, I have the honour to inform you that I have just shot a man who came to kill me. Your Obedient Servant, John Nicholson."

Then there was Nicholson's personality, described as "cool and reserved" by one fellow "political" (who liked him) and "stern and unbending" by another (who did not). No one recalled him as a man of warmth, wit, or charm—qualities that Nigel went out of his way to praise whenever he discerned them. Yet when Nigel first encountered him at the Lahore residency in the fall of 1846, he was positively smitten:

> [Nicholson] is tall and strong, with an unforced air of determination about him that excites admiration on the briefest acquaintance—a man of honesty and bravery and fine convictions, to be followed and trusted in the worst of conditions . . .
>
> After Cashmere is put right he wishes for political work in one of the outlying districts of the North-West frontier—Col. Lawrence has promised him as much. He has given a good deal of thought to the means of establishing justice there, and the attitude to be taken in governing under cir-

cumstances different from those present elsewhere in India. The great thing, he says, is to gain the favour of the inhabitants through fulfilling their desire for fair treatment, rather than enforcing co-operation based upon fear of force, or ill-use, or injustice. As we ourselves must lead by example, it behooves us then to master our own inmost fears, ruling ourselves individually in the manner we mean to rule Natives collectively. Such are his intentions and beliefs, as honourable as any expressed to me in India.

It was a philosophy of governance that by 1849 no longer held sway at the highest levels of colonial administration. Henry Lawrence's authority had been curtailed in the war's aftermath that spring, when the position of Punjab resident was abolished by Lord Dalhousie and replaced by a three-man Board of Administration, on which Lawrence sat with his brother John and another civilian. But the powers of Henry's Young Men in the field, unlike those of their mentor in Lahore, were extended, permitting them to operate in tribal areas as district commissioners with even greater latitude than before.

Nicholson was making the most of it, with exploits that thrilled the rough and ready tribesmen of the frontier. Fighting the Sikhs, he had led what he called "a very guerrilla sort of life, with seven hundred horse and foot hastily raised among the people of the country." Now stationed at Hasan Abdal, west of Margalla Pass, he had lately put paid to the anarchy of the Sind Sagar Doab by running a sword through the most rapacious of the local "robber chiefs," cutting off his head, and displaying it in his office after inviting every chief in the district to call on him. A few weeks before Nigel and S—— called at Hasan Abdal, an engineering officer named Alexander Taylor was relaxing in the dak bungalow there when a group of two dozen native men in saffron robes entered, saluted, and sat down silently before him. Upon asking their business, he learned that they were worshipers of Nicholson, whom they called "Nikal Seyn." These "Nikal Seynis" were en route to meet the object of their adoration, whose heroics during the recent war had persuaded them of his divinity. They had come to the rest house, they said, to pay their respects to Taylor as a member of Nikal Seyn's race.

Taylor, who was in charge of supervising the extension of the Grand Trunk Road from Lahore to Peshawar, heard afterwards that Nicholson had them all flogged when they appeared on his doorstep, and sent them packing with "most fearful imprecations."

Their reception — which proved to them that their deity was a just God and they were unworthy — served only to redouble their zeal, and, much to Nicholson's irritation, the Nikal Seynis flourished and gained adherents for the rest of his life. After his death, two of their leaders committed suicide by cutting their own throats, while the rest of the brotherhood were baptized as Christians, declaring that "Nikal Seyn always said that he was a man such as we are, and that he worshipped a God we could not see but who was always near us. Let us then learn to worship Nikal Seyn's God."

Hasan Abdal was an idyllic place, copiously watered by springs and surrounded by loquat orchards. Nicholson had established himself at a spot where a fountain gushed from a rock and became a rivulet, over which he built a platform of planks and pitched his canvas wall tent. Revealing a sensitive side that appealed to Nigel but remained unsuspected by the world at large, he christened the cooling flow beneath him Bendemeer, after the Romantic poem *Lalla Rookh*, by Thomas Moore:

> *There's a bower of roses by Bendemeer's stream,*
> *And the nightingale sings round it all the day long.*

Nicholson had never met S——. As a rule, he despised Afghans, whom he regarded as "the most vicious and blood thirsty race in existence." He had never forgiven himself for failing in his duty of care to his men during the Afghan War at the siege of Ghazni, where six hundred British officers and Indian troops were overwhelmed by twenty thousand Afghans. Under the surrender terms, only officers were promised honorable treatment, and Nicholson had argued passionately against abandoning their Hindu enlisted men. When his superior gave the order to lay down their arms after their food and water ran out, he refused to comply. At length he obeyed, and, wrote John William Kaye in *Lives of Indian Officers,* "gave up his sword with bitter tears and accompanied his comrades to an almost hopeless imprisonment." In short order, most of the native soldiers they left behind were hacked to pieces; those who survived were sold as slaves.

Though Nigel knew of Nicholson's capture and imprisonment during the Afghan War, he seems to have been unaware of an incident following his release, as he rode alongside Ensign Julian Dennys in the rear guard of the avenging army's withdrawal down the Khyber. Upon emerging from a narrow gorge into a small valley, Dennys spotted what appeared to be a naked body lying among the rocks on its far side. Cantering over, they found the corpse of a European, stripped of everything but a fragment of shirt, his genitals severed and stuffed in his mouth. Dennys, the first to dismount, remarked to Nicholson that the texture of the shirt was too fine to belong to a private soldier. Nicholson stared at the dead man.

"For a moment," wrote Dennys, "he could not speak." Nicholson stood gazing at the mutilated remains of his seventeen-year-old brother, Alexander.

Any awkwardness that Nicholson might have felt in welcoming S—— was dispelled when it emerged that both men shared a common acquaintance in the late Eldred Pottinger, who had served as a military adviser to the Afghans during the Persian siege of S——'s hometown of Herat ten years before.

"[Nicholson] is rather shy about telling 'war stories,'" wrote Nigel afterwards. "But he set aside his habitual reserve when it emerged that S—— had long enjoyed friendly relations with Major Pottinger, one of Capt. Nicholson's fellow captives when he was marched from Cabul to Bamiyan as a hostage during the Afghan War. They joined in reminiscence about the works and deeds of that gallant officer, now deceased, who left India for China some years ago, and contracted Fever there."

Nigel took advantage of Nicholson's loquaciousness to ask him about his recapture of Attock Fort the year before, perhaps the most far-famed example of his derring-do. With time of the essence, and Nicholson the only officer available to lead an expedition to regain control of the road from Lahore to Peshawar, he had risen from a sick-bed, so weakened with fever that George Lawrence judged him unfit to sit a horse. Yet he rode fifty miles under cover of darkness at the head of forty-odd Pashtun irregulars, setting so brisk a pace that nearly half of them fell far behind.

When the vanguard reached the bridge of boats that crossed the Indus to the fort, there was no question of waiting for the stragglers. Daylight drew nearer by the minute. Any chance of success depended on the element of surprise. What transpired, wrote Nigel, was "alto-gether miraculous" — the capture, without firing a single shot, of a for-tress enclosing an area as large as the City of London, garrisoned by a thousand Sikh troops. Nicholson had ridden boldly through the main gate, commanding the sentries to join his force and take up arms them-selves against the rebels within. He repeated the stratagem at an inner gate, only to encounter resistance at the final portal. When the sentries there aimed their rifles at him, he dismounted, seized the weapon of the nearest Sikh, and ordered his followers to arrest the captain of the guard. Ordered to lay down arms, the rebels obeyed to the last man.

"As strong and fine a word as 'Valour' does injustice to the conduct of such a one as Capt. Nicholson," wrote Nigel. "You will forgive me if I take the liberty of borrowing from Scripture, to aver that in this day too, it seems to me, there are 'giants in the earth!'"

When Nigel and S—— bade farewell to Nicholson, he told them that he was about to go on home leave. He had completed the requisite ten years of service with the Company that entitled him to a paid fur-lough in England. It meant losing his appointment as assistant com-missioner, but he was needed at home to comfort his grieving mother, a widow who had lost a second son in India earlier that year. William Nicholson, who was stationed at an outpost on the west bank of the Indus in Sindh, died there under mysterious circumstances on June 1, aged twenty. A few days before, after failing to appear at parade, he had been discovered semiconscious in his room. He had two broken ribs, and his body was covered with bruises. The only explanation he provided before lapsing into a coma was that he had dreamed of a fall from a great height. The officer who wrote to Mrs. Nicholson to inform her of his death suggested that William must have walked out of a window in his sleep, fallen from the veranda below and down a cliff, then crawled back somehow to his bed.

(Local natives took a darker view. Years later, when John's brother Charles visited William's grave, he learned that the house where he died was popularly known as "Murder House" and had remained uninhabited ever since.)

It was a melancholy leave-taking, and for Nigel the mood lingered on during an outing with S—— that followed. They rode out from Peshawar into a canyon that debouched from the mountains, accompanied by a dozen rough-looking men with incongruously exquisite manners. S—— identified them only as "friends." They reached their destination the following day, emerging into an upland of undulating ridges after navigating a succession of ever-steepening tracks through a vertical maze of rocky ramparts. This was Jagdalak, with its deposits of precious red corundum in a matrix of chalk-white marble.

We do not know whether Nigel entered one of the trenches where rubies were mined. Afterwards he wrote only of the "miners" at Jagdalak, without saying what they mined. But we do know what he saw there, because Jagdalak is also the site of the killing ground where the last of the Army of the Indus was slaughtered. He saw a hill of bones, and it unnerved him. He told S—— that he could not but fear for the future of his countrymen, so sure of themselves yet so vastly outnumbered.

20

A Crossing

WITHIN A FEW weeks of his visit to Hasan Abdal, Nigel decided to follow Nicholson's example and put in for home leave. Though he was just short of the decade of service in India that was usually required to qualify, paid leave was sometimes awarded earlier, on grounds of medical necessity or service in difficult conditions. It may have been Nicholson who advised Nigel that his work at Hoshiarpur and Kapurthala entitled him to special consideration. The Jullundur Doab had never been a war zone. But it qualified as a hardship post for civilians in peacetime, and life had only gotten rougher around the edges with the onset of the Second Anglo-Sikh War.

It probably did not hurt his chances that the dust had yet to settle from the reorganization of the Punjab administration. There were sure to be changes in the way revenue officers went about their business. But the nature of those changes remained in dispute—one that increasingly pitted John Lawrence against his brother Henry. For the rank and file caught in the middle, it was a convenient time to take a break, and at the end of January 1850, Nigel duly received leave to depart for England.

Most of those awarded leave made haste for the steamship docks of Calcutta, Bombay, or Madras. They hurried not only to escape the climate but to cut to the matrimonial chase in England, which was officially regarded as the main point of a Company man's first home leave. Marriage—to virtuous women of European descent—had been championed as a boon to empire since Richard Wellesley first advanced the idea that the British were a superior people who ruled most effectively by keeping to themselves. With the rise of the Evangelical movement and with parsons and missionaries flooding into India as never before, it was counted a Christianizing force as well. The dutiful memsahib who diverted her husband from giving vent to his "ungovernable passions" in the arms of a native mistress was also expected to compel his attendance at daily matins.

Young men who wanted to work for the Company, however, were still required to apply while in their mid-teens. They consequently arrived in India unattached, and the marriageable women of the "Fishing Fleet" that followed in their wake typically sought matches with bachelors whose griffinhood was long behind them. Home leave was the mechanism that corrected the imbalance of supply and demand. John Nicholson told Nigel at Hasan Abdal that the sole object of his upcoming leave was to comfort his mother in her bereavement. But Henry Lawrence had other ideas. "Get married, and come back soon," he wrote in approving Nicholson's request in October 1849.

Whether or not Nicholson meant to comply with Lawrence's wishes, he chose to tarry awhile in India after wrapping up his Company duties, and so did Nigel. Nicholson, accompanied by Herbert Edwardes, who was also bound for England, made a seven-hundred-mile river voyage in a rustic Indian houseboat down the Sutlej and the Indus in January 1850. It was a lazy interlude in which the two officers slipped into a companionable routine, exploring the shore after making fast to the riverbank each evening, searching for tiger tracks in the sand as their boatmen smoked "hubble-bubbles" and cooked simple meals. Nigel found himself on the lookout for big cats, too, on a detour that was far more challenging. On a fine winter morning in February, three days' journey out of Patna, still accompanied by S——, he alighted from a bullock cart on the bank of a poisonous-looking stream, its water black with rotting leaves. Eight or nine low-walled mud huts with shaggy mounded roofs like haystacks straggled up the opposite bank, interspersed with clumps of bamboo, tamarind, and mango trees. Beyond was a vivid green line of vegetation, running east and west to the horizon.

Nigel and S—— were bound for the heart of the Great Himalaya

Range, and there lay the way to hidden Nepal. There the mountain torrents met the lowland plain. There the plain's fine sediments and clays formed a natural dam for the groundwater flowing through the coarser soil brought down from the highlands, forcing it to the surface in marshes and springs. There was the Terai, a natural barrier twenty miles wide and a thousand miles long.

The "moist land."

Beneath its emerald canopy, everything seemed to be dissolving— the huge, shiny leaves, the tree trunks covered with dripping lichen, the slippery, squelching, rotting earth. It was a realm of fungi and ferns, worms and snakes, the Bengal tiger and the Indian rhinoceros, carnivorous flowers, indigo butterflies, mosquitos and malaria.

A no-man's-land.

The Terai had stymied would-be conquerors for millennia. The Mauryas. The Guptas. The Mughals. The British. Even the indige-nous Tharu, with their inherited resistance, fled the vicious malaria, called *awal*, that plagued the Terai from the end of April to the end of October.

Nigel addressed the heavily built driver in local dialect.

"Yo kun tao ho?"

What place was this?

The driver repeated the question, turning the answer over in his mind.

It was, he said finally, a Tharu place.

The last place.

Nigel had guessed as much. The terms negotiated the night before in Segowlee had provided for the driver's services as far as the *kalo pani*, a few miles distant. The "black water" could only be the unwhole-some stream before them.

It was also the boundary of British jurisdiction thereabouts, but that had nothing to do with the driver's reluctance to cross it. The stream marked the end of the road. No track or path traversed the jungle. There was only a route, a route known only to the Tharu.

But the village looked deserted. Where were the Tharu themselves? asked Nigel. Back in Segowlee?

No, said the driver. Those particular Tharu would reside in that village for a while yet, until the rains came. They were usually employed in the difficult and dangerous task of catching wild elephants. Even women and children joined in the pursuit, watching and waiting in the jungle.

Well before dark, they would make their way back. No one dared pass the night in the dread Terai, where ferocious beasts stalked unsuspecting prey, and the air itself was poisoned by the breath of serpents.

In that case, Nigel said, the Terai must be crossed in one day's time. Was that possible?

The driver thought so.

The Tharu were *thulo manche*, big strong men.

From time to time, other sahibs had made the journey, borne in hardwood litters bound with coarse hemp rope.

Or so it was said.

One heard many things, of course.

One did indeed. Nigel had already heard that the Tharu bearers were a stalwart lot. But he also heard of their profound unease in the jungle's depths. In the vaporous half-light with its malignant shadows, amid the pipings and squeakings, there was always the temptation to abandon Englishmen to their own devices. On more than one occasion, according to Company records, it had proved irresistible.

S—— was no better informed than Nigel about the way ahead. The dusty cargo of the bullock cart included two exquisite pony saddles of hand-tooled leather, crafted to order in Lahore. S—— had furnished the specifications. An accomplished horseman, he surmised from his experience of mountain tracks in his native Afghanistan that full-size mounts would prove unsuited to the still more treacherous terrain beyond the jungle.

They had planned to make their way to Kathmandu on sturdy po-

nies purchased in Segowlee. Upon arrival, though, they found no po-
nies to be had—even for hire.

It hardly mattered. The dissonant voices of the local bazaar spoke as
one in dismissing the notion of mounted travel to the sovereign kingdom of Nepal.

The track was too rough and too steep.

Too confined here, too airy there.

No horses could be led through those mountains, let alone ridden.

"We were assured that we must only proceed in doolies, borne by
coolies to be hired for each stage," wrote Nigel afterwards. "By no
means relishing the enforced separation, nor the discomfort of such
a jarring progress through the precipitous country, we privately resolved to walk."

All they really knew was that crossing the dismal stream meant entering forbidden territory. There was nothing complex about Nepalese foreign policy. Its sole object was the prevention of foreigners from
entering the country. So it had been since the kingdom's founding in
1768, and so it would remain until the mid-twentieth century. The Terai functioned as Nepal's main bulwark against the outside world. But
there was man-made reinforcement. Two or three days' journey into
the mountains beyond, loopholed walls marked the checkpoint and
choke point of Sisaghari. Its fortress-like facade commanded a defile
where the only track to Kathmandu dwindled into a traverse of a ledge
beside a precipice. The orders issued to its tenders brooked no disobe-
dience:

"If any person has constructed unauthorized tracks in your area,
discover and locate such tracks and install pikes or plant thorny bushes
there in such a manner that no persons can pass through them. If any
person tries to pass forcibly, capture him if possible or else fell him
with poisoned arrows . . . If you permit any person, irrespective of his
status, to proceed onwards without a document bearing the signature
of the passport authority, we will behead you."

The necessary signature could be obtained only in Kathmandu.

Lacking bona fides, Nigel and his companion hoped to substitute a letter of introduction to Maharaja Jang Bahadur, which S—— carried in the pocket of his jacket. They were counting on the literacy of someone at the checkpoint, someone moreover with fluency in Persian, the language of diplomacy in British India.

Which was counting on rather a lot. Nigel stood there peering into the rampart of jungle that checked the encroachment of the civilizing plain. No one would call him a novice at choosing a road less taken. He had forsaken the fast track to advancing his career at Government House in Calcutta. He had turned his back on the Bengal Club. He had invited Henry Lawrence to "borrow" him for service even farther afield than Patna, in locales so rustic and obscure that he was virtually certain to be overlooked for promotion. But this was different. Crossing the black water meant abandoning the road itself. Crossing the black water meant taking his life into his hands.

He might end up in the mouth of a man-eating tiger. Even if he made it as far as Kathmandu, he could hardly count on a welcoming embrace from the maharaja. He was just as likely to be handed over to a dungeon master or executioner—perhaps *more* likely, based on the stories he had heard in India of the murders attributed to Jang Bahadur in his ruthless pursuit of power.

More than murders, actually.

Massacres.

Anyone would feel uneasy. Nigel must have harbored second thoughts, but he kept them to himself. He scrambled down the bank and got his feet wet.

PART II

21

Chandragiri

1975

NOTHING LOOMED LARGER in the legend of Nigel Halleck than the palace he was said to have occupied in Kathmandu. There were footmen by the regiment, my mother had assured me, and a vast gilded ballroom. There was a dining hall crowded with hunting trophies big as houses, menacing tigers and charging rhinoceri, glass eyes glowering as he tucked into his tea. There was a bevy of maidens in tight black blouses and long pleated skirts, who daily brought in baskets on their backs the rhododendron wood that burned beneath the cauldron heating water for his splendid morning bath.

These details—and many more, all mined from the same gorgeous vein, polo grounds and palanquins and pink Italian marble—were preserved in the collective memory of his family and passed down the generations, but none were documented in the three surviving letters that chronicled his life there. When I thought about Nigel as I closed in on Kathmandu myself, on foot, following the same route through the Himalayan foothills that Nigel and S—— had taken in 1850, I could not help doubting every one of them. Some sounded a suspiciously personal note. Rhododendrons struck me as an unlikely source of firewood, but they were definitely my mother's favorite flower.

Nepal itself seemed an implausible setting for such extravagance. It had always been one of the poorest countries in the world. That morning I had awakened before dawn to the drumming of rain on the corrugated tin roof of the Sisaghari rest house, a few minutes' walk past the decaying fort whose officers had been charged with beheading any foreigners attempting to enter the kingdom without official permission. Before I left, I was careful to leave a few rupees in coins for the caretaker. Paper money had yet to catch on in those parts. Barter was as prevalent as cash. Prices might be quoted in eggs or needles or hard dried cheese.

The caretaker had promised me tea and a boiled egg for breakfast. But I was anxious to leave. The rain had stopped when the sun rose, leaving the green hills steaming under a blue sky dappled with thin silver clouds. A sign gave the elevation as 5,875 feet. I had grown up in the shadow of Mount St. Helens, then regarded as an "extinct" volcano. After climbing it several times, I had gone up most of the other great peaks of the Cascade Range, and I knew mountain weather. The clouds would fatten as the day wore on. I didn't want to miss the chance of seeing the Himalayas from the overlook of Chandragiri, high above Kathmandu.

After weeks of rattletrap buses and "hard class" railway cars, it felt good to be moving under my own power. Two days before, after leaving Patna and crossing the Terai on a narrow-gauge line to Raxaul, on the Nepalese border, I had parted company with my classmate. She boarded a bus bound for Kathmandu on the motor road completed in 1956, the first to reach the city. I started hiking.

The path stayed high for a mile or so, then plunged down the dry bed of a seasonal torrent. Pines gave way to a graceful forest of tapering sal trees, the forest to wild rose and pomegranate in the valley of a shallow river. Sometimes a scent like grape stole across the way, clean and sweet, carried from masses of blue *Vanda* orchids. The outcrops of hard clay that emerged here and there from the sandy soil were the deep red of *lungcha*, used by the Newars of Kathmandu for painting the walls of their houses.

Across the river was a mountain to climb. I zigzagged up a giant's staircase of cultivated terraces that ended in a vertical wall below the top. The wall was rent by a deep, narrow fissure, and the track followed the fissure. A carmine-daubed deity stood guard at the pass. Protruding from an excavation in the fissure beside it was a black stone phallus, brightened by a garland of marigolds. While I caught my breath, a laden bullock heaved into view, baskets of betel nuts lashed to its back. Another followed, loaded down with sheets of copper. A third carried bales of calico cloth. Their barefoot driver was a boy in tattered shorts. He stopped in his tracks and stared, surprised to see a sahib. Then he pressed his palms together in front of his chest and murmured, "Namaste."

I salute the god in you.

The caravan passed, heading south toward the plain. The track now angled toward the hidden valley like a needle swung by a lodestone. At the bottom of another long descent flowed a full-throated stream, its near bank grassy, the far a lustrous butte of blackest earth—eaten most greedily, I was given to understand in the village on the other side, by elephants when indisposed.

The face of the man who gave me directions was pitted from small-pox. He was renewing the thatch on the roof of his house when he saw me fording the river. He climbed down a notched-log ladder to point out the way up the mountain that loomed behind the village.

Or, in local parlance, the "hill."

Elevation, 7,500 feet above sea level, higher than any point in the United States east of the Rockies.

There were two routes to the top, he indicated. One, the old elephant track, was the prominent gash that gouged the mountainside from top to bottom. The other, well to the right, was an indistinct path, its airier sections interrupted with disquieting frequency by debris from rock avalanches. That the old way was nonetheless the greater of two evils he made clear despite the language barrier.

If I fell, I would die.

The new way was longer but not so bad.

Either way looked impossible to me without a rope. Fortunately, I had read the journal of a Scotsman who reported that he had been carried up the rightward path on the backs of coolies in 1947, at the age of sixty-three.

I was still climbing when I knew that there would be no glimpsing the Himalayas that day from the summit. The wind blew the smell of rain down the mountain ahead of the rain itself — the smell of wet earth and fiddlehead ferns. Before long, a mesh of clear water silvered the slope, mica flakes sparkling in the channels of its rivulets and rills. I unfurled my umbrella just as the gradient eased and walked fast in the downpour toward a gap in the forest on the other side of the mountain. I could almost taste the anticipation of my first view of Kathmandu, even as I mentally closed the book on the fable of Nigel's palace there. Coolies might have managed to haul a Scotsman up Chandragiri Hill, but slabs of Italian marble?

And yet.

A mile below lay the far-famed valley like a placid green lake, lapping at the bases of the mountains. Its twin holy rivers meandered through farmlands to converge in the center, where temples and pagodas rose high and stately from an upwelling clamor of redbrick tenements and serpentine bazaars. Atop a forested hill at the city's edge, the all-seeing eyes of Buddha gazed out from the gilded spire surmounting the hemisphere of an enormous stupa, the source of John Garstin's inspiration for the folly of the Golghar. At its base gleamed a monumental vajra, the thunderbolt that destroys all ignorance.

And gleaming, too, rising with neo-Gothic grandeur out of geometric garden parks in every district of the city, were the palaces.

Not two or three or five or ten, but dozens.

At that distance, all that distinguished them from their models in the ancien régime were roofs of corrugated iron. With their French windows and white plastered facades, they might have been the châteaux of a lost tribe of Bourbons, as fertile as they were forgotten.

There was even a replica Versailles.

I looked for a long time. Then I noticed the waterlogged blossoms on the glossy boughs that framed the view.

The forest of Chandragiri was a rhododendron forest.

22

A Maharaja

NIGEL'S FORAY INTO the Terai at the beginning of 1850 was the first of several, and he later wrote admiringly and enthusiastically about the jungle's flora, its solitude, and the "singular, deliquescent light" beneath its canopy. No record survives, though, of his impressions of the road to Kathmandu on that early, fraught journey with S——. From accounts by the few Europeans who preceded them, we learn mostly of the obstacles that the arduous track placed in their way. They portrayed the airy precipice and the dark defile in the resolute language of conquest, pushing and breaching and surmounting. The sole exception was the only woman among them, Honoria Lawrence. Enraptured by "the beautiful scenery and vegetation," Henry's wife scarcely mentioned the difficulties. Even those she described were presented in vignettes that made little of the passage but much of the forbidden land itself, in all its strange loveliness:

> *This difficult path, a mere foot-track, over ascents and descents, and along the beds of torrents, is the one mode of access to Nepaul, the only Pass entering their country which the jealousy of the Nepaulese has hitherto allowed strangers to see; and this one road is rendered apparently as difficult as possible to deter travellers. "Where the tree falleth there it lieth." In numberless places large trees had fallen across the path, and the path forthwith wound round them. Some had lain thus undisturbed till perfectly decayed, retaining the original form of the trunk, but transmuted into fine mould. Covered with sward they looked like gigantic graves.*

It was not the picturesque, however, that struck Mrs. Lawrence when she first gazed upon Kathmandu Valley from Chandragiri. "It was unlike anything I ever saw," she wrote, "more like an artificial model than any actual scenery, and suggested a crowd of new and strange ideas."

How did they ever get there?

How should they ever get away?

How could that "emerald, set in the ring of the hills," have been first discovered and inhabited?

"And being known at all, how comes it to be so little known?"

On that point, at least, she could turn to her husband for enlightenment. Save for the feudal theocracy of neighboring Tibet, no land in all the world was more xenophobic than Nepal. (Another eighty years would pass before the first white woman reached Lhasa, disguised as a Tibetan beggar.) Its rulers enforced its isolation the same way they wielded their power: with a vengeance. Nepal's history as a kingdom was a short one, no longer than a human lifespan. But it was a history so besmirched by bloodshed that it was cause for reproach even by the standard of savagery then prevailing at the courts of Central Asia.

The die was cast from the beginning. In 1768, Prithvi Narayan Shah set out from his tiny principality of Gorkha to conquer the city-states of the Nepal Valley, thirty-five miles to the east. No one expected him to succeed—least of all the Malla kings of Kathmandu, Lalitpur, and Bhaktapur, each of whose domains was larger, richer, and more powerful than Gorkha. But the cities of the valley had long located their only conceivable enemies on the plain of India and the high plateau of Tibet. To keep them out, they relied on the formidable natural barriers of the Terai and the Great Himalaya Range. Their local defenses were virtually nonexistent, their people—artisans, merchants, and traders—no match for the cutlass-wielding hillmen under Prithvi Narayan Shah.

"The conquest of Nepal by the Gurkha tribes was marked by revolting cruelty whenever opposition was encountered," wrote the Edwardian historian Frederick P. Gibbon, and the more valiant the opposition, the more barbaric the consequences for those who survived. Upon the surrender of Kirtipur, whose defenders had inflicted two humiliating defeats on the invaders before laying down their arms, Prithvi Narayan ordered his troops to cut off the noses and lips of every male inhabitant. The weight of these grisly trophies, according to a Jesuit who was present when they were presented to the prince of Gorkha, amounted to no less than eighty pounds. When Nigel Halleck arrived in the kingdom in 1850, there were still men alive whose skull-like faces bore witness to the brutality of its founding father.

At Kathmandu's Hanuman Dhoka Palace, on September 26, 1768, Prithvi Narayan Shah declared himself an incarnation of Lord Vishnu and placed a jeweled crown adorned with the three-foot plume of a bird of paradise on his head. His absolute, unchallenged rule as sovereign lasted until his death in 1775. After that, wrote Gibbon, "the court of that country was perhaps the most intriguing and treacherous in Asia. The only hope of retaining power appeared to lie in the destruction of all possible rivals, and no other method of rising to, or retaining, office seemed ever to enter the minds of the ambitious."

Infant kings. Scheming regents. Abdications, restorations. And, time and again, massacres. The murder of the third Shah king by his stepbrother, in 1806, provided a pretext for his prime minister, Bhimsen Thapa, to round up ninety-three nobles and army officers on charges of conspiring in the killing. All were executed, after which the senior queen and fifteen reputed mistresses of the late king were burned alive on funeral pyres. Shortly afterwards, Thapa, acting in the name of the three-year-old king, Rajendra Bikram Shah, persuaded tribal chiefs to march on the fertile lowlands of the Gangetic Plain, promising each a share of the substantial tax revenue that would flow into the Nepalese treasury after usurping the British. Defeat, he assured them, was impossible: "Our hills and fastness are formed by the hand of God, and are impregnable."

Thapa overplayed his own hand, but only just. The military outcome of the border dispute remembered grandly as the Anglo-Nepalese War was a stalemate. It was a stalemate, however, between twelve thousand irregulars and a disciplined force of thirty thousand equipped with far more modern weapons, and Calcutta took note. The Gurkhas

—who were actually drawn from several tribes in the Himalayan foot-hills, with disparate languages and traditions—clearly were a "mar-tial race," a distinction previously bestowed by the Company upon the Sikhs of the Punjab and the Pashtuns of the North-West Frontier.

The British could hardly permit the Nepalese incursions to pass un-challenged, but they were far from sanguine about their ability to cap-ture and hold the remote strongholds of Kathmandu Valley. Accord-ingly, they drafted a treaty that preserved Nepal as an independent buffer between India and China but forced the Nepalese to cede to Brit-ish India a third of the kingdom's territory—some of which proved so difficult to govern that it was returned to Nepal within months. They also negotiated the employment for mercenary service of five thou-sand Gurkha soldiers, and the acceptance of a British resident at Kath-mandu.

Bhimsen Thapa ruled Nepal as a despot for a generation, tortur-ing and beheading opponents real and imagined and keeping Rajendra under house arrest. The king got his revenge in 1837 by dismissing Bhimsen, who was charged with poisoning a young prince and im-prisoned soon afterwards; he committed suicide behind bars two years later. His successor as prime minister launched a short-lived occupa-tion of British territory and was sacked himself under pressure from Calcutta.

By the time Henry Lawrence arrived in 1843 to take up his duties as resident, a pro-British nobleman named Fateh Jang Chautaria was in nominal charge as prime minister. But neither he nor the king was actually calling the shots. Rajendra, confronted after the death of his senior queen with the conflicting ambitions of his junior queen, Lak-shmi Devi, and his son, Crown Prince Surendra, had issued a royal proclamation that assigned all his powers and prerogatives to Lakshmi Devi. Naturally enough, she wanted to depose Surendra and proclaim her own son the heir apparent. When Chautaria balked at changing the order of succession, she dismissed his government and nominated Mathabar Singh Thapa, brother of the late Bhimsen, as prime minister.

Upon taking office, Mathabar commenced a reign of terror, torturing and executing courtiers and army officers he believed responsible for his brother's imprisonment. Stealing a page from Prithvi Narayan Shah, he had one nobleman's lips and nose cut off on charges of giving false evidence. The queen watched his ruthlessness with approval, confident he would obey her orders to depose the teenaged crown prince at a suitable time.

Mathabar decided instead to serve his own ambitions. He wanted the king to abdicate so he might rule freely himself in the name of Crown Prince Surendra, just as Bhimsen had ruled in the name of Rajendra. From that point on, wrote Henry Lawrence, "The royal authority of Nepal . . . was shared by Mr. Nepal, Mrs. Nepal, and Master Nepal."

But it was Nephew Nepal who waited in the wings, intent on usurping them all. Jang Bahadur Kunwar was an army officer who had impressed the Lawrences with his solicitude for Honoria while leading the official party that escorted her to Kathmandu. He owed the assignment to his uncle Mathabar, and it was to Jang Bahadur that Mathabar turned again as the most trustworthy person he could think of after deciding to support the legitimate heir to the throne. Conscious that the average life expectancy of a Nepalese prince of the blood royal could be counted on the fingers of his hands, Mathabar appointed his nephew to serve as Surendra's personal bodyguard. Then he secretly urged the crown prince to challenge his father to step aside in his favor.

When the king refused, Surendra, with encouragement from Mathabar, announced his intention to go to Benares, smear his body with ashes, and live as a sadhu on the bank of the Ganges. Accompanied by three regiments of the army as an escort, he left Kathmandu for the Indian frontier.

Crossing the border with such a heavy escort, Mathabar advised the king, was asking for trouble. The prince was sure to be detained by the British government. At Mathabar's request, both the king and the queen set out to intervene. Mathabar followed with a regiment under his personal command. On November 25, 1844, encamped at the edge of the Terai, the king put his hand and seal to a document that revoked the transfer of his sovereign powers to the queen and assigned them instead to the crown prince. On Mathabar's orders, eighteen army officers who advised the king against issuing the proclamation were executed on the spot.

After a month of increasingly erratic and sadistic behavior by Surendra—he had a penchant for ordering young maidens thrown into wells—the king changed his mind and revoked the edict. Henceforth, he vowed, he would be the only ruler; no one would be placed in the position anymore of receiving conflicting orders from three different authorities. Lakshmi Devi, for her part, pressed the prime minister to fulfill his promise to declare Surendra's stepbrother the crown prince. Mathabar put her off, inflaming her suspicions further by raising three new army battalions in a bid to consolidate his power.

By this time Jang Bahadur had been transferred to the king's bodyguard, where he realized that the real power of the state remained in the hands of the queen, whatever Rajendra said publicly. And he could not help noticing that even Lakshmi Devi's lover, an army commander named Gagan Singh, exercised more authority than the prime minister.

Jang Bahadur, no less ambitious than his uncle, proved himself even more ruthless. By one account, he arranged to make Gagan Singh's acquaintance by first encouraging his brother in a romantic liaison with the commander's daughter. Once the introduction was made, he embarked on a successful campaign to ingratiate himself with Gagan Singh, who in turn introduced him to the queen. No proof exists that the three of them proceeded to plot Mathabar's assassination, which took place on May 17, 1845. But Nepalese historians agree that after the prime minister was summoned to the royal palace that evening, on the pretext that the queen had suddenly fallen ill, he was executed on her orders by a shot in the head from behind, fired at point-blank range by his nephew Jang Bahadur.

The next morning, Rajendra announced that he himself had executed Mathabar as a traitor. (Two years later, in a deposition addressed to the Government of India, he admitted that Jang Bahadur was responsible.) Then, in a show of independence that probably stemmed more from a cuckold's resentment than anything else, he defied the queen's wishes and refused to make Gagan Singh prime minister. Instead, both Gagan Singh and Jang Bahadur were promoted to the rank of general.

For the next year and a half, Jang Bahadur bided his time and plotted Gagan Singh's assassination. Upon learning of her lover's murder on the evening of September 14, 1847, the enraged Lakshmi Devi ordered the royal buglers to sound the call that summoned all civil officials and military officers to the palace courtyard. Once they had gathered, Jang Bahadur instigated their wholesale slaughter, on the pretext of protecting the queen and with the connivance of his brothers, assorted nephews, and trusted friends. As the queen looked on from a palace balcony, fifty-five unarmed nobles and army officers were slain so brutally that their blood flooded the gutters of the royal compound all night long, while bold packs of jackals howled beneath its walls.

The following afternoon, Queen Lakshmi Devi appointed Jang Bahadur supreme commander and prime minister of Nepal. Even as vultures wheeled slowly over the royal palace, temple bells rang out across Kathmandu, and an artillery battery of nineteen guns fired a feu de joie in honor of the new prime minister. But in two weeks' time the queen herself was plotting against Jang Bahadur. Like his uncle before him, he had promised to change the order of succession in favor of her son. Instead he posted a company of armed guards drawn from his own loyal regiments to protect the crown prince. After assuring Surendra's safety, he informed the queen that he could not support the disinheritance of the eldest prince. It was, he wrote primly, a matter of conscience. She then met with a group of officers hostile to Jang Bahadur and ordered them to kill him immediately.

That he learned of their plan to trap him in the palace garden was probably inevitable. Jang Bahadur, unbeknownst to the queen, had long enjoyed an ongoing affair with one of her maids, Putali Nani, who acted in concert with the palace priest to pass him urgent secret messages about what she saw and heard in the royal apartments. In the event, it was the conspirators who were trapped at the appointed hour in the garden, and twenty-three were executed there, in the second palace massacre in less than a month.

Afterwards, at an extraordinary meeting of the state council called by Jang Bahadur, the queen was formally accused of plotting to kill the crown prince and the prime minister. The surviving leaders of the kingdom's nobility, surrounded by heavily armed men charged with "protecting" them, convicted her of the charges. A proclamation issued in the name of King Rajendra stripped Lakshmi Devi of all royal powers, and on November 23 the royal couple departed for exile in Benares. In the absence of the king—who would spend the rest of his life under house arrest—Crown Prince Surendra became regent.

Jang Bahadur was twenty-nine years old. In one of his first acts after attaining absolute power and proclaiming himself maharaja, he installed the royal chambermaid Putali Nani in his own palace at Thapathali, declared her his wife, and honored her with the title of maharani. The son she bore him was ultimately made a general, and admitted to the roll of succession in the line of hereditary prime ministers who would rule Nepal for more than a hundred years, until the restoration of the Shah monarchy.

It was, perhaps, a sentimental gesture. But only in part. As much as Henry Lawrence deplored Jang Bahadur's lack of moral compass, he judged him "a man of exceptional intelligence," one who read almost instantly the lay of the land when it came to his own self-interest. It was the same intelligence—and self-interest—that assured Nigel Halleck and his Afghan companion of a milder greeting than a rain of poisoned arrows when they reached the strategic fort of Sisaghari.

We cannot be certain that Henry Lawrence was the author of the letter of introduction to Jang Bahadur that S—— presented to the commander there, though an aside in another letter written by Nigel suggests that he was. What is clear is that the two men were permitted to continue on their way, and that Jang Bahadur welcomed them with open arms. Just prior to their arrival, he had adopted the honorific surname Rana, which meant "brave with the sword of war." He was already contemplating the building spree that would raise, in all their gleaming dozens, what came to be known as "Rana palaces." And he shrewdly foresaw that the Englishman and the Afghan might both prove useful in making it come to pass.

23

Kathmandu

1975

I SPENT MY FIRST six weeks in Kathmandu learning to speak Nepali. I lived in the neighboring city of Lalitpur with a Nepalese family and commuted by bicycle every day to join my college classmates for five hours of intensive language lessons. Coming and going, I rode past several of the palaces I had glimpsed from Chandragiri, including Singha Durbar, the replica Versailles. Up close, their dilapidation threatened to eclipse their grandeur. Most, I learned, remained in the hands of the Rana family, who no longer ran the country but continued to exert their influence at the highest levels. Queen Aishwarya herself was a Rana. But when I tried to find out if one of them might once have housed a Victorian gentleman by the name of Halleck, I received the same blank look wherever I asked—the British Council, the American Library, Tribhuvan University—followed by the same succinct suggestion:

"Ask Boris."

There was only one Boris of Kathmandu. He had settled in Nepal in the early 1950s, and over time he'd achieved such renown that his last name became superfluous, like Cher or Madonna. In 1961, King Tribhuvan had entrusted him with the program for the visit of Elizabeth II and the Duke of Edinburgh. For the entrée at the state banquet he chose saddle of muntjac—barking deer. When it was served, the king summoned him to explain what it was, and it turned out that his reputation had preceded him even with the Windsors.

"Are you Boris?" asked Prince Philip.

Boris the tiger hunter, Boris the fighter pilot, Boris the trapeze artist.

Boris the White Russian raconteur, with a bullet in his thigh from fighting the Bolsheviks, aged twelve.

Boris who danced for Diaghilev, and at Balanchine's request broke the news of the impresario's death to Anna Pavlova, who swooned in his arms.

He made music with Stravinsky and paintings with Matisse, sang with Marlene Dietrich, acted in a film with Jean-Paul Belmondo. He was seventy when I first met him, stationed by a circular fireplace in the Chimney Room Bar of his Yak and Yeti restaurant, beneath a gleaming cone of beaten copper. But he looked a robust sixty, with a dazzling smile, bright, mischievous eyes, and graying hair parted carefully in the center. Even in his habitual striped cotton bush shirt with short sleeves, he had the aura of a man of fashion of La Belle Époque. His voice, deep and accented, made everything he said sound like a confidence. Boris Lissanevitch had no listeners—only co-conspirators.

No, he had never heard of Nigel. But he was certain that the stories were exaggerated. Boris knew himself to be the only European who had always lived in a palace there—Lal Durbar, courtesy of the late King Tribhuvan. If Nigel occupied a palace, he would have been a guest of its Nepalese owner. And if he took up residence in 1850 or thereabouts, there was no need for guesswork in identifying his host.

That would be Jang Bahadur himself.

"Founder of the shogunate," he said, and explained how the Ranas reduced the Shah kings to figureheads for a century, all the while treating the national treasury as their personal exchequer. As for their palaces, he didn't know which dated back that far, but Jang Bahadur was the one who started building them.

He was sure, he said, that some of the senior Ranas would receive me to talk about Nigel's connection with their forebear. If he thought it would help, he would make some introductions himself.

But he doubted that it would.

He smiled slyly.

Some might say that he had earned the Rana palace bestowed upon him by a grateful king. He first met His Majesty in Calcutta during the Second World War. Boris was running an exclusive social club, and Tribhuvan was in exile after fleeing Nepal. Since his enthronement as a child, the figurehead king had been kept in isolation and knew almost no one. Boris, who knew a great many Indian and Nepalese aristocrats through the shikar hunting circuit, had made certain introductions. One of these was to a close friend of his, a disgruntled member of the Rana family. The two countrymen began meeting discreetly in the flat Boris kept above the 300 Club, and one thing led to another. When Tribhuvan made his triumphant return to Kathmandu a few years later, and declared an end to the Rana usurpation, Boris was part of the entourage that followed him off the plane.

It was two in the afternoon. The copper chimney blazed with sun slanting down through high clerestory windows. Boris stepped behind the bar and set out two champagne flutes, chilled. He gripped an orange in the impeccably manicured fingers of one hand and expertly wielded a zester with the other. After he popped the cork on a bottle of Laurent-Perrier and poured out our cocktails, he led me down a marbled corridor to the music room. Atop the grand piano, in a heavy silver frame, stood an autographed portrait of Elizabeth II and the Duke of Edinburgh.

He had been granted British citizenship in the 1920s, he said. The queen herself had called him "our favorite Russian subject" at the end of her visit in 1961, which climaxed with a solemn and majestic salute from 376 elephants, decorated and painted under Boris' direction with gold and silver. As she drove by, each elephant raised its trunk, one after another, down a line a half mile long.

That, of course, was down in the Terai. He had organized a tiger shoot for the visiting royals there on the king's behalf. Unfortunately, Prince Philip had been obliged to forestall an outcry by wildlife conservationists by diplomatically begging off on the morning of the outing with a hastily bandaged trigger finger. (Another member of the party, an admiral of the Royal Navy, bagged a Bengal.)

Nigel hunted there, I told Boris. In fact, that was how his relatives in England believed that he had died. A tiger got him.

He considered this. He had bagged no fewer than seventy-eight of the species himself in the 1930s and 1940s, a total that secured his place as the top-ranked big-game hunter in India. And he had certainly done his share of shooting in the Terai, where the local history was almost exclusively oral. Sitting around the campfire with the beaters who flushed out the game, you heard tales dating back to the heyday of the Raj, passed down from one generation to the next. A sahib carried off by a tiger was a sahib to be remembered, all those years later.

Quite possibly Nigel had died in the jungle.

Many Englishmen did.

But like that?

Devoured by a Bengal?

Boris thought not.

He would have heard about it.

NOT LONG AFTER I spoke with Boris at Lal Durbar, I left Kathmandu on a trek to Mount Everest Base Camp. I returned in the fall, expecting to spend a few days in the city before departing on another trek to Dolpo, where I meant to winter over while working on my research project. After three weeks I was still there, waiting on a permit, and I decided to seek an audience with one of the leading lights of the Rana family, recommended by Boris as historically minded and a likely source of information about Nigel.

He was called General Samrajya Shamsher Jang Bahadur Rana, and I sought him out at his palace to ask about one of the more persistent family legends about Nigel: that he was an opportunistic jewel thief. One version of the story held that he had got his hands on the fabled Koh-i-noor diamond, which had been turned over to the Lawrence brothers in 1849 as a spoil of the Anglo-Sikh War. When the diamond was examined in London after it was presented to Queen Victoria, it was found to be eighty-three carats short of its historical weight of two hundred sixty-nine carats, lending credence to the theory that Nigel had conspired with a gem cutter to portion off a sizable chunk for himself before returning the mutilated gem to the treasure house in Lahore.

It was the subsequent discovery of the diamond's deficiencies, then, that explained his exile in Nepal, remote from the reach of British justice. Alternatively, he might have stolen the Koh-i-noor outright, substituting in its place a lesser diamond—obtained, perhaps, in Nepal? One way or another, believed the Hallecks, he had ended up selling the diamond to a blue blood in Nepal and lived sumptuously off the proceeds for the rest of his life.

Few Nepalese in modern times were as conscious of the azure in their veins as General Rana, a round, moustached gentleman in his fifties who spoke English with the cut-glass accent of the home counties. The first time he said "often," I heard "orphan." Only eight of his countrymen had ever been created honorary knights of the Royal Victorian Order, and he was one of them. He wore the order's rosette on his lapel—a silver Maltese cross with a central medallion depicting the royal cipher of Queen Victoria on a red background, surrounded by a blue ring bearing the order's motto and surmounted by a Tudor crown. The motto was simplicity itself: VICTORIA.

Elizabeth II had invested him during her state visit in 1961. The order, he told me, honored those who had personally served the monarchy.

The details of his service he left unspecified. It was not, at any rate, of a military nature. Though he insisted upon being addressed as "General," according to Boris he had never commanded any troops, let alone an army. Nor, Boris added, would his bearing strike one as military, except in the most elastic sense of the word. But this was Nepal, where the old ways died hard.

He received me beneath an art nouveau chandelier of Murano glass, in a room floored with pink marble. Both were imports from Italy, conveyed from Genoa to Calcutta by ship, and thence from the Indian border to Kathmandu by coolies.

"A great many coolies," he added pointlessly. I pictured them laboring up Chandragiri Hill beneath their burdens like Egyptian slaves in old engravings of the raising of the pyramids, their backs at right angles to the slope.

The enormous Belgian mirrors in gilded frames on the opposite wall were carried in as well. And so, over the years, were a number of automobiles, including a dove gray 1936 Standard Flying 8 saloon weighing twenty-five hundred pounds, by sixty-four men in twelve days.

The General, like Boris, had never heard of Nigel. He felt confident, nonetheless, in dismissing as "fantasy" the story of his diamond dealing, at least as far as it had anything to do with Nepal.

It was true that gemstones could be found in certain districts of the kingdom, if one knew where to look.

Not, however, diamonds.

Of that he was certain.

Nor was it probable that Nigel had entered Nepal as a trader in gems. Except for the General's forebears, there weren't any customers for luxury items in those days. (For the simple reason, I later learned, that his ancestors had murdered the rest of the nobility.) And the Ranas, for their part, had dealt only with a few trusted merchants, Muslims for the most part, from what is now Pakistan and, especially, Afghanistan.

Like Boris, too, he insisted that no foreigner in Kathmandu had ever built or occupied a palace of his own.

(Not while Ranas steered the ship of state; in the present day, he sniffed, all things were possible.)

Or her own, for that matter.

Not even the Queen of the Sikhs.

Did I know the story of Rani Jindan? In the Punjab? After the first

Sikh war, the British deposed her as regent and took away her power; after the second, they separated her from her son, the heir, and imprisoned her in India. When she escaped she fled to Nepal, and Jang Bahadur granted her political asylum. His government even granted her a pension.

But a palace?

No.

She was provided a residence in Jang Bahadur's Thapathali. It was the last of the old-style Oriental palaces, he said, built before Jang Bahadur visited England and France and acquired a taste for Occidental Gothic. It was really nothing more than a succession of gigantic square houses a mile long, fronting on the Bagmati River.

"Not very splendid" was the General's verdict.

"Not like Singha Durbar?" I asked.

He sighed.

"Nothing at all like Singha Durbar — as it was."

"Was?"

"You have seen it?"

I nodded. What I had seen, he informed me, was only the frontage. The frontage was all that remained of the seventeen wings constructed on orders of his grandfather Chandra Shumsher, longest-serving of all the Rana prime ministers. Two years before, a fire had gutted sixteen hundred rooms. A paltry hundred escaped the flames.

Among them, most fortunately, was the Hall of Mirrors.

No, there was nothing like that at Thapathali: no indoor fountains, no Carrara marble, no crystal windows, no stained glass doors from England. It was actually rather plain. He remembered Thapathali well, from his boyhood. Almost all of it collapsed in the earthquake that devastated Kathmandu in 1934.

What was likely, said the General, was that Nigel was a guest of Jang Bahadur's at Thapathali. He simply enjoyed the kingdom's hospitality, and for a good long time if he made for agreeable company.

That would not surprise him in the least.

"Jang Bahadur admired the English, you see."

Admired and liked.

Which, in a nutshell, was the difference between the Ranas and the Shahs.

(Historically speaking, he meant; now, with a Shah king and a Rana queen—his niece—a sort of equilibrium had been achieved.)

His forebears had embraced the English, and preserved Nepal's independence. The Shahs only wanted to fight them, a battle they could never win. Nepal would have ended up a colony. The country had done very well for itself under the Ranas.

As had the Ranas, I thought, but it seemed impolitic to say so. As for Nigel, the General invited me to look through the family archives in the personal library of the late field marshal, his father.

Like so much else in modern times, he said wearily, it was open to the bloody public.

THE LIBRARY OF Field Marshal H. H. Sir Kaiser Shumsher Jang Bahadur Rana was located, predictably enough, in a palace. Kaiser Mahal occupied twenty-odd acres directly across the street from Narayanhiti Palace, home of King Birendra and Queen Aishwarya. Its grounds, however, were nowhere near as immaculately kept as those of the royal residence—not so much overgrown as jungly, with fat, snaking vines smothering tree trunks and corrugating the surface of green-slimed ponds. No one lived there anymore, and high brick walls screened the neglect from the eyes of passersby.

From the librarian I learned that the field marshal's collection consisted of thirty-five thousand volumes, of which only those shelved at floor level had been gnawed by mice. I was told that His Highness had begun collecting books at the age of fifteen, when he accompanied his father, Maharaja Chandra, on a visit to England. I was told that "he was very much impressed by the ruling system of England," and also by "the proper management of books there." I was assured that His Highness could tell with uncanny precision where each of his holdings could be located.

"Every book," said the librarian admiringly. "Every document."

Unfortunately, His Highness had died in 1964. When I said that I hoped to learn whether a certain Englishman had once resided in Jang Bahadur's Thapathali Palace, he did not hold out much hope that I would find the answer. There were household ledgers, of course—

"Expenditures, inventories, rosters of servants."

That sort of thing.

He sighed.

But what with the climate, and the insects—

His voice trailed off and we took in the view, through a bay window thirty feet tall, to the grounds that surrounded the palace. In its original form, he said, the elaborate ensemble of formal gardens, fountains, pools, pergolas, balustrades, urns, and trellises included six freestanding pavilions, representing the seasons of South Asia: spring, early summer, summer monsoon, early autumn, late autumn, and winter. After three were demolished to make way for commercial development, the "Garden of the Six Seasons" became the "Garden of Dreams."

Whatever the condition of the ledgers, I said, the General had suggested that I should have a look.

He squared his shoulders so reflexively that a salute seemed imminent.

The General's wish, he made clear, was his command. If I would be so good as to allow him an hour or two—

By the slack reckoning employed in Nepal, that meant three or four, but I had time on my hands. Spending the winter in Dolpo was no longer in the cards. The Ministry of Home Affairs had denied my request for a trekking permit. After I got the news, I had stopped by the Yak and Yeti to console myself with a plate of *boeuf bourguignon*, prepared with buffalo meat in a country where even inadvertent "cow killers"— reckless lorry drivers, more often than not—were routinely sentenced to life in prison. Boris had advised me to keep my chin up. Prominent among the refugees in the "Little Tibet" of Bauddha, outside Kathmandu, were exiles active in a guerrilla movement called Four Rivers, Six Ranges. They could assist me in making a surreptitious visit.

He knew trustworthy people who would be happy to help.

Delighted, in fact.

Even if worse came to worst and I was taken into custody, he promised, foreigners in Nepal were treated well by jailers — rumors of flogging were greatly exaggerated.

After thinking it over — and recalling that Boris seemed to revel in speculation that he was some sort of secret agent without actually denying it was true — I chose to demur. I rented a small flat in a bucolic neighborhood on the outskirts of Kathmandu, about a mile away from Kaiser Mahal, and began casting about for a substitute research project. I had vague aspirations of writing a book. In the meantime I felt I owed it to my mother to try to find concrete evidence of Nigel's presence in Nepal.

When I returned to Kaiser Mahal, the refectory table was stacked with a dozen soiled pasteboard cartons, each marked boldly, though not sequentially, with a Roman numeral. There was a III and a VII and a XXX. What I took for a pebbled effect on the rotting leather covers of the ledgers turned out to be calcified remains of innumerable small snails. The librarian held out a pair of cotton gloves — to keep my hands clean — and a long, thin knife with a finely honed blade and full tang handle.

I mustn't hesitate to use it as necessary, he said.

It would only be a help to others.

For an uneasy moment I wondered whether patrons were expected to dispatch any vermin that intruded upon their research. But he was only encouraging me to separate pages that I deemed "intractable."

It took me most of that afternoon to ascertain which volumes might be worth perusing. It was not until the next day that I first came across a name that stood out to me, on the face of it unrelated to Nigel but seeming confirmation of the General's belief in the provenance of the Rana family jewels. Several ledger entries identified one Sa'adat ool-Moolk as the recipient of outlays for "dimond stones and rubees."

He was clearly a Muslim, one of the "few trusted merchants" the General had mentioned. Then, late that afternoon, came the eureka moment. There it was, in a lengthy list of guests invited to observe maneuvers of the Nepalese army in 1850: "Mr. Hillock."

Could it be? I wondered, but only for a moment.

It had to be.

The vowels were wrong, but the timing was right. And what was the likelihood, anyway, of both a Halleck and a Hillock turning up among the first few dozen Europeans to set foot in forbidden Nepal?

I had by then abandoned hope of finding Nigel's tombstone. Boris had agreed with the woman at the British Council library in Patna that there probably wasn't one.

(And he knew for a fact that Nigel had not been interred at the small British cemetery on the grounds of the old residency at Lainchaur, where Boris himself intended to be buried. It was where he took his daily walks, in an effort to make the acquaintance of his future neighbors. He knew the name on every tombstone.)

If Nigel died most anywhere in Nepal, he would have been cremated. In the unlikely event he met his end in the highlands, where firewood was at a premium, he would have been accorded a "sky burial." His remains would have been exposed to the elements on a mountaintop, to decompose or be eaten by carrion birds. If I was going to find anything of Nigel, his name in an antique ledger was probably the best I could do, and the sight of it thrilled me more than I ever could have guessed.

Suddenly, he seemed real.

And there was more. A couple of hours into my next visit to the library, there was "Hillock" again, the only European in a party that departed Thapathali for shooting in the Terai. And this time the name was linked by a bracket with that of another member of the party, whose name I recognized.

Sri Sri Sa'adat ool-Moolk, the supplier of Rana family jewels.

The two men's names were again linked by brackets in a third instance of "Hillock," posted four years later, in 1854.

What struck me at the time, of course, was the evident years-long connection between Nigel and a purveyor of "dimond stones and rubees."

Perhaps there was something, after all, to the Halleck family legend.

What was lost to me in the diamond dazzle was the significance of the dual honorific preceding the name of Sa'adat ool-Moolk. In the royal protocol of Nepal, only the king himself was entitled to a triple "Sri." The Rana prime ministers, for all their power, were obliged to settle for two, and they constituted an exception to the rule that "Sri Sri" connoted royal blood.

Nigel's friend was no ordinary jewel dealer.

24

A Prince

WHEN NIGEL FIRST mentioned his Afghan friend S—— in a letter sent from the Punjab, he called him "a Prince." For generations afterwards, Halleck family members who read it supposed that he simply meant "of a fellow." When they imagined him hobnobbing with royalty on the other side of the world, they thought only of Jang Bahadur, who pretended to come from an aristocratic background but never went so far as to claim descent from a monarch. But Nigel's Victorian penchant for random capitalization camouflaged unvarnished fact. In the archives of the India Office in London, the name of Sa'adat ul-Mulk is prefaced with "Shahzada," a Persian honorific meaning "son of the king."

Nigel's companion on his journey west from Ludhiana to Peshawar and then eastward to Nepal was none other than the great-great-grandson of Ahmad Shah Durrani, an Afghan cavalry commander in the Persian army who founded an empire in 1747 that came to encompass present-day Afghanistan, northeastern Iran, eastern Turkmenistan, most of Pakistan, and northwestern India, including the Kashmir region. At the time of his death, twenty-five years later, the Durrani Empire was the second-largest Muslim empire in the world, after the Ottoman.

Sa'adat's great-grandfather inherited the empire but proved too "humane and generous" to maintain a centralized government, and it began to contract. It dwindled further under his grandfather Mahmud Shah, who lost the throne to his brother Shah Shuja in 1803, reclaimed it in 1809, and fled to Herat, in western Afghanistan, in 1817. By then the Durrani Empire had shrunk to the limits of Herat, Kabul, and Kandahar, and only Herat remained in the hands of the Sadozais.

They were not a happy family. Father fought son, brother fought brother, half brother fought half brother, uncle fought nephew, in what ethnographer Louis Dupree called "a never-ending round robin of blood-letting and blindings." When Mahmud Shah died of poisoning in 1830, it was widely supposed that his son—Sa'adat's father, Kamran Shah—had administered the fatal dose.

"Kamran Shah can best be described as a human tiger," wrote the Victorian historian G. P. Tate. "A debauchee of the worst type, there ran through his disposition a strong vein of ferocity and cruelty. On occasion, during his early manhood, he displayed determination and the courage of his race; but in later years, after all avenues of action had been closed to him, he became a tyrannical ruler, and gave himself up to horrible vices."

However modest his reserves of compassion and charm, Kamran impressed the British intelligence officer Arthur Conolly with his dual act of patricide and regicide. Conolly, who had coined the term "the Great Game" as shorthand for the imperial contest for control of India's destiny, reached Herat after traveling in disguise all the way from Moscow. His four-thousand-mile reconnaissance mission had convinced him that only a reunified Afghanistan could halt Russian progress toward India. And after continuing on to British territory, he advised his superiors that "Kamran the Cruel" was the sole claimant to the Afghan throne who was up to the task.

Sa'adat was the third of Kamran's eight sons, collectively deemed "quite worthless" by one historian and dismissed as "degenerate descendants of the great Ahmed Shah" by another. But when their father was deposed in a palace coup by his prime minister Yar Muhammad in 1842, the four eldest of these "effeminate men" led five hundred others in seizing the citadel where Kamran was imprisoned and bravely held it for fifty days, repulsing five battalions with "the greatest intrepidity," until artillery and mines brought down the walls around them.

Yar Muhammad—unwilling, perhaps, to make martyrs—sent the princes out of the territory of Herat unharmed. Kamran was strangled; after his death, Sa'adat's mother was tortured daily for four years without revealing the whereabouts of a diamond-encrusted girdle that was famed throughout South Asia and would be worth an estimated $300 million today. Sa'adat fled with his elder brother Seif into the mountains of Ghor, in central Afghanistan, where they allied with two independent chiefs and plotted with Yar Muhammad's cousin to harass the usurper in Herat. When their attacks proved futile, the alliance soured, and he was imprisoned for a while in the onetime harem of a palace in Kandahar, quarters that a French officer and fellow inmate in 1845 judged "worthy of a prince."

Two of his brothers died of cholera in exile in Persia in 1846. Another sank there into opium addiction. Three or four of his sisters were sold by Yar Muhammad to the Turkmen, who disposed of them in the slave markets of Khiva and Bukhara. Sa'adat was said to have settled in Teheran, where doles paid out to Kamran's surviving sons by their cousin the shah went to finance lives that G. P. Tate described as "given up to low pleasures, and the indulgence of their depraved appetites."

Why Sa'adat decided to leave Persian protection in 1848 and settle in Ludhiana is unknown. Since he was reduced in Teheran to living on an allowance, it probably had to do with money. Perhaps the storied jeweled girdle had been entrusted to one of his relatives in Little Kabul, and his mother, whose ordeal at the hands of Yar Muhammad had ended with her ransom by the shah, sent him to retrieve it. Or, given the turbulence of internal Afghan politics, he may have held out hope that the ascendance of the rival Barakzai clan, which made the Sadozais personae non gratae in their own country, would prove short-lived. In the meantime, he may simply have wished to live closer to Afghanistan.

The Sadozais, unsentimental to a fault in most matters, were ever enthralled by the allure of their homeland. Ahmad Shah, the founder of the dynasty, invaded India eight times and installed a puppet emperor on the Mughal throne. He could have occupied it himself. If he had based his empire in India, with all its riches and resources, it might have lasted for hundreds of years instead of barely fifty. But Ahmad Shah demurred. The warrior regarded today as the father of modern Afghanistan was also a poet, who wrote in Delhi that grief clung to his heart "like a snake" when he remembered the mountaintops of his homeland.

Sa'adat's entry into Nepal as a dealer in "dimond stones and rubees" would explain his visit to Jagdalak before he set out with Nigel for Kathmandu. Sadozai nobles had long claimed the gemstones there as their shared patrimony. But he may have had another reason for asking Nigel to accompany him into that forbidding wilderness of rock without water. He may have wanted his English friend to gaze for himself on the mountains of Afghanistan.

25

A Welcome

S A'ADAT'S ARRIVAL IN Kathmandu presented Jang Bahadur Rana with an unexpected opportunity to enhance his own prestige. The maharaja understood that his past as a mere bodyguard was too recent to efface it from public memory. But he believed that the presence of foreign royalty in his household served to bolster his stature through association, and he had recently made a show of granting asylum to Rani Jindan Kaur.

As a prince of the blood royal, Sa'adat was even better suited than Jindan to Jang Bahadur's project of image building. The details of his illustrious lineage, moreover, were a perfect fit with the maharaja's aspirations. Jang Bahadur's ancestors were immigrants from India, who styled themselves as Rajputs upon arrival in Nepal. It was a claim supported by the flimsiest of genealogical evidence, and the established families harbored doubts from the beginning that the newcomers actually belonged to the highest Hindu warrior caste. If anyone could dispel the lingering air of the parvenu that clung to the maharaja's social status among the surviving nobility, it was Sa'adat. With the Afghan in residence at Thapathali, Jang Bahadur might remind his court at every opportunity that the prince's Sadozai forebears were Rajput Hindus, who converted to Islam and migrated west.

Influenced by word of Jindan's reception, which he seems to have received directly from Henry Lawrence, Sa'adat would have been reasonably certain that the maharaja would admit a fellow royal to his forbidden kingdom. But he surely never expected to be acknowledged as a distant cousin. Jang Bahadur's enthusiastic welcome must have come as a great relief after the successive bad patches of Sa'adat's recent past: living rough in the Hindu Kush, imprisonment in Kandahar, exile in Teheran.

There was also the matter of Sa'adat's complicated relationship with his ostensible protectors, the British. They may well have instigated his departure from Little Kabul in Ludhiana, simply because they had reason to wish him elsewhere. As a plausible claimant to the Afghan crown, he was capable of causing trouble on the North-West Frontier, already seething with trouble caused by the British themselves as they abandoned the policy of indirect rule championed by Henry Lawrence. Nor would the British have been confident that they could guarantee Sa'adat's safety there, which they valued less for his sake than for their own, in case they decided to back him at some later date as a candidate for the throne.

His blood must have run cold at the prospect. He would have needed no reminding of the final, ignominious reign of Shah Shuja, which ended with a bullet to his uncle's head as soon as British backing was withdrawn. If he harbored doubts about settling in Kathmandu, his remoteness there from British interference could only have quieted them. In the closed society of Nepal, he would neither be stalked by his enemies nor watched by his friends.

Except, that is, for the newest one. Jang Bahadur, rightly suspected of clandestine dealings with Calcutta by the anti-British faction in the Nepalese army, had pointed to his reception of Jindan as proof of his independence. In truth, the maharaja had secretly promised to keep a close eye on her. If he came across any evidence that she still plotted to revive the Sikh dynasty, he assured Lord Dalhousie, the governor general would be the first to know. Sa'adat would have been accorded similar surveillance.

The extent of British involvement in the rise of Jang Bahadur will probably never be known. The future maharaja had called regularly on Henry Lawrence during his term as resident, and solicited his advice. Though promoted to the rank of general not long before Henry received his summons to the Punjab, he had continued to maintain a low profile. "He takes no very prominent part just now," wrote Honoria Lawrence at the time, "and seems to spend his energies in devising new uniforms." But she went on to predict his future distinction, and even his means of achieving it, through "another slaughter in the Durbar."

After Lawrence's departure, Jang Bahadur thought it prudent to publicly distance himself from the British, a policy influenced by his dislike of the new resident, Colonel George Ramsay. But even as he declined to receive Ramsay except on official occasions, he maintained regular back-channel contact with the residency surgeon, James Dryburgh Login. Like his brother John, who had been appointed guardian of Duleep Singh upon Rani Jindan's imprisonment, Login owed his position to the exertions of Henry Lawrence, with whom he stayed in close touch.

According to Login's sister-in-law, Lady Lena Campbell Login, the young surgeon's influence over Jang Bahadur was "remarkable," and it had reached its zenith not long before Sa'adat and Nigel presented themselves at Thapathali Palace. It was Login, she wrote, who inspired Jang Bahadur with "a great desire to go to England to judge for himself what sort of people they were who ruled India." In defiance of Brahmin priests who threatened him with loss of caste for crossing the ocean, the maharaja had decided to present himself at Buckingham Palace and ask Queen Victoria for her personal assurance that the sovereignty of Nepal would remain unchallenged by the East India Company.

It was a bold, unprecedented move. For 250 years, the only constant at the tumultuous courts of the subcontinent had been the chronic irritant of the British in one guise or another, beseeching and wheeling and dealing and finally commanding. Yet in all that time, not a single native potentate had troubled to return the favor. Religious scruples had discouraged Hindus, who were taught that leaving India meant cutting themselves off from the regenerating waters of the

Ganges and thus entailed the end of the reincarnation cycle. Muslims and Sikhs lacked doctrinal constraints, but they joined with Hindus in fearing a more immediate temporal outcome. It was one thing to relinquish direct authority for a year or more to relatives or allies, quite another to reclaim it.

Jang Bahadur felt confident that he could minimize the risk to his power by carefully apportioning military commands so that no one or two of his brothers might bring sufficient force to bear to overwhelm the others in his absence. To safeguard the state of his eternal soul, he would see to the inclusion in his luggage of huge casks of water from the Ganges for his daily ablutions. He outlined his plans in a letter to Dalhousie, seeking permission for the journey and official leave for James Login to accompany him.

Both requests were granted. But by the time word reached Kathmandu, James Login was dead from cholera.

Jang Bahadur clearly required a cicerone for the journey, and despite the dearth of companionable Englishmen in Nepal, he was not long in finding one. There is no record of Nigel or anyone else receiving sanction from the Company to take Login's place. Nor is there evidence that Henry Lawrence put forth a candidate — unsurprisingly, since he had fallen out of favor with Calcutta and knew that anyone he suggested to Government House would be a marked man. He nonetheless remained adamantly opposed to further expansion of the Indian Empire, and wished Jang Bahadur every success on his mission to England. Though there was nothing Lawrence could do about the death of his protégé Login, there was nothing to prevent him, either, from putting in a private word with the maharaja for another young Company man, one he knew to share his views and one moreover who was already on leave and required no dispensation to depart.

Whether Lawrence played a role in securing his place or not, Nigel was the only European in a party led by the maharaja that departed in March 1850 for shooting at a hunting camp in the Terai, the first stage of a journey that would proceed to Calcutta and the steamship docks on the Hooghly. There, at the end of the first week in April, he joined Jang Bahadur and twenty-three other members of his party in embarking for Southampton.

After nine years in India, Nigel was headed home.

26

A Showcase

J ANG BAHADUR'S VOYAGE by paddle sloop to England seems to
have been uneventful. (Unlike that of two British officers who departed Calcutta on the long journey at about the same time, entrusted
with conveying the Koh-i-noor diamond to Queen Victoria; after cholera broke out on board, the ship received a hostile welcome in Mauri-
tius and was nearly sunk, then narrowly averted the same fate afterwards in a monumental gale as it rounded the Cape of Good Hope.)
But the maharaja's arrival was front-page news. As the first prince of
the East to visit Britain, he created a sensation.

One newspaper account described him as athletic, dark, and handsome, dressed in splendor, "like most Oriental despots," with special
reference to his *sarpech* headpiece adorned with rubies, pearls, and
diamonds. Waltz king Johann Strauss II composed "The Nepaulese
Polka," with sheet music featuring a half-page lithograph portrait of
"General Jang Bahadur Koomwur Ranajee." On an evening out at Cov-
ent Garden with Queen Victoria, Jang Bahadur tossed gold coins on-
stage at the conclusion of an aria, calling out "Pick up!" in Nepali, and
his countrymen believe to this day that this is how the word "tip" entered the English language.

Jang Bahadur failed, however, in his mission to obtain a pledge that
Britain would respect Nepalese sovereignty. At the insistence of the
East India Company, he was refused direct negotiations. Despite increasing dissatisfaction in Parliament with the Company's management of India, the sovereign powers granted by its charter remained in
force. If Jang Bahadur was to treat with anyone, maintained the Court
of Directors, it must be the governor general in Calcutta.

Though the maharaja was left to wonder why, then, he was encouraged to set out for England in the first place, the rebuff was precisely what Government House had counted upon in granting his wish to travel. No one in Calcutta expected him to make diplomatic headway on British soil. They endorsed his sojourn there in the belief that it would shatter any illusions he might cherish about opposing British ambitions, including the annexation of his country if it ever came to that. Once Jang Bahadur saw for himself the full extent of British wealth and power, went the thinking, he would realize the futility of resistance.

Of wealth and power he duly received an eyeful. He spent his days reviewing troops, inspecting armories, and touring factories. Accompanied by Victoria's husband, Prince Albert, he visited the gargantuan framework of iron rising in Hyde Park, 1,851 feet long and sheathed with a million square feet of glass — a "Great Shalimar" to some, and to others a "Crystal Palace." Upon completion, it would enclose full-grown trees and thirteen thousand exhibits devoted to modern technology and design: steam engines and carriages, surgical instruments and "philosophical instruments," the electric telegraph and the illuminated microscope. Organized by Albert himself, the upcoming Great Exhibition of the Works of Industry of All Nations made much of its attention to the achievements of countries around the world, and would serve as the prototype for a succession of world's fairs that continues to the present day. But it was conceived above all as a showcase for the supremacy and superiority of the people who were just then beginning to know themselves as Victorians.

Over there: cotton cloth made by the slaves of the king of Dahomey.

Over here: the first working version of a fax machine, made by a physicist in Hampstead.

England had the world at her feet. It was impossible for Jang Bahadur to come away with a contrary impression. But what Henry Lawrence and James Login had wanted him to see for himself about the British was not their material preeminence but, as Lady Login put it, "what sort of people they were."

They wanted to expose him to the masters of India's masters. And these, by and large, did not share the bloody-mindedness of those who ruled on their behalf in India. Staunch opponents of conquest for its own sake, the governing classes supported not the subjugation of native peoples but rather their elevation. Their lofty conception of empire was rooted in the conviction, as Jan Morris put it, that "British skill and science was ready to usher mankind into a golden age." And, thanks to science itself, it was a mind-set that could now be imposed from afar. The telegraph wires first raised in Britain in 1846 already extended to Egypt and the Levant. Calcutta still clung to its remoteness from oversight, but its grip would not last long. Unauthorized wars and injudicious proclamations would soon go the way of suttee and Thuggee and the sacrifice of infants on the shore of Sagar Island.

It was up to Jang Bahadur to make of these English what he would. Events proved his judgment astute, for his dynasty's rule of Nepal outlasted the British Raj in India. In the meantime, he succeeded at ingratiating himself with all the right people, just as Henry Lawrence imagined he would after experiencing firsthand the queen's keen interest in the East and its natives during his stay at Windsor Castle two years before. All society took its cues from the royal couple, and their attentiveness to Jang Bahadur opened every splendid door in London at the maharaja's convenience. He was feted so tirelessly that during his three-month stay he graced only one other English city with his presence: Nigel's hometown of Coventry, in the West Midlands.

What Nigel's family thought of Jang Bahadur was lost in the German raid that destroyed more than four thousand homes and made its own contribution to the English lexicon: "coventrate." Nor do firsthand accounts survive of their reaction to Nigel himself. Judging from the stories told and retold for decades afterwards, he was anything but reticent about his life of luxury in Kathmandu, which he seems to have hinted was somehow connected with the conveyance of precious gems. Another story out of India that vied with the visit of Jang Bahadur for prominence in the news during Nigel's leave was the arrival of the Koh-i-noor diamond, which reached London on July 2. That he returned East just as doubts about the diamond's provenance surfaced publicly evidently gave rise to the legend that Nigel "owed everything" to that gemstone in particular.

What clinched it for his family was that he stayed there. He stayed there and maintained sporadic contact for a few years, and then there was none. They could only conceive of a nefarious explanation.

Whether it could stand up to scrutiny probably seemed less consequential to the Hallecks of the mid-nineteenth century than it would to a distant relative in the latter part of the twentieth. He was concerned with the vagaries of history. What mattered to Nigel's immediate family in Coventry was incontrovertible contemporary fact.

He was gone. They said their goodbyes and wished him bon voyage in April 1851. They never saw him again.

27

Tipling

1976

YOU WILL NOT like Tipling," said the constable. "It is necessary to bear the presence of the Christian communities."

There were seven churches thereabouts, he added.

Seven churches and no trekking.

No one trekked there.

No one.

"The trekking you will find in Langtang."

He was a thin, nervous man in a moth-eaten navy tunic with powder blue epaulets. His sidearm clattered loosely in its holster. The police check-post was made of corrugated steel. It stood where the pine forest abruptly ended, at the outermost edge of the terraced fields of wheat, rye, millet, and oats surrounding the village.

He faced me from the doorway. I fixed my eyes above his shoulder, on the rotogravure portrait of King Birendra and Queen Aishwarya pasted to the wall behind him.

Langtang was undoubtedly well worth seeing, I said. Unfortunately, my time was limited — I was leaving Nepal in a few short weeks.

I nodded at the portrait, and lied.

It was Her Majesty's uncle General Rana, I said, who suggested that I visit Tipling.

"General Rana knows Tipling?" he said doubtfully.

"We were talking of jewels. He said that if I wished to learn about gemstones in Nepal, I must go to Tipling, in the Ganesh Himal."

Actually, the General had volunteered a hint only when I pressed him for details after he told me that precious gems could be found in Nepal if one knew where to look. I should find a rhyme, he said, for "Kipling."

The constable stepped down from the threshold onto the packed-dirt path.

"My home is Lalitpur," he said, sweeping his urban eyes disdainfully across the green, lush fields, moist with rain.

"I know nothing of these things."

In the steaming rhododendron forest that cloaked a hillside a thousand feet above us, a tin roof glinted in the afternoon sun. There, he said, lived a man who might help me.

A pensioned Gurkha, then. The roof gave the game away. In up-country Nepal, no one else could afford the luxury of roofing that held its own against the elements. His monthly remittances from London would have brought a species of prosperity to his neighbors, too. A village that counted a tin roof among its housetops was a village where Nebico biscuits might be purchased, and bottled Star beer from the brewery in Baneswor, and perfumed basmati rice.

As I neared the house, a long hour later, the rhododendrons gave way to solemn deodars that overhung the steep track. Stone steps led from the path to a terrace planted with fenugreek, where a dozen plump hens scrabbled and squawked. A copse of birches screened the house on the terrace above. A large dog barked.

"Identify yourself!" called a stern voice. "Friend or foe?"

"*Saathi!*" I replied automatically, even as his clipped English consonants hung crisply in the earth-smelling air.

I was a friend.

"*Angrezi saathi!*"

An English friend.

"Come then, welcome! Do not worry, the dog is chained. Well chained, I tell you! Links of steel!"

He laughed.

"The British steel, you may be sure. Not the Indian. Oh, no."

Corporal Rajendraman Tamang, 1st Battalion, 2nd King Edward VII's Own Gurkha Rifles (retired) had a bit of a belly, but plenty of parade ground still in his posture. His face was burnished bronze and he wore khaki shorts. He led me up to a pair of spindly wooden chairs on the edge of a wide veranda of rough-sawn cedar boards.

The chairs, he said, converted from walking sticks. He demonstrated how the legs opened and closed automatically when the leather seats were folded. They came from England.

He had a folding table, too. He erected it between the chairs, then excused himself and went inside.

Far below, Tipling lay deep in shadow. A long, round-shouldered bank of mist floated lazily over terraced fields and shrouded the pine forest beyond. I could see the green tops looking like a bed of moss when wind eddies thinned the cloud.

He returned with two glasses, sparkling clean, and a bottle of Khukri rum. He permitted himself a daily peg and was pleased to have company in taking it.

"It ages a man, the drinking alone."

He had married late, and survived his wife. He feared he might survive his sons, settled in Kathmandu and addicted to their motorbikes. They had gone to the boarding school in Pokhara—he did not think highly of the local Christian establishment. His daughter had wished to do the same, to the dismay of her grandparents.

But who was he to deny her?

He who knew the world!

London and Hong Kong, of course. But also Brunei, Iran, Malaysia. Nowadays even the Muslim girls were allowed to think for themselves.

She had promised to return.

But she would not.

For a visit, yes. To stay, no. There was nothing for the young people there. Only the beauty, and they were used to that. They did not see it. They saw only the lack of opportunity.

While he spoke, the sun was driving saffron shafts through the

down-drooping branches of the deodar beside the house, and its light
turned crimson as it dropped behind the peaks above. Then the night
fell, drawing a veil of blue haze across the face of the country.

I said I had heard that there were mineral deposits in the district,
with precious gems. There were no opportunities of that sort?

Indeed there were such gems, he replied, and of the best quality.

But mines?

No.

Mining of the gems posed three great difficulties. The first was the
difficulty of access. There was much danger in reaching the deposits,
high in the mountains. The second was the difficulty of ownership. It
had lately been decreed that His Majesty owned the mountains. On
that principle had been created the national park, in Langtang. On it,
too, were charged many lakh rupees to foreign expeditions, for their
climbing permits. These funds went directly into the royal coffers. It
would be no different with proceeds from the gem deposits.

"A king's jewels, a Gurkha's rifle, peas in a pod. Such things are
taken by fighting only."

The third was the difficulty of belief. They were most of them Ta-
mangs in those parts, who followed the Buddha's teachings. For the
Buddhist, the sinful occupations were the butcher, the blacksmith, and
the miner. For that reason there could be no mining of the precious
gems. Of course there would always be men who had some knowledge
of them, and a need for money for one reason or another, or a greedy
nature. And they would take the risk of obtaining such as they could,
in secret, then making some kind of arrangement. So it might be that
now and again a helicopter would make a flight from India to land at
an unknown place, and be met there.

"Then very quickly an exchange takes place, or so the rumors tell."

He stood.

"A moment."

A match lit up the darkness inside the house. I caught the purr and
fizzle of grains of incense. In attending to me, he had neglected the

household shrine. He reappeared with a spirit lamp of heavy glass and placed it on the table. Then he laid out four pouches of soft patterned cloth.

He opened the pouches one by one, carefully turning them inside out and handling the stones through the cloth. They were lumps of white marble the size of darning eggs, coursed with veins of red corundum.

The test of a ruby, he said, was that it lost none of its beauty in artificial light.

That was not the case with other red gemstones. Stationed in Teheran, guarding the British embassy, he had visited the National Museum, which housed the storied Peacock Throne of the Persian emperors.

He made a wry face.

"Garnets, I am sure."

The rubies in matrix blazed in the mellow lamplight, their fire acid pink instead of carmine or crimson.

It was a hue "characteristical" of the Nepalese ruby, he said.

A hue most valuable.

A hue most unusual, found nowhere else in the world save a single deposit in Afghanistan.

A deposit that I later learned was called Jagdalak.

A deposit visited by Nigel with Sa'adat ul-Mulk a few months before he returned to England on home leave, bearing gifts.

A hue that I had seen once before, as a child, in the dim electric light of my aunt's dressing closet in Coventry, on a heavy old brooch inscribed YOUR LOVING NIGEL.

There was no mistaking that hue. When I asked my aunt about the brooch after I returned home from Nepal, she remembered it. She doubted anyone had ever worn the thing, cheap as it looked. What sort of son would wish it on his mother?

He never told her it was a ruby. If he had, it would have been passed down with all the other fabulous stories. Nigel kept his own counsel, and I think I know why. His mother was a clergyman's daughter. She might have asked how he had come to afford such a bauble, and might not have accepted it.

When my aunt told me it had long since gone to a jumble sale, I took my cue from Nigel. I kept my mouth shut, too.

28

A Lark

NIGEL WAS NO LONGER bound by the terms of his ten-year covenant with the East India Company when he returned to Kathmandu in October 1851. He easily could have renewed it. His superiors recorded no complaints about his performance as a revenue officer. He had been singled out for recognition for his fluency in Urdu. More than once, he had demonstrated the sort of mettle that the Company not only valued in its civil servants but prized all the more because none of them could count on material reward for it.

Volunteering for Dacca, one of the unhealthiest postings in India. Serving in the newly British territory of the Jullundur Doab. Training native revenue clerks in what had lately been a war zone. He had shown himself a trooper. John Lawrence would have wanted him back. John, a billiard player and cigar smoker who was neither as refined nor as sensitive as his older brother Henry, had a horror of what he called "cakey men." He steadfastly refused his officers permission to decamp for the hills in the Hot Weather and preferred that they remain unmarried. His ideal subordinate, according to one of them, was a man who "worked all day and nearly all night, ate and drank when and where he could, had no family ties, no wife or children to hamper him, and whose whole establishment consisted of a camp bed, an odd table and chair or so, and a small box of clothes such as could be slung on a camel."

But Nigel demurred. When he said his farewells in England, he left no one with the impression that he might leave the Company's service. That might have been pragmatism. The Company strictly controlled the admittance of Europeans to India, limiting it to those it employed and those it invited to serve its commercial, scientific, and religious interests. Visits by relatives were tolerated, but not tourism for its own sake. Nigel would have known that if he ended his affiliation with the Company in England, he would have a devil of a time getting permission to return to India as a free agent.

He also would have known that those who separated in-country were under no particular compulsion to hasten back to Blighty. India had a way of absorbing outsiders. As far as the Company was concerned, going native meant a lapse of discipline and a descent into chaos. But if it was chaos that Englishmen wanted once they were off the Company books, far be it from Calcutta to stand in their way. No one traveled very far in the subcontinent without running into one of the innumerable models for Kipling's retired color sergeant Kimball O'Hara, who took up with a half-caste opium addict after his wife succumbed to cholera, acquired a taste for the pipe himself, and died "as poor whites die in India."

Nigel had already spent three months with Sa'adat enjoying the sumptuous hospitality of the sovereign kingdom of Nepal. It is hard to imagine a more luxurious retirement destination for a man who had gone beyond the English notion of propriety—particularly in the company of a jewel trader.

A jewel trader, it has to be said, with his own personal connection to the storied diamond that featured in the Halleck family legends about Nigel. Sa'adat's grandfather had owned the Koh-i-noor, which subsequently ended up in the hands of his uncle Shah Shuja until it was extorted from him by Ranjit Singh as the price of his protection when Shuja was forced into exile. After the diamond's presentation to Queen Victoria in 1850, her husband Prince Albert arranged an inquest into its perceived deficiencies, which revealed two cleavage planes in the gemstone. It was a mutilation that lapidarist James Tennant attributed to the Sadozais of Afghanistan, "whose necessities may have caused one of them to have pieces removed to furnish him with money."

Nigel's friendship with a scion of the Sadozais undoubtedly helped persuade some of his relatives that ill-gotten gains from such a transaction had somehow financed his splendid exile. They also knew of his connection to the Lawrence brothers, who featured in newspaper accounts of the diamond's surrender as a spoil of the Anglo-Sikh wars. He never came home, they later guessed, because he couldn't.

They surely guessed wrong. Jang Bahadur would have handed Nigel over in a heartbeat if the British really wanted him. His travels abroad had shown him the wisdom of Nepal's isolation — the less its people realized what they lacked, the likelier they would be satisfied with what they had. But the splendor of London and Paris had also sharpened his appetite for spending such wealth as his kingdom possessed. Upon his return, he decided on a policy of depriving his subjects of any foreign influence while rewarding his family with every foreign luxury. The trick was persuading the British to go along with it. For, as any fool could see, if the British wished, Nepal was theirs.

What most gives the lie to the legend of Nigel's forced exile, though, is that he spent several months in British India in 1854 without encountering any difficulties with the authorities. At the end of the Hot Weather, he set out from Nepal on what he called a "merry lark," traveling westward on the Grand Trunk Road with Sa'adat, whose obligations in the Punjab seem to have been the reason for the journey. With those taken care of, they proceeded to Bannu, the district south of Peshawar that Herbert Edwardes had cleared of its four hundred native forts in 1847. Since Bannu was en route to nowhere else, and since there was nothing of particular interest there, it is safe to say that the sole object of their visit was to pay another call on John Nicholson, then serving as deputy district commissioner.

Two and a half years had passed since he took over from another protégé of Henry Lawrence, Reynell Taylor, who had unwisely attempted to govern the unruly Bannuchis with fatherly indulgence. Nicholson established at the outset that he favored the wielded stick over the dangled carrot and, according to one of his successors, was hated at first as a "hard-hearted, self-willed tyrant."

The result of his exertions was neither riot nor rebellion nor religious upset. Bannu under Nicholson instead enjoyed a tranquility it had never known, one to be remembered fifty years later as having never recurred since. This comity came at a cost to Nicholson of at least one assassination attempt, the subject of his famous one-line dispatch to John Lawrence that he had shot a man who came to kill him. But the greater threat to achieving it was a falling-out between Lawrence and his brother Henry not long after Nicholson took up his post. Both men sat on the three-member Board of Administration for the Punjab, a body that Henry had long maintained should be replaced by a single commissioner. As the architect of British rule there, he considered himself the only man for the job. When a fierce dispute erupted over imposing a new system of land rights that John favored and Henry opposed, Dalhousie resolved the matter by doing away with the board and appointing John as commissioner. For the second time in his career, Henry was exiled from his beloved Punjab, this time to a ceremonial position in Rajputana.

Herbert Edwardes wept when he learned the news; Nicholson despaired of carrying on at Bannu. "I don't know how I shall ever get on when you are gone," he wrote to Henry. "If there is any work in Rajputana I am fit for, I wish you would take me with you. I certainly won't stay on the border in your absence. If you can't take me away, I shall apply for some quiet internal district like Shahpur."

Henry advised Nicholson to remain at his post. The best way to support him, he wrote, was to continue his work. Nicholson rose to the occasion by remaking Bannu in Shahpur's placid image. But by the time he received Nigel and Sa'adat there, it was apparent to all that the era of Henry Lawrence's Young Men was drawing to a close. Telegraph wires connected Calcutta to Lahore. In both their missions and their methods, the Company's officers on the frontier were subject as never before to stricture and supervision. "I know that Nicholson is a first rate guerrilla leader, but we don't want a guerrilla policy," fumed the governor general in a complaint to John Lawrence.

In the fragment from Nigel's correspondence that touches on his visit with Sa'adat, he alludes only in passing to the taming of Bannu, saying that the settled state of the district permitted Nicholson to ease his isolation by visiting Herbert Edwardes in Peshawar on his leave days. It was Henry's banishment from Lahore that dominated their conversation. Nicholson, unable to shake his abiding gloom over the situation, joined Sa'adat in forecasting trouble:

"S[a'adat], having known [Henry Lawrence] as one whose word could be relied upon in matters of import to himself and his relations, believes that esteem for the Government can only suffer from his absence, and the loyalty of Native Chiefs might thus waver, reverting the Tribal Areas to their prior state of mistrust and confusion. As does Maj. Nicholson, he fears unhappy consequences."

In the event, their fears proved unfounded, owing to what turned out to be the final hurrah of Henry Lawrence's onetime lieutenants on the North-West Frontier. Convinced that the security of the Punjab depended on harmonious relations with the Afghans, Edwardes spent the next few years negotiating treaties that bound them to be friends of Britain's friends and enemies of Britain's enemies. In return, the East India Company would promise to expand no further westward than its existing boundaries. John Lawrence, however, opposed any such agreements, forcing Edwardes to go over his head—not once, but twice—to secure support from Dalhousie in Calcutta. The telegraph, after all, worked both ways.

John Lawrence remained so hostile to the idea of coming to terms with the Afghans that it required a direct order from the governor general to compel his attendance at the signing of the final treaty. Yet it was John Lawrence who ultimately received credit when the Afghans lived up to their obligations and fought for the British during the Indian Mutiny. In gratitude for securing their alliance, he was created a baronet. Herbert Edwardes received no official recognition at all.

The true unhappy consequence of the change in Lahore was a disregard for happiness itself. Henry Lawrence, who believed that the well-being of natives ought to be the principal objective of British rule, had always commanded his lieutenants to "make the people happy." He repeated the refrain in a letter to his brother from Rajputana:

"If you preserve the peace of the country and make the people happy, high and low, I shall have no regrets that I have vacated the field for you."

John Lawrence replied with a promise that was also the empire's, and, in all its cool majesty, so was his rebuke:

"I will give every man a fair hearing, and will endeavour to give every man his due. More than this no one should expect."

29

A Mutiny

SIX YEARS AFTER he first gazed upon the Terai jungle with Sa'adat
—and five after he returned East from England to settle in Kathmandu as a guest of Jang Bahadur—Nigel again surveyed the steaming wilderness of the Terai, scribbling notes about flora and fauna. Natives armed with rifles stood guard around him. Somewhere behind them was the main hunting party, led by Jang Bahadur. Their quarry was a Bengal tiger—a man-eater blamed for a hundred deaths. The day before, in a village near the jungle's edge, they were shown a bitten-off lower arm, all that remained of its latest victim, a teenaged boy taken while gathering firewood. The ruler of Nepal regarded the killing of man-eaters as an obligation as well as entertainment, and, never one to leave matters to chance, favored a robust approach to discharging his duty. On one occasion, Jang Bahadur had taken to the bush with thirty-two thousand soldiers, fifty-two guns, two hundred fifty horse artillery, three hundred horsemen, a hundred elephants, two thousand camp followers, and seven hundred ration officers.

Nigel's letter, preserved because it mentioned John Nicholson, was written in November 1856. Sa'adat had recently returned from another trip to the Punjab, this time by himself, bearing sketch plans of a formal garden in Peshawar that he had commended to Jang Bahadur. This was surely Wazir Bagh, established in 1810 under the patronage of Sa'adat's grandfather Mahmud Shah, then reigning for the second time as king of Afghanistan. Its spacious lawns and flower beds, shaded by apricot, peach, and pomegranate trees, remained in Afghan hands for only three years, until the city's conquest by the Sikhs under Ranjit Singh. Responsibility for their upkeep now rested with the Brit-

ish. In charge as district commissioner was Herbert Edwardes, who—
as Sa'adat learned in Peshawar—was about to be joined by Nicholson
as his deputy.

When Nicholson arrived, he declined to move into the house assigned to him. He took up residence instead with Edwardes, in the
commissioner's bungalow. It was there that an officer found them
on the afternoon of May 11, 1857, when he burst in with a signal just
telegraphed from Delhi. Sepoys of the large Company army based at
Meerut, northwest of the city, had risen the day before and massacred
the Christian population. Now, after riding all night, they were swarm-
ing through the gates of the old Mughal capital.

Some had seen it coming. As far back as 1850, General Charles Napier had warned that the British were in "great peril" from native unrest within the army. When Lord Dalhousie dismissed his concerns as
unjustified, Napier resigned as commander in chief. The sepoys had
a long list of grievances. No matter how long they served, few could
hope for commissions as regimental officers. Their base pay was relatively low, and after the annexation of the Punjab and Oudh (the region in north India centered around Lucknow, in present-day Uttar
Pradesh), they no longer received bonuses for duty on "foreign missions." The influx of Gurkhas and Sikhs, who were favored by the British for their fighting qualities, made it harder for the sons of serving
sepoys to break into the ranks. High-caste Hindus—the majority of
sepoys in the Bengal Army—were distressed by the Company's new
emphasis on recruitment of the lower-born, a deliberate strategy to reduce the complications caused by ritual sensitivities. An article attributed to an invalided sepoy that was published in the *Delhi Gazette* in
May 1855 warned the British to desist from enlisting "men we cannot
know and whom 1000 of the 1120 people in the village despise."

Then there were the larger issues.

The increasing gulf between the rulers and the ruled was one. Sahibs shut themselves off from India and retreated into their canton-

ments and clubs at the price of the camaraderie that once forged bonds of trust between British officers and their native men.

Evangelism was another. Proselytizing, long proscribed by the Company, was now exalted by an increasing number of Englishmen as their highest calling in India. The Reverend Midgeley Jennings, appointed chaplain of Delhi in 1852, invoked the Koh-i-noor diamond in calling for the transmission of Christian doctrine to the farthest reaches of the subcontinent. Now that the British Crown possessed that splendid jewel, he wrote, it behooved the British themselves to show their gratitude and "give in return that 'pearl of great price.'" More often than not, a commander like Colonel Steven Wheler, who took it upon himself to preach the Gospel to "natives of all classes . . . in the highways, cities, bazaars and villages," was no less eager to brandish his Bible in the barrack-room, reading Scripture to his sepoys on a regular basis in hopes of rescuing them from eternal damnation.

It was the belief that the Company was intent on caste breaking and Christianizing that finally led to revolt. In August 1856, the Indian Army began testing the new Enfield rifle, which used pre-greased paper ammunition cartridges that sepoys were obliged to bite open. After the rifles were issued, rumors spread in the ranks that the cartridges were defiling to Hindus and Muslims alike. They were greased, it was said, with a mixture of tallow and lard, animal fats derived from beef and pork.

Though denied at the time, the rumors were true, at least at first. The Company made haste to change the ingredients, and officers told sepoys they were free to make their own grease from beeswax and vegetable oil.

Almost to a man, they refused to have anything at all to do with the new weapons. Their hostility persisted even after the Company went further and modified the loading drill to permit tearing open the cartridges by hand. Most sepoys believed the defilement was no accident. They accused the British of violating their ritual purity in order to forcibly convert the entire army to Christianity. When word reached Meerut of the execution of a sepoy who had tried to incite rebellion at Barrackpore, they turned on their officers—the first of all but 7,796 of the 139,000 sepoys in the Bengal Army to mutiny.

Nicholson's first response to the bad news was to ask its bearer who else had heard it. Told that the signal was first brought to the officers' mess by the telegraph operator, he hurried over and told those present to keep word of the rebellion to themselves. He then asked Fred Roberts, a twenty-four-year-old ensign in the Bengal Artillery, to take the minutes at a council of war the next morning.

It was Roberts who witnessed the genesis of Nicholson's plan for a fast-moving force of Pashtun and Sikh irregulars that could strike anywhere in the Punjab at the first sign of trouble; Roberts who accompanied that column to Delhi in August, when it constituted the last British hope of saving the Indian Empire; Roberts who found Nicholson's mortally wounded body after he led the charge that carried the main breach of the city walls and heard him say, "I am dying; there is no chance for me."

And it was Roberts—the future Field Marshal Lord Roberts of Kandahar, one of the most successful British commanders of the nineteenth century—who would remember him in terms that echoed those of Nigel, captivated by the "honesty and bravery and fine convictions" of a then-unknown lieutenant at the residency in Lahore in 1846.

"Nicholson impressed me more profoundly than any man I had ever met before, or have ever met since. I have never seen anyone like him. He was the beau ideal of a soldier and a gentleman. His appearance was distinguished and commanding, with a sense of power about him which to my mind was the result of his having passed so much of his life among the wild and lawless tribesmen, with whom his authority was supreme. Intercourse with this man amongst men made me more eager than ever to remain on the frontier, and I was seized with ambition to follow in his footsteps."

Nicholson survived his injuries long enough to learn that Delhi had been taken, and to dictate a farewell message to Herbert Edwardes. "Tell him that, if at this moment a good fairy were to grant me a wish," he said, "my wish would be to have him here next to my mother." He died on September 23, 1857, six weeks after a rebel artillery shell killed Henry Lawrence during the siege of the Lucknow residency. Among the last words of Lawrence, who had been appointed chief commissioner of Oudh upon its annexation the year before, were instructions for his epitaph:

"Put on my tomb only this: HERE LIES HENRY LAWRENCE, WHO TRIED TO DO HIS DUTY."

Both would pass into history as paragons of Victorian chivalry. And so, at least officially, would Jang Bahadur, after taking personal command of an army of twenty-five thousand Nepalese troops in the Hot Weather of 1857 and rushing to the aid of British garrisons besieged in Gorakhpur and Lucknow. Queen Victoria rewarded him for his loyalty by creating him a Knight Grand Cross in the Order of the Bath, one of Britain's highest chivalric orders. Her government further showed its gratitude by restoring to Nepal the territory it had ceded to India as the price of ending the Anglo-Nepalese War.

Reprisals were the first order of business in the rebellion's aftermath. Many were enacted to cries of "Remember Cawnpore!" There, after a Company garrison numbering nine hundred men surrendered under a guarantee of safe passage, all but four were killed by mutineers, who then hacked 120 European women and children to death and dismembered their bodies with meat cleavers before tossing them into a well. The British took their revenge with equal savagery, and far greater loss of life. Entire villages were burned to the ground, their inhabitants hanged. Delhi became a charnel house. Among those taking part in the slaughter there was Edward Vibart, a nineteen-year-old company commander whose brother, sister, and parents had been slain in the Cawnpore massacre. They "cry aloud for vengeance," he wrote to his uncle afterwards, "and their son will avenge them." But the scale of the carnage unnerved him:

I have seen many bloody and awful sights lately. But such a one as I witnessed yesterday please God I pray I never see again. The regiment was ordered to clear the houses between the Delhi and Turkman Gates . . . and the orders were to shoot every soul. I think I must have seen about 30 or 40 defenceless people shot down before me. It was literally murder and I was perfectly horrified. The women were all spared, but their screams, on seeing their husbands and sons butchered, were most terrible.

The town as you may imagine presents an awful spectacle now . . . heaps of dead bodies scattered throughout the place and every house broken into and sacked — but it is the townspeople who are now falling victims to our infuriated soldiery . . . Wherever you go, you see some unfortunate man or other being dragged out of his hiding place, and barbarously put to death.

Heaven knows I feel no pity — but when some old grey bearded man is brought and shot before your very eyes — hard must be that man's heart I think who can look on with indifference.

It was John Lawrence who acted to end what he likened to "a war of extermination." After the administration of Delhi was transferred to the Punjab government in February 1858, he complained to the new governor general, Lord Canning, that the magistrate in charge of Delhi was guilty of "wholesale slaughters" and requested that he be sent back to England.

"I stopped the different civil officers hanging at their own will and pleasure," wrote Lawrence at the end of April, "and appointed a commission, since when matters have greatly improved and confidence among the natives greatly increased." He persuaded Canning to oppose the wholesale demolition of Delhi proposed by Lord Palmerston, the prime minister, as punishment for the city's central role in the rebellion. Lawrence also argued for a general amnesty for all who had not personally murdered British civilians in cold blood. He was no more willing to make natives pay for crimes they had not committed than he was to take responsibility for making them happy.

Opposition to amnesty ran deep among the British in India. But it gained support at home once remorse set in about the reduction of officers and gentlemen to the same brutish level as "heathens." The British, after all, were a superior people.

"I protest against meeting atrocities with atrocities," Benjamin Disraeli told the House of Commons, and on November 1 a general amnesty was proclaimed in the name of Queen Victoria. It followed by two months the effective date of the Act for the Better Government of India, which transferred to the British Crown all territories possessed by the East India Company, and all powers exercised by the Company over them.

On that day, meeting for the last time at their headquarters in Leadenhall Street, the directors of the Honourable East India Company issued a statement of farewell to all their many servants. "The Company has the great privilege," it began, "of transferring to the service of Her Majesty such a body of civil and military officers as the world has never seen before."

It was only the truth. But it surely seemed anticlimactic to one civil officer who had already said farewell to the service and everything it stood for. Nigel Halleck's privilege, for the next twenty years, was to continue to enjoy the life he had made for himself apart from the Company, in all its splendid isolation.

PART III

30

Rosi Bagh

1976

WHEN I RETURNED to Kathmandu from my trek to Tipling, I called on Boris at the Yak and Yeti. He listened with interest to the tale of helicopters touching down to spirit away gemstones that rightly belonged to His Majesty King Birendra. His own relations with the royal family had cooled since the halcyon days of the Shah restoration. In 1970, he had lost the catering contract for state functions to the new Soaltee Hotel, owned by Prince Gyanendra. He naturally made his displeasure known, and the next thing he knew he had been detained during an investigation into the theft and illegal export of ancient art objects.

Jailed!

He himself!

Boris!

He was cleared, of course, but the message was plain: one crossed the Shahs at one's peril. He hoped that was understood fully up in Tipling.

The first thing he said when I told him that my visa was up and I would be returning to the States was that if I wanted to stay in Nepal, he would be happy to give me a part-time job teaching English to his employees. That would take care of the visa extension. The second thing he said, after I demurred because I had another year of college to complete, was that since I was traveling across Afghanistan again, I ought to look up a fellow he knew in Herat.

An Englishman, one of those archaeologists who couldn't sit still.

Digging, digging, always digging. Not one to bother with papers and permits. He'd show me a proper ruin or two, my eyes only. That I could depend upon. He would write him straightaway.

Relying on the post between Nepal and Afghanistan, though — that would be foolish. One didn't place wagers on a horse gone lame in two legs. I had better take a copy of his letter with me.

The Englishman, whom I'll call Hendricks, turned out to be a donnish loner in his forties. He insisted that Boris had over-egged the pudding in calling him an archaeologist. He was nothing of the sort. Bog-standard amateur was more like it. (Later, after the Islamic revolution in nearby Iran and the invasion of Afghanistan by the equally nearby USSR, he would strike me as a likely professional in a more clandestine line — one that would have accounted for his fluency in Farsi, Dari, Pashto, and Russian as well as the vagueness of his explanation for his presence in Herat.) As promised, he chauffeured me by Land Rover to wild, unknown ruins on the outskirts of the ancient city, termed "the breadbasket of Central Asia" by Herodotus and captured by Alexander in 330 B.C. But he also showed me the spires and domes clad in luminous mosaics that brought Herat its greatest fame as the capital of the Timurid Empire, whose rulers bestowed lavish commissions on artists, architects, and men of letters.

Here were the towering minarets of the Musalla, tiled with blue lozenges filled with flowers. There was the azure mausoleum of Empress Gohar Shad, described by Robert Byron after his visit in 1934 as "the most beautiful example in color in architecture ever devised by man to the glory of God and himself."

At the zenith of Herat's magnificence, in the fifteenth century, it was one of the most cultured cities in the world, larger than Paris or London. It was a place where it was said that if you stretched out your feet, you were sure to hit a poet.

The greatest was the beloved Persian Jami. On a bright, clear morning, we drove out a dusty road lined with pines to his simple tomb, sheltered by a spreading pistachio tree in the garden of a mosque. The poet had written his own epitaph, and I copied Hendricks' translation into my notebook:

> *When your face is hidden from me,*
> *Like the moon hidden on a dark night,*
> *I shed stars of tears and yet my night remains dark*
> *In spite of all those shining stars.*

Later we wandered through the ruins of an old royal hunting lodge at Rosi Bagh, a few miles south of the city. The sand-blown grounds of the adjacent necropolis were littered with shards of the exquisite glazed tiles that had given the monuments of Herat their celestial luminescence. The two largest tombs contained the remains of father and son. Hendricks called them Sadozais. The father's name was Mahmud Shah. He was once the king of Afghanistan, once held the Koh-i-noor diamond. He was thought to have been poisoned by his son Kamran, whose name was on the other tomb.

After the bloodline ran out, Hendricks said, most of the lesser royal tombs had been stripped of their mosaics by grave robbers. Only a few forlorn tiles with inscriptions remained. He drew my attention to one, shaped as a twelve-pointed star and decorated with fine faience mosaic — small pieces of turquoise, saffron, and green ceramics fitted together to form designs of flowers, leaves, and calligraphy.

The curious thing about it was the calligraphy. It quoted from Jami's epitaph, which was well-known in the Islamic world. But the inscription concluded abruptly with "I shed stars," as if the artisan's thoughts had turned elsewhere and, upon resuming his work, he'd forgotten there was more to the poem.

It was the sort of lapse, grumbled Hendricks, that never would have happened in the glorious reign of Gohar Shad.

He pointed out the pattern of arabesques on another tile. It consisted entirely of repetitions of the word for "mercy."

That, he said drily, was the rarest of qualities among the rulers interred there. Then he told me a story about "Kamran the Cruel," who maintained a pride of lions to which he fed his enemies alive.

YEARS WOULD PASS before the story signified. I had not yet connected Sa'adat to the Afghan ruling family and the vivid pink-hued rubies of his birthright. There was no way of knowing then that the truncated stanza from Jami on the star-shaped tile in that bleak dusty boneyard outside of Herat was the crucial missing piece of the puzzle that was Nigel.

31

Khyber Pakhtunkhwa

1982

WHEN I RETURNED to the United States, I regaled my mother with stories of the Ranas and their palaces. She had always been an ardent monarchist, of the sort found these days mostly among expatriates like herself, who revel in the glory without paying for the privilege, and I wondered at first how she would receive the news that Nigel had so long enjoyed the hospitality of the usurper Jang Bahadur. But it pleased her immensely that he had moved in such exalted circles. And she was relieved that Boris had dismissed the family legend that Nigel met his end in the mouth of a man-eater. She resisted the idea of Nigel's cremation, though, however much sense it might seem to make with benefit of hindsight.

No, she said—he had been buried. He must have been, because she remembered hearing there was some kind of marker, emplaced by the same friend who sent word of Nigel's death to his family in England. She was sure its location had been known, if left unvisited, until the letter describing it went up in flames in 1940. All anyone remembered was that the place had something to do with a tiger. Perhaps the idea that he'd been killed by one arose out of that. Was there a town in Nepal that was famous for tigers, or named after them in the native tongue?

All I could think of was Tiger Tops, where guests took in the wild-life of the Terai from a rustic lodge perched on stilts. But it had been in business only since 1965, and no town or village names came to mind that incorporated the word *bāgha*. None came up later, either, when I consulted a gazetteer at my college library.

I had better luck researching Nigel's friend John Nicholson. I learned, in the first place, that his name is immortalized in English usage. When we say "in the nick of time," we pay homage to the hero of the Indian Mutiny, who had the habit of turning up just when his help was needed most. Then I read about the cult of the Nikal Seynis and discovered that the sect has survived to the present day in remote parts of northwest Pakistan. Finally, I learned that the man behind the myth had lately been cut down to size by revisionist historians.

That they accused him of racism and religious bigotry was only to be expected. In applying the standards of the late twentieth century to the attitudes of those who lived in the mid-nineteenth, the same would have to be said about virtually all of his contemporaries, including the benevolent Henry Lawrence. There was more to it than that, though. Nicholson, they asserted, was a guilt-ridden homosexual bully, so disgusted by his orientation that he sought release in manic violence. One called him a sadomasochist.

Though Nicholson never married—instead of heeding Henry Lawrence's advice to find a wife on his home leave, he spent much of it inquiring into weaponry and military training in Prussia and Russia—there is no hard evidence that he found solace in men or boys. Some of the smoke that has led to the presumption of fire may be traced to his closeness with the son of Hassan Karam Khan, a tribal chieftain who rode with the force he led in the ill-fated attempt to reclaim the watchtower at Margalla Pass. Accounts differ on Khan's fate. One holds that he was among those who died at the base of the Margalla watchtower. According to another, he was murdered afterwards by a rival chief, in revenge for siding with the British. What is certain, wrote Nicholson's fellow "political" James Abbott, is that he left a young son named Muhammad Hayat Khan, "upon whom Nicholson lavished much care and attention."

Abbott reported the boy's age as "about seven," but it was probably closer to ten or eleven; nine years later the lad was fighting at Nicholson's side as a leader of irregular troops himself. On the face of the surviving evidence, at least to a casual reader, there is nothing to suggest that Nicholson's interest in Muhammad Hayat Khan was anything but paternal. But such a reading, in the minds of modern historians, fails to account for the cultural context of such a connection.

Then as now, the practice of sodomy was endemic among Pashtun men. (A study conducted by an American military research unit in 2010 would conclude that the entire Pashtun ethnic group was experiencing a "sexual identity crisis" after finding that Pashtun men commonly had sex with other men, admired other men physically, had sexual relationships with boys, and shunned women both socially and sexually—yet completely rejected the label "homosexual.") When adults "lavished" their "care and attention" on adolescent boys, there was only one possible interpretation of its nature. It wasn't just Nicholson's fearlessness that natives admired. Time and again, the grizzled warriors of the North-West Frontier voiced their conviction that in the core of his being, "Nikal Seyn" was one of them.

There was also the matter of Nicholson's friendship with Herbert Edwardes. During the several years Nicholson served at Bannu as deputy district commissioner, he had given over his leave days to riding nine hard hours each way to spend one night a week at Edwardes' bungalow in Peshawar. When he was transferred to Peshawar himself, he moved in with Edwardes rather than occupy the house assigned to him. Though the two officers had known each other since the Battle of Sobraon, in 1846, by all accounts their mutual fondness dated to their voyage down the Sutlej and the Indus after they set out for England from Ferozepore at the end of 1849. It was a long way to Karachi—almost seven hundred miles—and the enforced intimacy of a rustic Indian houseboat might easily have become what Nicholson's Victorian biographer called "one of those ordeals which test the strength of human friendship." Instead, wrote Lionel Trotter, "the days flowed by in the easy intercourse of two fine noble spirits bound together by com-

mon aims, sympathies, experiences, and by a certain lack in each of that
which the other could best supply."

Instead, they bonded into soul mates.

"In the sunshine of the elder man's cheery nature and bright, tren-
chant, easyflowing talk, Nicholson's heart grew lighter, his coun-
tenance less stern, and his tongue found readier utterance for the
thoughts that filled his brain. Edwardes, too, knew how to hold his
tongue on fit occasion, and to serve his friend by the silence that is often more eloquent than any words."

Twentieth-century authors would imagine the outing as a homosexual idyll. Trotter's rather abrupt insistence that "other incidents of
this voyage remain matters for guess-work" may or may not suggest
that there was gossip at the time. Whether Nicholson ever wrote about
the river trip is unknown. A great many of his letters were destroyed
in an "accidental" fire in the study of Sir John William Kaye, author of
Lives of Indian Officers; coincidentally or not, similar fires flared up in
the studies of Victorian biographers of Lord Byron and Sir Richard
Burton, other heroic public figures whose private lives flouted the con-
ventions of the day.

Edwardes, for his part, told Emma Sidney, whom he married in
England in 1850 — with Nicholson standing as best man — that they
spent their time "beguiling their way with books and talk." We owe
the assurance that afterwards the two men were "welded together" in
"strong, true love and friendship" to Lady Edwardes herself, who had
accompanied her husband on his return to India but found the climate
unbearable and returned to England:

"Knowing each other most intimately, they were more than brothers
in the tenderness of their whole lives henceforth, and the fame and interests of each other were dearer to them both than their own."

I learned of Nicholson's voyage down the Indus with Herbert Edwardes from Rasheed, the Pashtun admirer of John Nicholson whom
I first met at Margalla Pass. After we re-boarded the segregated bus
there, he had given me his address, and we exchanged letters while I

lived in Kathmandu. On my way back to Afghanistan, he put me up for a few days at his place in Peshawar. I kept his account of the houseboat journey—minus the modern interpretation—in the back of my mind until 1982, when I decided to pitch the idea of emulating Nicholson and Edwardes' journey to my editor at the outdoor sports magazine that had been publishing my stories since I graduated from college.

By then Rasheed had graduated, too; he was practicing dentistry up in the Hazara country at Abbottabad, the hill station named after James Abbott. He wrote to me that the construction of barrages—diversion dams for irrigation—on the lower Indus had made it impossible to float the river as far as Nicholson and Edwardes had, all the way to the Arabian Sea. But there was a significant stretch of free-flowing water downstream from Attock, passing through roadless country that was little changed from the days of Henry Lawrence's Young Men.

And there we were, a few months later, perched on a low drystone wall beneath a mulberry tree that canopied out from the corner of a teahouse on the riverbank, somewhere nameless in Khyber Pakhtunkhwa. Fine pink sand spilled down the bank to the shore. It showed no tracks. Behind the teahouse rose a ridge of shattered rock. The boatman leaned over the gunwale of a fishing boat tied to a piling on the shore. The water was smooth pink glass that mirrored the patched hull of the boat and the bald black tires nailed to the piling. A teenaged boy slouched in the shade of the arched doorway of the teahouse. It was very hot.

"Did you hear that?" asked Rasheed. "What the boatman said?"

Rasheed called out in Urdu to the boatman. The boatman looked up and smiled. Then he turned back toward the boy in the doorway.

"*Te zan ta Nikal Seyn wayat?*" he repeated.

It was a catchphrase, Rasheed told me, for exasperation.

The boatman wanted the boy to bring him a glass of tea.

The boy told him he was a doorkeeper, not a waiter.

The boatman impugned his upbringing; the boy replied in kind.

The boatman said:

"Who do you think you are, Nicholson?"

After all these years, said Rasheed, the common people still remembered him.

"How lovely is that?" he asked.

That night, sitting beside me at our campsite on a sandbar, Rasheed told me that he hoped the modern historians were right—that the two Englishmen had been lovers, that life without tenderness was possible but miserable, that the frontier was a lonely and dangerous place that either drew men together or tore them apart.

England was another planet.

These men lived for years among the Pashtuns, he said, whose ways were not the English ways. Nor were Pashtuns ashamed of their attachments. They spoke of their loves and conquests. They teased and joked. They showed their affection.

Rasheed supposed that what had shocked and offended the Englishmen at first ceased, finally, to trouble them. Did they not let it be known time and again that they liked and admired the Pashtuns above all other natives? They could not, of course, permit their liking for a Pashtun to become an attraction—there was too much risk of lowering their status. If they lowered their status, they weakened their authority. For men in their position, there was always the color bar.

But what was to stop the physical expression of their attraction to one another?

So far from home, so remote even from their countrymen in India, so needy in their loneliness.

Surely they would have been tempted to follow the Pashtun example.

If they needed one.

Perhaps they did not.

But if they did, what, after all, had provided it?

What had placed temptation in their way?

What, indeed, had promised privacy if it proved irresistible, by posting them to the farthest fringes of its back of beyond?

There was no better label for what happened between them than the words stamped into the handle of the battered tin kettle that hung from a tripod over our cooking fire.

He flashed his million-rupee smile and read them out:

EMPIRE MADE.

32

Lal Durbar

1982

ONLY NINETY YEARS separated the Indian Mutiny from Indian Independence. In the rebellion's aftermath, racial attitudes hardened and the British isolated themselves more than ever from contact with their subjects. Sahibs and memsahibs settled into a routine that a Victorian critic summed up as "duty and red tape, tempered with picnics and adultery." Evangelism fell out of favor as the notion took hold that the spiritual progress of natives would follow naturally from material progress. Public works eclipsed social reform as the professed objective of empire. Among them were the universities founded in Calcutta, Bombay, and Madras that taught the principles and practices of Western democracy to a new class of anglicized Indians. The political parties they formed and the strikes they organized not only undermined the Raj but convinced the British that its demise was only a matter of time — and not so much of it, either.

Neither party politics nor protest movements would flourish in Nepal until well into the second half of the twentieth century. Jang Bahadur founded no universities. And his staunchness during the Mutiny removed any possibility of British interference in the ongoing plunder of the mountain kingdom by the maharaja and his family. Most unusual for a ruler of Nepal, Jang Bahadur lived past the age of sixty and died of natural causes in February 1877, at the same hunting camp in the Terai where he had entertained Albert Edward, the Prince of Wales, the year before.

The staunchness of the Pashtuns, on the other hand, served only to

postpone for a generation another round of bloodletting and barba-
rism on the North-West Frontier. Forty thousand British and Indian
troops invaded Afghanistan again in the fall of 1878, after the Barakzai emir welcomed Russian envoys to Kabul but turned their British
counterparts away. As before, the Forward Policy demanded action.
As before, the British swiftly occupied key Afghan cities. As before,
the Afghans signed a treaty that ended the fighting, accepted a British
resident, and relinquished control of foreign affairs to Calcutta. And
as before, an uprising in Kabul a year later led to the slaughter of the
resident and his staff, which ushered in a second and crueler phase of
the conflict.

The British, reprising a practice employed against the Indian mutineers, took to blowing their prisoners from guns. The victim was tied
to the mouth of a cannon with the small of his back resting against the
muzzle. When the gun was fired, the birds of prey that circled above
the killing ground swooped down to catch pieces of flesh in the air.
(More than once, witnesses who failed to sufficiently withdraw were
injured by whizzing fragments of bone.) Afghans, for their part, had a
tradition of bleeding captured soldiers to death by castrating them—
the fate of young Alexander Nicholson during the First Anglo-Afghan
War. Now they sought to further humiliate their British prisoners by
turning the task over to women, who also served as instruments of
vengeance in another method of execution. After British captives were
spread-eagled on the ground, with sticks inserted in their mouths to
prevent swallowing, Pashtun women took turns squatting over the
prisoners and urinating into their open mouths until they drowned.

You will find no mention of the historical antecedents of water-
boarding in *Counterinsurgency in Afghanistan*, a report prepared by the
RAND Corporation for the United States Office of the Secretary of
Defense in 2008. You will read of the need to improve the quality of local governance. You will read of the need to focus American resources
on developing indigenous security forces that are "competent and legitimate." And you will read of the need to come to terms with the pre-

vailing culture of the tribal areas that straddle both sides of the boundary with the North-West Frontier Territories of Pakistan.

Settle the country.

Make the people happy.

Take care there are no rows.

Henry Lawrence had yet to be recognized as the father of counterinsurgency in those parts when I floated down the Indus with Rasheed in 1982. The Soviets had invaded Afghanistan three years before. It was too early to foresee the consequences of American support for the mujahideen who opposed them, too early to anticipate the founding of Al Qaeda and the rise of the Taliban, too early to understand that the British in the middle of the nineteenth century engaged with the inhabitants of India's western frontier for the same selfish reason that Americans would take on some of their descendants at the beginning of the twenty-first. They feared an external threat to their power and their people. Their motives were anything but humanitarian. But they got to know the leading troublemakers, and worked with them to improve both the quality of their leadership and the conditions of everyday life for those they led.

Boris Lissanevitch, however, thought it was high time to recognize another side of Henry Lawrence. When I visited him in Kathmandu after I left Pakistan, we sat in the music room at Lal Durbar and I ran down what I had learned since I last saw him about the details of Nigel's life in India and Nepal. He listened intently, then connected sundry dots with his habitual gusto and identified Lawrence as a consummate player in the politics of Nepal long after the kingdom had ceased officially to concern him, working his will and England's through the clandestine agency of my ancestor.

"Of course," said Boris admiringly. "Of course."

His own role in ending Rana rule had heightened his interest in its advent, and there were things about it, he said, that had never been adequately explained. He greeted the intelligence that Nigel had sailed to England at the same time as Jang Bahadur with compliments on my detective work.

It was certainly an interesting coincidence.

If that was what it was.

Perhaps Nigel had only pretended to throw over his career with the East India Company.

Perhaps he was some sort of secret agent.

Perhaps he was working for Henry Lawrence.

Lawrence, Boris pointed out, was posted to Nepal in the aftermath of the Afghan War, ostensibly charged with doing nothing. But with benefit of hindsight, his mission was obvious: to curb the expansionist ambitions of the ruling Shah dynasty. Before Lawrence could finish the job, he was called to the taming of the Punjab. Yet the job had got done. It had got done so well that by 1850 an obscure artillery captain with British sympathies had consolidated all power in his own hands as prime minister, installed his own candidate on the throne, appointed his brothers and cronies to all important administrative posts, and eliminated all his major rivals. It had got done so well that in April of that year, Jang Bahadur made his boldest move yet and set out for England to make the case for his ongoing rule to Queen Victoria herself.

Upon his return, Jang Bahadur made an unexpected concession to Calcutta. As the sole exception to his policy of strict isolation for ordinary Nepalese, he permitted a vast expansion in the recruitment of Gurkha mercenaries to serve in the East India Company army. It was a bold—and risky—departure from past practice, but also a brilliant one. In the first place, pensions and remittances sent home provided a country that exported nothing with foreign exchange. In the second, it created opportunities to escape a closed society that amounted to a safety valve, releasing pressure that otherwise might have posed a threat to Rana rule.

It seemed to Boris that Jang Bahadur's flexibility on that point was curious indeed. He had an obsessive interest in all things British, but he harbored deep misgivings about the men who succeeded Lawrence as resident, whom he deigned to receive only when diplomatic protocol required it. They were hardly in a position to influence his thinking. But someone clearly had — someone, perhaps, whose undercover assignment was to ensure above all that the "martial race" of the Gurkhas fought for the British interest instead of against it. If there was such a someone with such an assignment, the history of the Mutiny amounted to proof that he had carried it out. In decisive engagements with the rebels at Lucknow and Delhi, Nepalese troops helped carry the day for the British. Afterwards, when mutineers fleeing retribution sought sanctuary in the Terai, kukri-wielding Gurkhas led by Jang Bahadur himself cut them to pieces, sparing no one.

There was something else he had always wondered about. The provisions of the Nepalese legal code promulgated in the 1850s reflected sympathies not usually associated with despots like Jang Bahadur. It abolished torture and corporal punishment, reduced the number of capital crimes from hundreds to a handful, empowered the peasantry with economic rights, and raised women to a status that, though less than coequal with men, was closer to it than in India and indeed parts of Europe. For the time and the place, it was really quite astonishing.

It might have been drafted by Lawrence himself — or someone in a position to exert the sort of influence on Jang Bahadur that Lawrence undoubtedly exercised when he was resident.

Someone like the residency surgeon James Login, to begin with.

Someone like Nigel, after Login died.

It certainly would explain things, would it not?

It all made so much better sense when you saw the hand of Nigel in the improbable outcome of Jang Bahadur's ambition, so beneficial for so long to both England and the Ranas.

And then there was the curious coincidence of Nigel's arrival in Kathmandu just three months before Jang Bahadur packed up for his sojourn abroad, just weeks after Login's death.

I refrained from rolling my eyes, but Boris caught my skepticism and laughed.

Everyone in Kathmandu, of course, thought that *he* was a spy.

The Russians thought he spied for the Americans. The Americans thought he spied for the Russians. The Indians thought he spied for both. In one of the framed photographs on the music room wall, Jawaharlal Nehru addressed a banquet. To his left sat Queen Ratna of Nepal. Behind Nehru, with one hand resting on the back of his chair, stood Boris in black tie, dominating the tableau.

In another, the commanding figure was a husky blonde—Valentina Tereshkova, the first woman in space. Beside her was her husband, Andrian Nikolayev, also a cosmonaut. They had honeymooned in Kathmandu in 1963. When the Soviet embassy asked him to arrange a reception, he naturally complied.

That, one might say, was the extent of his perfidy. Communism was decidedly not his cup of tea. He was born in a palace on his mother's ancestral estate in Odessa. He joined the Imperial Cadets before he was ten, and when he was wounded five years later fighting the Bolsheviks, it steeled his resolve to cover himself in glory in those days that shook the world. His greatest ambition was to join his great-grandfather Grigory Ivanovich, a general whose portrait hung in the Military Gallery of the Winter Palace.

But it was not to be. His second-eldest brother, a naval officer, went down with his ship in the Baltic rather than face a revolutionary tribunal on shore. The eldest was condemned to death by a tribunal in St. Petersburg. His dispossessed parents required looking after. When Odessa fell to the Reds, he escaped retribution by obtaining a certificate that identified him as a member of the ballet troupe of the Odessa Opera. He never doubted where his duty lay. But he never forgot his chagrin at the charade that had damned him to ballet school.

I told him that I saw a flaw in his theory about Nigel. His letters suggested that he wasn't very patriotic, not by Victorian standards.

The longer he worked for the East India Company, the more he questioned colonial rule. By the end of the 1840s his sympathies lay more with the natives than with his own countrymen. Why, then, would he dedicate himself to preserving the empire?

He considered this.

What was the primary motivation of any secret agent?

Was it idealism, or self-interest?

The same might be asked about a king. With Tribhuvan, for example, it was hard to say. He truly wanted to better the lives of his people by opening Nepal to the rest of the world. But he also wanted to wield power for its own sake—he considered it his birthright. With Tribhuvan's son Mahendra, on the other hand, the answer was clear enough. Boris recalled that when I lived in Kathmandu, I had taken a minibus trip up the Chinese-built road to the Tibetan border with a Nepalese friend, a Sherpa I had met near Mount Everest. He wondered if I had noticed the bridges.

No, I said, I had not.

They certainly were massive, said Boris.

Rather over-engineered for lorries, he thought.

Had I seen any lorries on the road?

No?

Well, no surprise there. No trade, either, not between China and Nepal via that road, though that was why the road was said to have been built.

He didn't suppose that I had seen any tanks, either.

Nor troop carriers.

Not yet.

He happened to know (and later I confirmed) that China's offer to build the road had been accepted only after a deposit of $7 million into the London bank account of the late King Mahendra.

Personal account, needless to say.

He laughed again.

As for Nigel, perhaps he simply wanted to live out his days in the lap

of luxury. Men had betrayed their ideals for less. But what if Nigel saw
a way to have his cake and eat it, too? What if he decided to become, in
effect, a double agent? What if the last thing on his mind was exerting
his influence on behalf of the empire? What if he exerted it on behalf
of what he thought were the best interests of Nepal? What if he saw
Jang Bahadur not as a native to manipulate but as a man with whom he
shared a common cause—keeping the empire at bay? What if the price
of saving Nepal from the British was saving India for them?

If that was the bargain, Boris said, Jang Bahadur got the best of it.
The British never challenged Nepalese sovereignty, and the kingdom
remained in the hands of his family until 1951, almost five years after
Indian Independence.

He asked me what I thought.

The idea of Nigel as a consummate player in the Great Game struck
me as a large leap to make, if a predictable one from a self-conscious
mover and shaker like Boris. The first time I spoke with him, he wondered why Nigel would have chosen the Company's civil over its military service. He thought that a man who hunted Bengal tigers was,
ipso facto, a man of action. He simply could not picture a man like that
bent over a ledger in an opium warehouse. And I knew it pleased him
to imagine that I shared his reckless temperament, simply because I
climbed mountains.

If Boris felt a superficial sense of kinship with me, the same had to
be said about my own connection with Nigel. I liked him, because he
threw down the white man's burden and boldly went where he was not
supposed to go. For no good reason—a misdemeanor here, a trespass
there—I fancied a bit of outlaw in myself. It was easy to identify with
a renegade sahib—especially one whose sensibility seemed so refresh-
ingly modern. The veneer of Nigel's dense Victorian diction camouflaged the same sort of free spirit that I admired in my favorite companions on climbing ropes and road trips. I didn't have many—any,
really—friends among my relatives, but I felt sure that Nigel would
have been one if we were contemporaries.

What made him a renegade, though, was a tougher nut to crack. And I couldn't help thinking that Boris was inclined to set a stage for Nigel to act as he himself would have done, or wished he might have done.

But I didn't say so.

I said it sounded like something out of Kipling.

I said I hoped it was true, and if it wasn't it deserved to be.

If only for poetic justice.

If only because the Great Game, for the British, was always about the Russians.

33

Now Is the Waiting

1982

A BAD DAY FOR an exorcism.

Of that the seeress was certain. Every sign was inauspicious
—the phase of the moon, the alignment of stars, the temper of Lord
Pashupatinath in his temple on the Bagmati River on the far side of
Kathmandu. To cast out the spirit of the ancestor who troubled me was
beyond her capabilities, there and then.

It was the end of May 1982, a few days after the conversation with
Boris that turned out to be the last time I saw him. He died in Kathmandu three years later, aged eighty. When I told the friend with
whom I was staying that Boris thought Nigel had been a secret agent
for the British, I said that I was resigned to never sorting out what had
really happened to him. Seven years into my search for an answer, I had
run out of sources.

Not necessarily, she said.

Not if I stopped thinking like a Westerner.

What about supernatural assistance?

Had I thought of that?

No, I said, and she asked why not. Kathmandu was the world capital
of the occult, seething with sortilege and sorcery of the deepest dye in
every hue of magic. It was like looking for a taxi in Manhattan and ignoring the yellow cabs.

My friend was an expatriate Brit who had lived there since shortly
after the visit by the Beatles in 1968 that turned Nepal into a mecca

for seekers of Nirvana and fine hashish. She said she knew just the woman to see. Her rates were reasonable, and I could always write about it.

She lived across the Bagmati River in Lalitpur, not far from the home of the Nepalese family who hosted me in 1975 during my Nepali language lessons. We sat in her flat on cushions on a floor the color of café au lait, plastered with mud and cow dung mixed with rice straw. She lowered her kohl-rimmed eyes to a steaming glass of milky tea. She skimmed the surface with a deckle-edged Nebico biscuit. As she rushed it to her lips, her varnished nails caught the light, a lurid flash of shocking pink.

A pink very close to that of Jagdalak rubies, and also those of the Ganesh Himal.

She was a seeress, a medium, a witch. Nepali is a pithy tongue. One word—*bokshi*—covers them all. But if I needed an exorcist, it was news to me.

I told her that I must have misspoken. I required information, not intervention. This was not a personal matter.

Not personal at all.

There was no misunderstanding, she insisted, and disposed of my qualms about exorcism with the same vigorous flick of varnished nails that banished biscuit crumbs from the table between us.

Like any professional, she had made her diagnosis. In her judgment, the matter of this man Nigel-sahib was more personal than I was letting on.

Her eyes searched mine.

"You feel no torment?" she asked. "All these many years?"

Torment?

"From your ancestor, alive in your thoughts? Making them—like his own?"

No, I said.

"Sometimes?"

No torment.

"Many times?"

Never.

Just—

She pressed her glossed lips together and leaned forward expectantly. I started to say "Confusion," then caught myself from owning up to something a demon might sow.

"Curiosity."

It was only the truth. Talking with Boris had piqued it anew, and when I gave my British friend the go-ahead to arrange a session with the seeress, it wasn't just for the novelty. When I lived in Kathmandu myself, I had twice experienced what seemed to be paranormal phenomena. The first time I was alone. The second time I had company, and my companions were as sure as I was that something strange and inexplicable had occurred as we made our way down a narrow walled lane one night on our way home from the Yak and Yeti. Not to put too fine a point on it—we saw a ghost.

A faceless—but not soundless—being.

Saw and felt and heard, independently, without speaking of it until it had passed.

And disappeared, in a place where nothing could hide.

I was skeptical that a seeress could tell me more about Nigel. But my friend was right: if there was any place where such a one might, it was Nepal.

The *bokshi* regarded me in silence. She looked genuinely puzzled. Then, after hinting again that I was holding back, she relaxed a little. She dipped another biscuit. She permitted herself a small smile and said that she was satisfied, at any rate, that torment was wanting.

Nothing so drastic as an exorcism was on the cards after all.

We would proceed.

She left the room and returned with a school exercise book. After she opened the pasteboard cover, she asked me to write down the years

of Nigel's birth and death. I dashed off the numerals 1822 and 1878
with a flourish, anxious for her to start.

She gave me a look.

"By the Nepalese reckoning, Sahib."

I shot back a look of my own. The conversion was no trivial affair.
The Bikram Sambat calendar is 56.7 years ahead of the Gregorian and
begins each year with a date that usually corresponds to the thirteenth
or fourteenth of April.

Usually.

She shrugged.

"In this world, Sahib, we can only walk one step at a time."

After I finished laboring over the figures, she examined my work
with the stern absorption of a ninth-grade algebra teacher, thumbing
through the wide-ruled pages and *hmm*ing to herself. Then she handed
back the book and asked me to convert my own birthdate.

"Why?"

"It is necessary, Sahib."

She ushered me into a stifling windowless kitchen, where sparks
leaped randomly from banked coals in a pit recessed in the floor. Resting on the hearth was the flask-shaped shoulder bone of a recently
slaughtered goat.

It would serve, she murmured, as a link between the land of the living and the land of the dead.

Despite the heat, I felt a chill. The apparition I had seen with my
friends seven years before had later seemed to us exactly that: an omen
of a disaster in the mountains that came close to taking some of our
lives.

She squatted on her hams in the firelight and carefully copied the
vital dates for Nigel onto a small square of rice paper, block-printed
with a crudely drawn image. I moved closer and gazed down upon the
three-eyed Lord of Death.

His hair stood on end. He was haloed in flames. His upraised right
hand brandished a club surmounted with a human skull. His left hand

held a lasso at his waist. His legs were extended in a striding posture. He was naked from the waist up; below he wore a skirt of tiger skin.

Another chill.

"There was a story that Nigel was carried off by a tiger," I whispered. "That was how he might have died."

To this intelligence she responded with the deftest of role reversals. "Coincidence only, Sahib."

From an adjoining pantry she fetched a clay pot of paste and affixed the baleful image to the shoulder blade, flicking away bits of sinew as she pressed it into place. All the while I fretted over her penciled notation of my birthdate.

Would necessity demand its last-minute inscription on the Lord of Death?

Were we not perhaps playing too literally with fire?

Was it too late to back out?

There was no breathing easy until she reached for blackened fire tongs and thrust the bone deeply into the shimmering coals, muttering incantations.

The features of the image contorted hideously as they flamed, then swiftly burned to whitest ash. Soon the bone began to crack. Each sharp report she greeted with a satisfied "La!"

When the fusillade died down, she withdrew the bone and dropped it on a copper tray. I followed her to an altar at the base of a tall wooden grain storage container that formed a partition between the kitchen and what she called "the house gods room." There, she lit a twist of braided incense and made an offering of rice grains and rose petals to two divinities.

The first, represented by a flat human-shaped figure made of leather, hung from a hook on the storage bin high above the altar. She explained that he was Guru Babà, the first human being in the world.

He lived in the mountains to the north, with all our ancestors.

Directly below him, in the center of the altar, sculpted in bronze, was the mother goddess Devi.

She lived on the great plain to the south, in her temple at Patna, the navel of the world.

The plain, said the seeress, was the land of the living.

The mountains were the land of the dead.

She knelt before the altar, holding out the bone on the tray in her hands. After a moment of silence, she addressed the mother goddess in a monotone.

I stood a step behind her, comprehending nothing, wondering at the common residence of Devi and Nigel in the navel of the world.

Did it signify?

Or was it like the tiger skin, coincidence only?

When she rose, she motioned toward the doorway of the room with the cushions.

"Please, Sahib," she said softly. "Now is the waiting."

I ducked beneath a lintel the height of a pillar-box and settled down with my back to the *locus dei*. Of the esoteric goings-on there, I heard only murmuring now and again, faintly beseeching, with the cadence of prayer. The time passed neither quickly nor slowly, simply without tension, without further contemplation of my personal relationship with the fearsome Lord of Death.

When she rejoined me, she carried steaming glasses of tea. She placed them on the table without speaking, left the room, and returned with the fire-cracked bone, covered with a scrap of calico. Gathering her sari with one hand, she sank to the cushion.

"You know the place already," she announced with an air of satisfaction.

"The place of his grave?"

"Place of this man Nigel-sahib's death."

She said that whether he was buried or not remained unclear.

She took a sip of tea.

"But I think—no grave."

"I have been there myself? In person?"

"Yes."

She unveiled the shoulder blade, reviewed its fissures with a critical eye. "Not self only. With one other."

"Do you know who?"

"One man," she said confidently.

It was the same with Nigel, she said, when he was there.

"Exact same, sahib with other man. Two men only. Two men going to this place. No tiger is coming. This man Nigel-sahib, he died. Other man died other place. Far place. Nigel-sahib's death place, no jungle."

I asked if she could judge the direction, from Kathmandu.

"Not north," she said quickly.

"South?" I asked. "Patna?"

Her eyes widened.

"You have looked for this man in Patna?"

I explained that he had lived there before he came to Kathmandu.

"And that decision, it was made in Patna?"

There was no way of knowing, I said. He had come from Patna, and he could have changed his mind there and stayed in India. But he didn't. So I supposed it was likely that he did make his decision there, the final one.

"A large decision," she replied.

"Yes."

For such a large decision, she observed, there would be a large explanation.

"Large explanation?"

"Nothing was said? Nothing written?"

"No."

She assayed the bone thoughtfully. It was a type of divination, I later learned, that dated back to the Neolithic Longshan culture. The bones used by its practitioners were incised by markings that constitute the earliest known form of Chinese writing.

She raised her eyes.

"These men, very much friends."

And there was one more thing.

I stared.

Only one?

"You are not his reincarnation."

That was all.

34

Stars of Tears

1996

THESE MEN, very much friends."

Looking back, it seems that the seeress had made the connection that finally explained what happened to Nigel. But it was one that would continue to elude me—somehow—for many years to come.

Somehow, because during my first stay in Nepal I had become "very much friends" with another man myself. One brisk fall evening in 1975, in a village a few days' walk from the base of Mount Everest, I joined a raucous crowd gathered round a tipsy, beaming Sherpa couple. (What I took for a lively wedding turned out to be a devil-may-care divorce.) When I noticed another onlooker staring at me, I thought I knew why —we were the only Europeans present. He was tall, bearded, and muscular, a little older than me, with eyes of pale cornflower blue.

But he turned out to be a Sherpa, and after an awkward encounter I wondered whether his father had been one of the first white men to pass through the area, with the 1953 British Everest expedition. A few days afterwards, in another village, there he was again, staring, and we talked again, just as awkwardly, and then, weeks later, when the cold weather came and the hill people came down to Kathmandu for the winter, I saw him in a barley beer shop by the great stupa at Bauddha.

Somehow, because finally, over *chang*, the unresolved tension between us vanished. We understood each other perfectly, and my increasing fluency in conversational Nepali had nothing to do with it. One weekend we took a bus up the Chinese road to the Tibetan border. We got off in the only town it passed through, hiked for several hours to the shrine at Namobuddha, and braved the arctic chill of a tumble-down lodge to spend the night—one of the warmest, I have to say, that I ever spent.

Somehow, because I had looked him up again on my return to Nepal in 1982, not long before my session with the seeress. He ran his own lodge catering to foreigners on one of the newly opened trekking routes. After he greeted me, he said that he already had enough business to employ his whole family.

"Splendid!" I said in Nepali.

He considered this longer than he ought to have, eyeing me gravely. Then he flashed the smile I remembered, bright as sun on snow.

"Sisters!" he said in English. "Brothers!"

His blue eyes pierced mine.

"No wife! No kids! Never!"

He hugged me fiercely, then said he was taking off time for a trek he had planned for the two of us, the destination a surprise. He kept me guessing for four or five days, choosing tracks that were sure to confuse, until finally I recognized the only path up the Mukti Kshetra (Salvation Valley). It led to a shrine in the heart of the Himalayas called Muktinath, sacred for millennia to Hindus and long regarded as a "wish-fulfilling jewel" by Buddhists too. There we bathed beneath each of 108 faucets, cast in the shape of a bull's head, closely arranged in a semicircle. Gasping—and shriveling—in the icy water, we joked of dire consequences later. (As pilgrims in a state of grace, of course, we suffered none at all.)

Somehow, because what, after all, had my companion said in Lahore in 1975 when I showed her Nigel's letters that mentioned John Nicholson?

"They sound like love letters."

By the time I returned to Nepal in 1996, I knew that historians had begun to speculate about John Nicholson's supposed homosexual attachments. I had stopped writing for magazines and taken a job writing speeches for the chancellor of a university. It called for long days in the research library, which I habitually broke up with trips to the stacks concerned with British India and its luminaries. I had long since abandoned hope of finding out anything more about Nigel. But I was curious about the documented lives of people he had known. And when I thought about it, the most striking thing about Nigel's regard for Nicholson—apart from its fervor—was how little the two men had in common.

Unlike Nigel—and the officers at Barrackpore who befriended him when he lived in Calcutta—Nicholson cared nothing for Persian poetry or Mughal architecture. Apart from the Holy Bible, the only book he ever mentioned reading in his letters was a tome on military tactics. And while Nigel came across in his correspondence as outgoing and sociable, Nicholson, according to an ensign who served with him, "was reserved almost to moroseness." Under the circumstances, it seemed reasonable to wonder if what drew the two men together was mutual attraction rather than shared interests and compatible temperaments, if the bond between them was identical to the one that Nicholson might have forged with Herbert Edwardes and Muhammad Hayat Khan.

Who could say? No one living, certainly. The closest thing I found to supporting evidence when I reread Nigel's correspondence was a letter he wrote in 1846 that described a Hindu festival. It began with the ritual slaughter of livestock in a public square, followed by a raucous parade in which a young girl costumed as a goddess was borne through the streets to a temple on a riverbank, where feasting and drinking continued long into the night and reflections of bonfires danced on the water. It reminded him, he wrote, of the festivities of "low-born Egyptians," harvesters of dates and olives, who on "periodic occasions" enjoyed the "freedom of the town." Consumption of palm wine worked to the detriment of their singing and dancing, but seemed not to compromise the "sweet melodies of their flutes," which he found "strangely pleasing."

The passage drew my attention because I was trying to fill in the

gap in Nigel's letters after he met with Louis Linant about visiting
the oasis of Siwa, in the Western Desert; whether he made it there or
not was one of the enduring mysteries about his life after he left England. In reading up on Egyptian cultural observances, I discovered
that the Egyptian "festivities" he described did not correspond with
any holiday celebrated in Cairo or Alexandria. But Nigel's description
—and his comparison to the Indian festival—evokes the character of
one unique to Siwa, called *moulid*. Émile Laoust, who helped organize
schooling for native Berbers there, published an account of it in 1924:

"The fellahin go into the gardens where they feast upon a sheep,
whose throat has been cut the evening before in the citadel, and get
drunk on palm wine. They gather in groups to the sound of flutes, and
pay court to a young boy whom they have dressed in women's cloth-
ing. They return by the light of torches in the evening after having
visited Tmussi spring for ritual ablutions."

Until the mid-twentieth century, Siwa's agricultural laborers practiced another observance. When Nigel wrote home about calling on
Egyptian civil servants shortly after arriving in Alexandria, he provided no details of the "immoderate" habits they attributed to Siwans.
But Siwa, I learned, was notorious for "dubious morals," with special
reference to the homosexual inclinations of its male inhabitants. Single men and adolescents, barred from residing within the walls of the
town, lived a communal life in the gardens surrounding it. Most were
landless peasants, who were not permitted to take wives until the age
of forty. They passed their evenings playing music and drinking fer-
mented palm sap. It was anything but a chaste existence. When enduring attachments formed, genuine wedding contracts were drawn
up, awarding dowries to the families of the younger partners. The
wedding itself was the occasion of a large public celebration—so out-
wardly similar to Laoust's description of *moulid* that Nigel, if indeed
he visited the oasis, might have attended not a harvest festival but a
male marriage.

Male matrimony was not the sort of local color he would have shared with his parents. Even if his correspondence was intact, I doubted it would provide further insight into the nature of the oasis' appeal for him. What is certain is that he knew of its reputation for "immoderate" goings-on, a reputation that did not deter him from the prospect of a taxing journey there. It was tempting to speculate that Siwa's reputation might actually have served to entice him.

But, once again, who could say?

What I could say, though, was what I told a Japanese graduate student on a spring day in Kathmandu at the Unity Restaurant in 1996, after he handed me a photograph of an unusual star-shaped tile of faience mosaic, inset between the roots of an ancient tree. He said that it supposedly memorialized an Englishman.

"Do you know Namobuddha?" he asked.

I said that I did, without saying why.

Without saying I had been very cold there, but also very warm.

What I said was:

I remember it well.

Even after twenty years.

What I said was:

I know this poem.

From somewhere.

Without remembering Herat.

Without remembering the poet Jami's epitaph in Rosi Bagh.

> *When your face is hidden from me,*
> *Like the moon hidden on a dark night,*
> *I shed stars of tears and yet my night remains dark*
> *In spite of all those shining stars.*

"Like a head without a trunk," said the spurious archaeologist who was probably a spy, after he translated the incomplete stanza of the poem on the mosaic tile of the derelict royal tomb.

Without knowing then that Nigel's friend Sa'adat was a prince of the blood royal, credited by the Afghan Royal Genealogy with "no issue," a conspicuous exception to the rule for Sadozai nobles who lived into manhood.

Without recognizing then that the words in English on the star-shaped tile of the *chautara* at Namobuddha completed the truncated stanza in Persian on the star-shaped tile fifteen hundred miles distant at Rosi Bagh, and could only serve as a private memorial to the lives shared for twenty-eight years by two men, a Muslim and a Christian, a prince and a clerk, an Afghan and an Englishman.

Not the only Englishman who was different from the rest. Not the only Englishman for whom the empire made a bed and beckoned him to lie in it. But a rare one nonetheless, who permitted his liking for a native to become so much more than just attraction that there was no turning back, no going home, no darkening the love-lit nighttime sky until death did them part.

The revelation finally came later, back in America after my encounter with the Japanese student. One day, as I was looking for something else, I unearthed a school exercise book that had served as my daybook when I lived in Kathmandu. It also contained my journal from Afghanistan, which quoted the lines from Jami as translated by Boris' friend beneath the spreading dusty leaves of a pistachio tree, once upon another time.

What I remembered in the moment that I read them was the seeress, saying that I already knew the place.

Saying:

"Exact same, sahib with other man."

Saying:

"These men, very much friends."

Saying, finally, in answer to a question I never asked:

"You are not his reincarnation."

How could I be? I thought. If I was Nigel's reincarnation, I surely would have known it when I found it, the place I thought I could not find.

But that was then.

Now I think that she was speaking of another man, the man with him when he died.

Now that I know who he was.

Now that I know that Sa'adat was what happened to Nigel.

Now that I know that everything she told me turned out to be true.

It wasn't personal, I told her.

Not personal at all.

She knew better.

It would have saved me time and trouble if I realized it then. But in this world we can only walk one step at a time.

A NOTE ON SOURCES AND FURTHER READING

The most difficult part of researching this book was knowing when to stop. Victorians abroad in India were prodigious letter writers and journal keepers. Much of their output survives in the stacks of university and public libraries and, increasingly, in digitized form, freely available online. It amounts to an embarrassment of riches for anyone interested in sahibs and memsahibs and how they went about the business of ruling a sizable portion of the world's population for two hundred years. One attempts to fix undivided attention on a governor's prosecution of a war in Afghanistan, only to encounter the beguiling distraction that his wife deserted him to live in a Bedouin harem.

Nor was the historical quicksand confined to the British. The plots of William Shakespeare—and the librettos of Giuseppe Verdi—seem pedestrian compared with the documented histories of the royal dynasties that rose and fell in eighteenth- and nineteenth-century Nepal and Afghanistan. Behind every beheading and blinding and servant girl made queen lurks a story demanding to be told. That it was tough enough telling Nigel's was a lesson I learned through trial, tribulation, and many months of unforced error.

In addition to the period correspondence and archival research described in the narrative, I relied on the sources that follow in re-creating Nigel's world.

The Company

Confronted by the sweep and scope of the affairs of the "Company of Traders" chartered by Elizabeth I, it is only natural to yearn for a historical masterwork on the order of Edward Gibbon. Such a book, alas, remains to be written. John Keay's *The Honourable Company: A History of the English East India Company* (London: HarperCollins, 1991), though light on details about the social side of life for Company employees, goes further than most popular histories toward filling the vacuum. A briefer and equally readable introduction is Brian Gardner's *The East India Company* (London: Marlboro, 1971). Most of my principal sources date back to the Company's heyday:

Anonymous, *Facts and Reflections by a Subaltern of the Indian Army* (London: James Madden, 1849).

John Beames, *Memoirs of a Bengal Civilian* (London: Chatto & Windus, 1961).

Francis John Bellew, *Memoirs of a Griffin; Or, a Cadet's First Year in India* (London: William Allen & Co., 1880).

Kathleen Blechynden, *Calcutta: Past and Present* (London: W. Thacker & Co., 1905).

Francis Hamilton (formerly Buchanan), *An Account of the Districts of Bihar and Patna in 1811–1812* (Bankipore, India: Bihar Research Society, 1936).

Rev. John Cormac, *Account of the Abolition of Female Infanticide in Guzerat, with Considerations of the Question of Promoting the Gospel in India* (London: Black, Parry, & Co., 1815).

William Dalrymple, *White Mughals: Love and Betrayal in Eighteenth-Century India* (New York: Penguin, 2004).

Frederick Danvers, Monier Williams, Steuart Bayley, Percy Wigram, and Brand Sapte, *Memorials of Old Haileybury College* (Westminster, UK: Archibald Constable & Co., 1894).

Sara Graham Mulhall, *Opium: The Demon Flower* (New York: Montrose, 1928).

Fanny Parkes, *Wanderings of a Pilgrim in Search of the Picturesque* (London: Pelham Richardson, 1850).

John Pinkerton, ed., *A General Collection of Voyages and Travels: Hindostan* (London: Longman, Hurst, Rees, Orme & Brown, 1811).

Narendra Krishna Sinha and Nisith Ranjan Ray, *A History of India* (Hyderabad, India: Orient Longman, 1973).

Joachim Stocqueler, *The Hand-Book of British India: A Guide to the Stranger, the Traveller, the Resident, and All Who May Have Business with or Appertaining to India* (London: William Allen & Co., 1854).

Jean-Baptiste Tavernier and Valentine Ball, *Travels in India* (Cambridge, UK: Cambridge University Press, 2012).

Horace Wilson, *The History of British India* (London: Madden & Malcolm, 1846).

The Empire

The memoirs and correspondence of British India's supreme rulers make for heavy going. Steeped in cultural arrogance and overt racism that is profoundly distasteful to modern sensibilities — or so it would have seemed, in America anyway, prior to November 8, 2016 — they nonetheless provide insights into decision-making and contemporary politics available nowhere else. Here and there, too, emerge striking vignettes of the imperial progress, as when Governor General Charles Hardinge whispers to the Sikh foreign secretary to remind him that, by the terms of the Treaty of Lahore, the Koh-i-noor diamond is to be delivered to Queen Victoria, and must be submitted for his inspection:

> *Another pause, and more whispers. At last, a small tin box enveloped in a shabby cloth was brought in, containing the diamond which is now worn by the Empress of India on state occasions. Many have since seen it; to us it appeared to be wanting in that brilliancy which is the charm of lesser stones.*

James Andrew Broun-Ramsay, Marquis of Dalhousie, *Private Letters* (London: Blackwood, 1911).

George Nathaniel Curzon, *British Government in India: The Story of the Viceroys and Government Houses* (London: Cassell & Co., 1925).

Byron Farwell, *Queen Victoria's Little Wars* (New York: W. W. Norton & Co., 1985).

Charles Hardinge, *Rulers of India: Viscount Hardinge* (Oxford, UK: Clarendon Press, 1891).

Lena Campbell Login, *Sir John Login and Duleep Singh* (London: W. H. Allen & Co., 1890).

Robert Pearce, *Memoirs and Correspondence of the Most Noble Richard Marquess Wellesley* (London: Richard Bentley, 1846).

Frederick Sleigh Roberts, *Forty-one Years in India: From Subaltern to Commander-in-Chief* (London: Richard Bentley & Son, 1897).

Ernest Sackville Turner, *Gallant Gentlemen: A Portrait of the British Officer, 1600–1956* (London: Michael Joseph, 1956).

The Lawrences and Henry's Young Men

In the aftermath of John Nicholson's heroic death during the Siege of Delhi, John Lawrence remarked that his name would not be forgotten, "as long as an Englishman survives in India." Surely enough, everyone from Rudyard Kipling to authors of adventure stories for boys worked to ensure the immortality of "Nikal Seyn." But Lawrence might have said the same about himself and his brother Henry, as well as several of the larger-than-life officers who served under them. Charles Allen's *Soldier Sahibs: The Men Who Made the North-West Frontier* (London: John Murray, 2000) began as an attempt by a Nicholson family descendant to sort out the truth from the hagiography, then expanded into a riveting account of the exploits and personalities of his forebear's colleagues and mentors. There is no better introduction to the time, the place, and the players. Other—mostly period—sources include:

Maud Diver, *Honoria Lawrence: A Fragment of Indian History* (London: John Murray, 1936).

Herbert Edwardes, *A Year on the Punjab Frontier, in 1848–49* (London: Richard Bentley, 1851).

Herbert Edwardes and Emma Sydney Edwardes, *Memorials of the Life and Letters of Major General Sir Herbert B. Edwardes* (London: Kegan Paul, Trench & Co., 1886).

Herbert Edwardes and Herman Merivale, *Life of Sir Henry Lawrence* (London: Smith, Elder & Co., 1872).

Frederick P. Gibbon, *The Lawrences of the Punjab* (London: J. M. Dent & Co., 1908).

John William Kaye, *Lives of Indian Officers: Illustrative of the Civil and Military Services of India* (London: A. Strahan & Co., 1867).

Harold Lee, *Brothers in the Raj: The Lives of John and Henry Lawrence* (Oxford, UK: Oxford University Press, 2002).

Peter Lumsden and George Elsmie, *Lumsden of the Guides* (London: John Murray, 1900).

Reginald Bosworth Smith, *Life of Lord Lawrence* (London: Smith, Elder & Co., 1883).

Lionel Trotter, *The Life of John Nicholson: Soldier and Administrator* (London: John Murray, 1898).

Afghanistan

A great many books about Afghanistan have been published since the Soviet invasion in 1979. None approach Louis Dupree's magisterial *Afghanistan* (Princeton, NJ: Princeton University Press, 1983) as a definitive survey of the country's history and culture. Rory Stewart's *The Places in Between* (London: Picador, 2004), a Scotsman's personal narrative of his walk across Afghanistan shortly after the fall of the Taliban in 2002, provides a memorable portrait of Ghor, the mountainous province where Sa'adat ul-Mulk and his elder brother plotted revenge on the traitorous vizier who imprisoned and murdered their father, Kamran Shah.

Henry Bellew, *Afghanistan and the Afghans* (London: S. Low, Marston, Searle, & Rivington, 1879).
———. *The Races of Afghanistan* (Calcutta: Thacker, Spink & Co., 1880).
Human Terrain Team AF-6, "Pashtun Sexuality" (Washington: U.S. Department of Defense, 2009).
Seth G. Jones, *Counterinsurgency in Afghanistan* (Santa Monica, CA: RAND National Defense Research Institute, 2008).
John William Kaye, *History of the War in Afghanistan* (London: William Allen & Co., 1878).
George Rawlinson, *A Memoir of Major-General Sir Henry Creswicke Rawlinson* (London: Longmans, Green & Co., 1898).
G. P. Tate, *The Kingdom of Afghanistan: A Historical Sketch* (Bombay: Times of India, 1911).

Nepal

Francis Hamilton (formerly Buchanan) wrote the essential work in English. One of the first Europeans to venture beyond the dread Terai jungle, he spent fourteen months in the vicinity of Kathmandu in 1802–1803. His *Account of the Kingdom of Nepal, and of the Territories Annexed to This Dominion by the House of Gorkha* (Edinburgh: Archibald Constable, 1819) provides a detailed overview of Nepalese geography, natural history, and ethnography, coupled with recent history gleaned from informants who personally experienced the momentous rise to power of Prithvi Narayan Shah. Other principal sources:

Michael Peissel, *Tiger for Breakfast* (New York: E. P. Dutton & Co., 1966).

Pramode Shamshere Rana, *Rana Intrigues* (Kathmandu: Pramode Shamshere Rana, 1995).

Mahesh Chandra Regmi, *A Study in Nepali Economic History, 1768–1846* (Kathmandu: Mañjuśrī Publishing House, 1971).

Tulasī Rāma Vaidya, Triratna Mānandhara, and Shankar Lal Joshi, *Social History of Nepal* (Kathmandu: Anmol Publications, 1993).

The Mutiny

In the interest of historical accuracy — as well as fidelity to eyewitness accounts — I have avoided the current fashion of referring to the Indian Mutiny of 1857–58 as the "Indian Rebellion" or "India's First War of Independence." The uprising began as a series of mutinies by native soldiers serving in the Bengal Army, who were joined by former soldiers as prime movers in hostilities that were largely confined to the Gangetic Plain. Most of the sources listed above for "The Lawrences and Henry's Young Men" include accounts of the Mutiny relevant to the lives — and deaths — of those individuals. The following sources depict the Mutiny from the viewpoints of less illustrious survivors.

Anonymous, *The Story of the Indian Mutiny (1857–58)* (Edinburgh: William P. Nimmo & Co., 1885).

Edward Vibart, *The Sepoy Mutiny as Seen by a Subaltern, from Delhi to Lucknow* (London: Smith, Elder & Co., 1898).

ACKNOWLEDGMENTS

To the many Nepalis, Indians, Pakistanis, and Afghans who showed such kindness and hospitality to me during my travels over the years, I owe a debt impossible to repay in words. To protect the privacy of certain inviduals mentioned in the text, I have changed their names and identifying characteristics.

My special thanks go to Kathy Robbins, who has represented me since 1982. No author could hope for wiser counsel or stauncher advocacy. I also want to thank everyone else at the Robbins Office.

Andrea Schulz acquired *Empire Made* and saw the manuscript through two drafts before leaving Houghton Mifflin Harcourt. My dismay at her departure proved short-lived once Nicole Angeloro took up the reins. Working with editors of their acumen and judgment was the best part of making this book.

This project owes its genesis to a book proposal completed on assignment for Nicholas Christopher's seminar on travel writing in the MFA program at Columbia University. It was Nic who encouraged me to run with the idea in the real world, and I am grateful for both his belief in my writing and the inspiration of his own artistry in fiction, poetry, and nonfiction.